MBA
FUNDAMENTALS

STATISTICS

Kaplan MBA Fundamentals Series

MBA Fundamentals Business Law

MBA Fundamentals Statistics

From the #1 graduate test prep provider, *Kaplan MBA Fundamentals* helps you to master core business basics in a few easy steps. Each book in the series is based on an actual MBA course, providing direct and measurable skills you can use today.

For the latest titles in the series, as well as downloadable resources, visit:
www.kaplanmbafundamentals.com

MBA
FUNDAMENTALS

STATISTICS

Paul W. Thurman

KAPLAN

PUBLISHING

New York

Vice President and Publisher: Maureen McMahon
Editorial Director: Jennifer Farthing
Acquisitions Editor: Shannon Berning
Development Editor: Joshua Martino
Production Editor: Fred Urfer
Production Designer: Pamela Beaulieu
Cover Designer: Rod Hernandez

January 2008
10 9 8 7 6 5

ISBN-13: 978-1-4277-9659-2

For my darling wife, Andrea,

and for our beautiful princesses,

Lisa and Vanessa

And in loving memory of my mother, Velma

Table of Contents

Introduction

IS THIS BOOK RIGHT FOR ME?

As a businessperson, executive, or aspiring MBA student, you work with lots of data. Every day, you read charts, graphs, and market research reports that contain the results of surveys, samples, summary statistical analyses, comparative tests, and predictive models. You're responsible for reviewing these analyses, crunching the numbers, and approving them for distribution. And though you didn't generate these statistics, you will certainly be held accountable for the results.

By learning how to be a critical reader of data and perform basic statistical analyses, you can face the crush of numbers without hesitation. The basic statistics training in this book will enhance your management skills in almost any area of business, from marketing, finance, and human resources to accounting, strategic planning, and operations. In the pages to come, you'll find the most vital principles of typical MBA core courses.

Rigorous professional data analysis requires years of study, research, and practical application of the lessons in this book and many others beyond the scope of this text. This book is written primarily for *consumers* of statistical information and data analysis, not for *producers* of such analyses.

As such, *MBA Fundamentals in Statistics* was developed with three goals in mind:

1. To help you become more critical of what you read, see, and hear in news reports, magazines, at work in meetings, and from other so-called official sources. This is not to imply that everything you read is wrong, but many charts, graphs, and statistics in headlines and business reports ought to be more carefully scrutinized.

2. To teach you some basic statistical tools that can be used to solve some simple problems. Not every analysis of data or statistical study can be conducted completely using the tools in this text. However, some basic tools—and more importantly, their limitations—are introduced, with plenty of examples and practice problems

3. To learn when to call a professional. From simple regression to complex surveying and sampling methods, so many statistical analyses are best left to data analysis professionals. You won't be able to solve every data analysis problem alone, and it's important to recognize a statistical challenge that requires professional consultation.

This text is intended to introduce managers, executives, and graduate students, particularly those in MBA degree programs, to the basic data analysis tools and techniques commonly used in business applications. Most MBA programs have a core requirement in statistics and quantitative analysis, and this book covers many of those topics. I have developed these lessons, practice problems, and real-world examples from my career, which spans business and educational spheres. The chapters that follow come from lectures, course notes, and professional development seminars from 10 years of teaching business graduate students (including more than 3,000 students in U.S. and international master's degree programs) and more than 15 years of management consulting and advisory work. I hope you find this book practical, useful, and readable.

DESCRIBING UNCERTAINTY AND POPULATIONS OF DATA WITH NUMBERS AND PICTURES

Summarizing the "Center," "Wobble," and "Shape" of Data

INTRODUCTION

Newspaper articles, TV stories, radio updates, and Internet Web pages are full of statistics: average salaries in technology jobs are up; average weight of American children is climbing; global average temperatures are rising; median home prices are falling; markets showed more volatility this week than in previous weeks; the Dow Jones Industrial Average is down; Alex Rodriguez's batting average is up.

It seems statistics are everywhere, and wherever they are used, writers and commentators use them to speak authoritatively. But are we always using the right statistic for the job?

WHAT'S AHEAD

In this chapter, you'll learn:
- How to use only a few numbers or one graph to represent lots of data
- Statistics to measure the central tendency, variability, and graphed appearance of a dataset

- The difference between mean, median, and mode
- How to describe the shape of a dataset
- The difference between populations and samples of data

IN THE REAL WORLD

Your real estate agent is on the phone, and she's thrilled. For months, she's been helping you look for a house. You've seen a lot of nice homes, but all of them were located in bad neighborhoods. Several times, the agent has shown you a beautiful, new house next to small, rundown homes with overgrown yards. Now your agent says she's found a great house in a neighborhood with an average home price of $250,000. As you drive into the neighborhood, you notice promising signs. You pass two mansions—huge, million-dollar homes. Yet when you reach the street with the house for sale, your heart sinks. You find yourself among small, dilapidated houses clearly worth no more than $75,000.

Has your broker lied? Can the neighborhood's average home price actually be $250,000?

THE KEY CONCEPTS

Statistical analysis means summarizing a lot of information with only a few shorthand quantities or *statistics*. For example, if someone asks you how your customers feel about your current product, you could answer by explaining how each and every customer likes or doesn't like your product—but that would be very difficult to do! Statistics offer ways to describe a large set of data in a short summary using pictures or numbers.

Using statistics, we can describe three important features of a set of information (or a *dataset*): the central tendency or "center" of the data, the variability or "wobble" of the data, and the geometry or "shape" of the data. Key measures that you may have seen or heard include the following:

- The center or central tendency can be described by three statistics: the average (or *mean*), the *median*, and the *mode*.
- The wobble or variability of a dataset can be described by the *variance* and the *standard deviation*.
- The shape or geometry of a dataset can be described by the *skewness* or *kurtosis* of data that has been represented visually on a graph or histogram.

Now let's define how to measure these features of a dataset by considering two sets of midterm scores from a statistics courses. The scores range from 0 to 100, and we have selected 13 scores from last year and 13 from this year. Let's examine which group did better on the midterm—this year's class or last year's class—by looking at the average score.

What Does *Mean* Really Mean?

A common way to summarize data is to find the average or *mean* score. The mean is the sum of all the scores divided by the number of scores. We can write this mathematically using the Greek symbol sigma (Σ) as the sum and the lowercase letter n to represent the number of scores in the dataset.

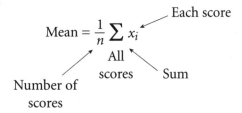

$$\text{Mean} = \frac{1}{n} \sum x_i$$

Each score — All scores — Sum — Number of scores

Notice that based on the mean midterm scores, this year's group did better than last year's group.

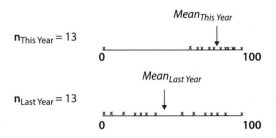

But the mean is not the only way to represent the center of a dataset. We can also use the *median* or "middle" value. When the dataset has been sorted, the median is the actual middle value with an odd number of data, values, or the mean of the two middle values in an even number of data points. For example, in a set of 11 test scores, the 6th score is the median; but in a set of 10 scores, the median is the average of the 5th and 6th scores.

Because it sits in the middle of the dataset, the median is also often referred to as the 50th percentile, the 5th decile, and/or the 2nd quartile.

So where is the median test score for each dataset? If we have 13 test scores in each year's dataset, then the median will be the 7th test score when the results are sorted in order. Although some people use the terms interchangeably, the median is not necessarily the same as the mean—in fact, they are often different:

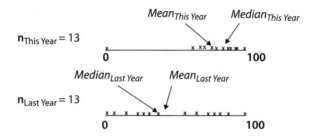

When we look at medians, the difference between the two classes is even greater—this year's students performed even better than last year's.

A third statistic used to describe central tendency is the *mode* of a dataset, or the most frequently occurring value. Modes are most often helpful when trying to determine which response—or score, in this case—was most frequent or popular. In the charts above, because it appears that each test score (for each dataset) is unique—that is, no score appears more than once—these distributions have no modes.

What Is the Best Statistic to Summarize Central Tendency?

Thus, we have an interesting dilemma—which statistic best describes central tendency? Is it the average? The median? Maybe the mode? If we look at news reports, we see the average used most often in stories—average income, average age, average profit, and batting averages. So is the average (or mean) the best statistic since it seems to be so common?

No! In fact, we have to be very careful with the average statistic. Because the average is the sum of all the data points divided by the number of data points, any very large or very small data point could significantly affect the average.

For example, in the charts above, note that this year's scores are mostly high except for one zero score. This single score, which sits far away from the rest of the data points, causes the mean to be lower than it would be without this extreme value in the dataset. In fact, if we removed this score, the mean of this year's data would likely be very close to the median score.

A value that is far from the rest of the dataset is called an *outlier*. Outliers, which are often determined subjectively, are values with small frequencies (small in number) that occur away from most of the other data. Thus, the presence of these outliers will have a significant effect on the mean statistic.

When it comes to describing the central tendency of a dataset, we have a choice; the average is not necessarily the best statistic.

TIP: *If a dataset has outliers, the median is often a better statistic to use than the mean. The median is less influenced by outlying values; therefore, it may be a better, more reliable descriptive statistic to use. However, if the dataset is a mirror image around its median, also called* symmetric, *the mean (which will equal the median) is the better statistic to use.*

But how can we determine if the mean is being heavily influenced by outliers? The simple answer is: Don't just look at one statistic—look at several. If the mean and median are not close together, then the mean may be affected by outliers.

Is there a case where the mode might be better than the mean and median? Take a look at the example below. In this case, the horizontal x-axis is salaries of one company's employees, and the vertical y-axis is how frequently these salaries are reported. Thus, a higher frequency means that more employees earn that particular salary amount.

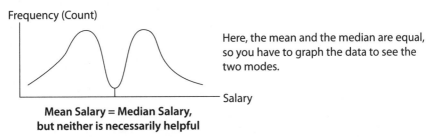

Here, the mean and the median are equal, so you have to graph the data to see the two modes.

Mean Salary = Median Salary, but neither is necessarily helpful

On the graph for this dataset, you can see that the mean salary and median salary are very close. Thus, you might be led to think the average salary would be the better summary statistic to use.

But wait—look again. The mean and median salaries are some of the least frequently reported values. These salaries appear to be *bimodal,* which means there are two modes. (Perhaps in this case both staff and executive salaries have been collected.) Because there are two frequently occurring salaries, the mode salary values may be the best way to summarize the dataset.

We could not have determined the best statistic to report central tendency in this dataset until we graphed the data. This is a critical point!

TIP: *When deciding what statistic is most appropriate to measure central tendency of a dataset, always graph the data! Numbers and statistics are not enough; we must actually "look" at the dataset to see the complete story. "Running the numbers" to get mean, median, and mode is simply not sufficient. Always look at numbers and pictures before deciding how best to summarize a dataset.*

Rule #1 of Statistics: Graph the Data!

How do we draw a picture of a dataset? The answer is to create a distribution like the one above. A chart shows the variable we are measuring (test scores, for example) on the x-axis and the frequency of the test scores on the y-axis. Such a chart is called a *frequency distribution* or *histogram.* Such charts can be easily created in Microsoft Excel (with the use of the included Data Analysis Toolkit add-ins) and with many other popular statistical packages/programs.

HISTOGRAM

- A histogram is also referred to as a *frequency distribution*.

- A histogram graphs quantitative data in contiguous ranges, often called *bins* or *buckets*, along the x-axis

- You can order a histogram in order of frequency; this is called a *Pareto distribution* if you order the frequency bars from highest (most frequent) to lowest.

- A histogram will let you "see" the descriptive statistics such as mean and median.

- A histogram is *not* the same as a bar chart; histograms have continuous values along the x-axis. Bar charts do not necessarily (see example below). In a bar chart

  - the data are not related (States not related; FL not "greater" than MO),

  - bin size is not a factor, and

  - there is no quantifiable relationship among bins.

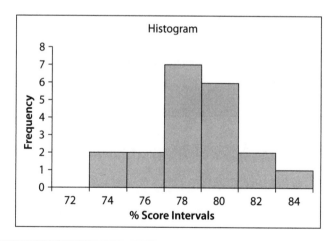

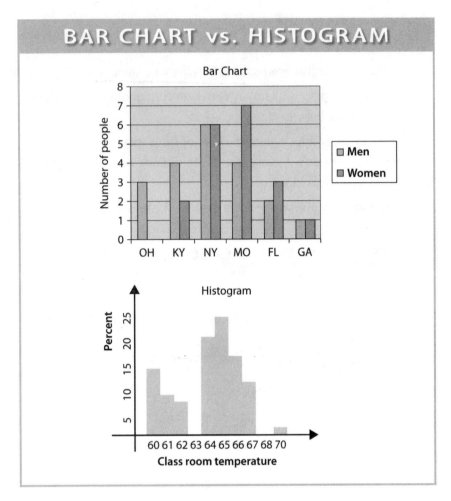

This brings us to our first rule of statistics: *Always graph the data!*

How Do We Measure the Variability or "Spread" of a Dataset?

When we have more than one dataset, how can we tell which dataset is

- more variable,
- more volatile,
- more "spread out,"
- less consistent, or
- less predictable?

We are trying to measure the spread or "wobble" of the dataset. Let's return to our test scores example (see charts below). Which group—this year's or last year's—had more variability in its test scores? Which group had less consistent scores or less predictable scores? Let's consider the simplest way to measure how datasets can be spread out (or narrow).

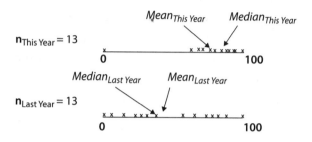

The easiest way to think about spread or volatility of a dataset is literally to consider how "wide" it is. This is called the *range* of the dataset, or the distance between the minimum and maximum values. Note that in the two datasets above, the ranges are identical; that is, the distance from the minimum score (0) to the maximum score (100) is the same range, or 100 points.

Thus, the range doesn't help us much here. We need to look inside these end points of the data distribution to figure out which dataset is more or less variable.

Maybe one way is to find out how far away each test score is from the mean score. If a set of scores is further away from the mean, the dataset with the higher average distance from the mean should be more spread out or variable.

Let's write this in a simple equation as we did before when we created the formula in "sigma" notation for the mean of a dataset. To express the average (signed) distance (or *deviation*) of one test score from the mean score, we must first find that score's distance from the mean. Then we do this for all the test scores, adding up all of these deviations (some positive, some negative). Now, find the average of all these individual deviations from the mean. We can express this using the following formula:

$$\frac{1}{n}\sum(x_i - \mu) \qquad \leftarrow \text{ average deviation from the mean}$$

This equation represents the average distance that a value, x_i, is from the mean of the dataset, μ. We add up all the deviations from the mean and then average them (or divide by the total number of scores in our dataset).

Of course, this formula always equals zero! But why? The average (signed) distance from the average is zero—on average, we are at the average. We must improve this formula slightly so that the deviations on either side of the mean don't offset each other in the aggregate. To get rid of the offsets, we could remove the signs of the deviations by taking the absolute value of the distance between a test score and the mean of all scores. But an even easier way to get rid of the signs in front of the deviations is to square them.

To do so, we can simply *square* the deviations to create the *mean squared deviation* from the mean. The further the data points are from the mean, the larger this quantity becomes. And the larger the dispersion or "wobble" of the dataset being studied! We call the mean squared deviation from the mean the statistical *variance*.

$$\frac{1}{n}\sum(x_i - \mu)^2 \quad \leftarrow \text{mean squared deviation} = \text{variance (in units squared)}$$

But along comes a problem with variance. This quantity is in units of the data, squared. Wouldn't it be better to use a spread or wobble statistic that is expressed in the same units of the data we are studying, just like the mean, median, and mode?

The answer is yes. So how do we get variance into a form that is in units of the data? Simple—just take the square root of the variance. This will give the root mean squared deviation from the mean, or *standard deviation* of the dataset.

$$\sqrt{\frac{1}{n}\sum(x_i - \mu)^2} \quad \leftarrow \text{root mean squared deviation}$$
$$= \text{square root of variance}$$
$$= \text{standard deviation (units of the data)}$$

This quantity is in units of the data now (or in units of points when considering the midterm scores problem, above). This standard deviation quantity is the preferred measure of the variability of a dataset, because it's in the units of the data and we don't have to worry about potential mathematical issues with the absolute value function.

Using our two examples above, although the two datasets have the same range, this year's test scores are *less variable* or *more consistent* than last year's scores. Note that this year's scores cluster more closely around the mean—save for one outlier—while last year's scores are somewhat all over the place. The standard deviation, then, of this year's test scores will be lower—and will indicate less wobble or variability in the data—than the standard deviation of last year's test scores.

How Can We Describe the Shape of a Dataset?

Because we now have a way to graph the data—using the histogram—we can use some additional statistics to describe the "shape" of the data distribution. Recall the effect that outliers can have on the mean. If a high-value outlier exists—like one or two perfect test scores—and these scores are well above most others, the mean test score will get pulled or *skewed* to the right (see chart at left, below). On the other hand, if most scores are high but a few low scores exist, the effect is to skew the mean to the left (see chart below).

However, if no significant outliers or long "tails" exist at either end of the data distribution, the graph is said to be *not skewed*. Note in the middle picture, below, that in a symmetric distribution, the mean and median are equal to each other. In both the right- and left-skew cases, note that the skewness or *tail* of the distribution is in the direction of the outliers. Right-skewed distributions are *right-tailed* while left-skewed distributions are *left-tailed*.

SKEWNESS

Skewness is the measurement of the deviation of the distribution from symmetry. It is defined by the location of the outliers—a symmetric distribution has no skewness. Skewness can be positive or negative.

Rightward Skewness	Symmetry	Leftward Skewness
Relative frequency — Median, Mean — Rightward skewness	Relative frequency — Median, Mean — Symmetry	Relative frequency — Mean, Median — Leftward skewness
Skewness > 0	Skewness = 0	Skewness < 0

Mean 7 Median

Thus, the *skewness statistic* will be positive when the distribution is skewed to the right (and the mean is greater than the median) and negative when the distribution is skewed to the left (and the mean is less than the median). Note that a symmetric distribution has no or zero skewness. Therefore, if we know the skewness, we can immediately know whether the mean is to the left or right of the median. And as we've learned, in skewed distributions, the median is often the preferred statistic because it is less susceptible to skewing effects.

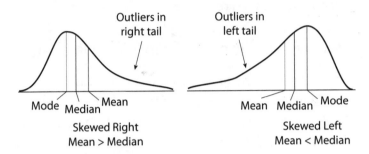

But what about the "hump" in the distribution? Is there a way to measure how pointed or flat the peak of the distribution is?

The answer lies in the *kurtosis statistic*. Kurtosis measures a distribution's "peakedness," the height of the hump. The narrower the hump, the more compact are the data points in relation to the mean. A highly kurtotic curve is also said to have *fat tails* due to more outlier behavior further from the mean (caused by the higher, thinner peak in the middle).

In most statistical programs, a descriptive statistics tool is available that can produce several standard descriptive statistics for a dataset. From these tools, a kurtosis of three is the dividing line between a tall, peaked distribution (*leptokurtic*) and a flatter distribution (*platykurtic*). A kurtosis of exactly three describes a bell-shaped or *normal* distribution. The bell curve is said to have no kurtosis or is *mesokurtic* even though formulaically the kurtosis is equal to three.

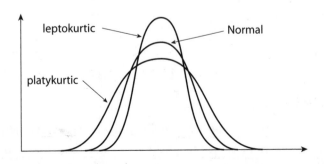

Note that in some tools, like Microsoft Excel, three is subtracted from the kurtosis formula so that a bell-shaped distribution has zero kurtosis. In general, however, a kurtosis of three is the bell curve and the dividing point between leptokurtic (high) and platykurtic (low) distributions. See the following table for a comparison of kurtosis results from a popular tool, STATA, and from Microsoft Excel.

STATA	Description	Excel
Greater than 3	Peaked, leptokurtic	Greater than 0
Less than 3	Flatter, platykurtic	Less than 0
Equal to 3	Bell-shaped or normal, mesokurtic	Equal to 0

What Is the Difference between Populations and Samples of Data?

A *population* of data is essentially the entire set of individuals or objects of a particular group, such as all students in MBA programs worldwide. A *sample*, on the other hand, is just a part of a population, such as African-American females over 25 years of age in this year's entering MBA class at a particular school.

In general, getting populations of data—and summary descriptive statistics—is difficult, if not impossible. In some cases, population data are possible, such as in a drug study where only 100 people in the world have tried a new cancer treatment. This is not usually the case in business. We cannot survey every customer, audit every transaction, or inspect every product we produce. Thus, we perform *sampling*, and samples are used to infer population behaviors. The average overdue amount for credit cards held by a sample of cardholders age 25 to 35 may be used to infer how the population—all cardholders in this age range—behaves in terms of average overdue amount. So why do we sample?

- *Cost*: Only need enough data to be "sufficiently" accurate.
- *Accuracy*: Maintain better control of data collection errors.
- *Timeliness*: Business decisions are made in real time; we cannot wait for perfect information.

- *Amount of information*: Process and model more detailed information using samples to get to population inferences more quickly and efficiently.

- *Destructive testing*: If we need to destroy a product we are inspecting to test its quality, we do not want to destroy the entire population for one analysis.

Therefore, it becomes important to differentiate population statistics (often referred to as *parameters*) from sample statistics (measurements or descriptions made of a sample). When we write statistical formulas, we generally use Greek symbols for population parameters and Roman characters for sample statistics as in the Symbol Summary below.

Symbol Summary		
Descriptive Statistic	**Symbol for Sample (A piece of the population)**	**Symbol for Population (All data over all time, categories, etc.)**
Mean	$\bar{x}$	μ
Variance	s^2	σ^2
Standard Deviation	s	σ
Median	$x_{0.5}$	$x_{0.5}$

STATISTICS IN ACTION

Look at the two investment funds below:

<u>MBA Student Fund</u>
Average return over
 10 years = 5%
Median return = 7%
Standard Deviation = 10%

<u>Faculty Fund</u>
Average return over
 10 years = 5%
Median return = 2%
Standard Deviation = 1%

In which fund would you invest? Note that the average returns over the past ten years are the same; does that mean that the funds are equally good investments? Not at all—don't consider just the average. Notice that the median return is higher for the student fund. Perhaps a bad year or two has pulled down the average return while the median return has stayed relatively high.

The opposite for true for the faculty fund. The mean is higher than the median. This may mean that a very good year or two has pulled up the average but left the median (a lowly 2 percent return) relatively unchanged.

It's still not clear which is the better investment. Maybe we should look at the volatility of the returns or "risk" of each fund (as measured by volatility or variability from the average return). This may help us decide: the faculty fund has only a 1 percent standard deviation (or risk) as compared to 10 percent for the student fund.

If we like steady, predictable returns, we want to pick the less volatile faculty fund (even though a good year may have affected the average return quite a bit). But if we are looking for higher returns—and we are willing to assume the higher risk that comes with them—perhaps the student fund is a better choice.

TEST YOURSELF

Look at the data below on student expenditures. These data are student expenditures per capita for every state in the United States.

State	Expenditure Per Student	State	Expenditure Per Student
NJ	$12,428.71	SC	$7,988.55
NY	$12,087.10	WA	$7,825.26
CT	$11,530.56	TX	$7,799.66
AK	$10,395.06	IA	$7,799.49
DE	$10,242.85	MO	$7,601.18
VT	$9,791.73	CO	$7,561.11
MA	$9,758.17	NV	$7,540.11
MI	$9,706.44	FL	$7,539.73
RI	$9,604.36	NC	$7,480.77
PA	$9,436.55	HI	$7,421.80

Continued

Continued

State	Expenditure Per Student	State	Expenditure Per Student
WI	$9,343.26	KS	$7,412.11
MD	$9,248.83	SD	$7,333.20
MN	$9,138.28	NM	$7,309.57
ME	$9,004.43	MT	$7,182.06
IL	$8,989.23	AL	$6,744.91
OH	$8,732.32	TN	$6,711.61
WY	$8,608.02	ND	$6,700.84
IN	$8,544.66	LA	$6,614.54
OR	$8,328.51	AZ	$6,595.01
VA	$8,298.51	OK	$6,491.74
CA	$8,167.40	KY	$6,403.51
WV	$8,162.72	ID	$6,257.05
NE	$8,157.35	AR	$6,117.58
NH	$8,107.08	MS	$5,669.75
GA	$8,086.15	UT	$5,571.30

1. Why are the data presented as expenditures per student and not as total, statewide numbers?

2. Describe the data in terms of the basic descriptive statistics (mean, median, and so on). Are the data normally distributed? Why or why not?

3. Create a histogram of the data. Describe the histogram. Are there any outliers? Which states/expenditures appear to be outliers?

4. What bin size did you choose for your histogram and why? Can you compare histograms of different bin sizes?

KEY POINTS TO REMEMBER

In this chapter, we have examined some basic descriptive statistics—in both number and chart form—that are commonly used to represent a great deal of data succinctly:

- Central tendency
  - *Mean*: The sum of all the scores divided by the number of scores
  - *Median*: The actual middle value in an odd number of data values or the mean of the two middle values in an even number of data points
  - *Mode*: The most frequently occurring value
- Variability
  - *Variance*: The measure of statistical dispersion in a dataset in units of data squared
  - *Standard deviation*: The measure of statistical dispersion in a dataset in units of the data
- Geometry
  - *Skewness*: The direction and relative magnitude the mean is pulled and/or the direction the tail of a graphed dataset is pulled
  - *Kurtosis*: The measure of how peaked or "pointy" a data distribution is in a graph. Also a measure of how "fat" the tails of the distribution are.

2

Measuring and Managing Uncertainty

INTRODUCTION

The papers say that there's a 60 percent chance of rain today here in Atlantic City. I guess we'll have to stay in the casino instead of enjoying the beach. But all of the casino games seem so unfair. Can we really win? How long do we need to play to win back our losses (or lose back our winnings)? Perhaps we should just watch television in the hotel instead. Maybe the TV news anchor will explain how eating chocolate may reduce my risk of a heart attack (even though a clever advertisement I heard on the radio says that my risk of a heart attack is just as likely to be determined by my family history as my diet).

Probability is all around us: a small chance of this, a big chance of that. Forty percent chance of snow on Saturday followed by a 20 percent chance on Sunday. So does that mean there's a 60 percent chance of snow this weekend? How do weather forecasters get these numbers, anyway? And the casinos—why do people even go if all the games are "rigged" to make the gambler lose? And those studies we hear about on the evening news—where do those numbers come from? The concepts of likelihood, expectation, payoff, and odds aren't just for gamblers—they're practical tools we can use to assess risks, determine preferred choices, and measure potential net impacts of business decisions. This isn't your high school math teacher's probability.

WHAT'S AHEAD

In this chapter, you'll learn:

- How to put a number or probability on uncertainty
- Simple probability concepts and calculations
- The importance of (and the difference between) mutually exclusive events and independent events

- How to numerically calculate what should happen and compare this "expectation" with what actually happens
- A practical decision-making tool that incorporates all of these calculations and concepts

IN THE REAL WORLD

Your record company is doing quite well—you've just signed a hot young singing sensation, and she's agreed, in principle, to release two albums with your label. Based on market research, there's a 70 percent likelihood that her first album will be a hit, and a hit album can result in $1 million per month in profit. If her first album is a hit, then there's a 90 percent chance her second album will also be a hit. If her first album is unsuccessful, however, the likelihood that her second album will be a hit is cut in half. Note that an album that does not become a hit often loses money—as much as $500,000 per month in profit.

Given this market research, can we figure out how likely it is that both albums will become hits? What about the probability that just the second album will be a hit? Can we calculate how much this two-album deal might be worth to us in terms of profit per month? These results will be important as we negotiate the terms of this two-album deal with the artist and as we determine how broadly to distribute her albums.

THE KEY CONCEPTS

The concept of *probability* helps us measure—and assess the impact of—the likelihood of results or outcomes that are *stochastic*; that is, unknown in advance. For example, when we flip a single coin, we know we'll either get a head or a tail when it lands, but we don't know—before we flip the coin—what the outcome will be. (If we did, we would call these outcomes *deterministic*.)

Because business is full of possible outcomes, decisions, and results—very few of which are known in advance of trying new strategies, implementing new policies, or changing existing operations—we need some tools to allow us to work with—and to measure, quantitatively—the inherent uncertainty in business decision making. In this chapter, we will discuss the following concepts related to uncertainty and how to measure it:

- How to compute probabilities of compound events, such as the likelihood of its raining today *or* tomorrow versus the likelihood of its raining today *and* tomorrow

- How to measure expectations—or what should happen—and compare them to what actually happens

- A simple yet powerful tool called *probability trees* that can be used (in certain circumstances) to map out probabilities, calculate them, and assess expectation

How Can We Measure Uncertainty?

Though probability doesn't seem like it belongs with statistics, understanding how to measure uncertainty—and then to reduce it, if possible—is a critical business skill. Few business processes, plans, or functions have predetermined outcomes. Thus, knowing how to measure and compute probabilities is helpful for creating better strategies—and better contingency plans.

Let's start our discussion with the classic coin-flipping example. Two outcomes are possible—heads or tails—but we don't know which one we'll get before we flip the coin. The likelihood, or *probability*, that we will get a head is the same as the probability of getting a tail. Thus, we have a 50 percent chance of the coin's landing heads and a 50 percent chance of the coin's landing tails.

But if we flip the coin only once, does this mean we'll get half of a head and half of a tail? This is impossible, of course. Let's look at a simple chart that shows the percentage of one outcome—heads, in this case—as we flip this coin over and over again. Note the x-axis is the number of flips—starting with one flip—and the y-axis is the percentage of flips that results in heads. As we can see, the first flip must have resulted in tails because the percentage of heads on the first flip is zero.

Example: Coin Toss

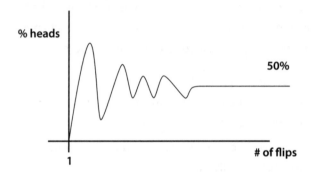

A few clarifications will be helpful, here. The *experiment* we are conducting is flipping a coin over and over again and monitoring the number of heads we get as a percentage of the total number of coin flips. The outcome—or *event*—we are measuring is getting heads. Note a few key concepts that we can determine from this simple picture:

- Probability is a long-run, theoretical concept. Although we could get several tails with the first few flips, in the long run, we would expect to get about 50 percent of the flips recorded as heads.
- Probability (in our examples) is the result of this long-run convergence. In the short run—as in a casino—we could see streaks that might lead us to believe this coin isn't fair. However, flipped enough times, this coin will give us, over the long run, 50 percent heads (and thus 50 percent tails).

This chart also illustrates the simple fact that if we repeat an experiment a large number of times, we should see some convergence or "stability" in the percentage of times an outcome occurs. This is often referred to as the *law of large numbers*. Although you might get on a winning streak at the casino, in the long run, with enough hands of blackjack or rolls of the craps dice, you should expect losses.

Now, we can distinguish what does happen from what should happen. In other words, the connection between probability and statistics is the following: Data (or outcomes) tell us *what actually happened*; for instance, we got four tails and two heads when we flipped a coin six times. Probability, on the other hand, tell us *what should happen*; we should get three heads and three tails when flip a coin six times (though not necessarily in that order).

Three different definitions of probability are important for us to understand. Note that we can assign probabilities that events will happen based on several qualitative and quantitative ways:

Three probability definitions

1. *Subjective*: "You tell me," or an educated guess or estimate of the likelihood of an outcome. For example, you may think there is a 30 percent chance of rain today, but I may think the probability of rain is closer to 50 percent. These are both subjective probabilities since they are based on nothing more than our intuition and/or experience.

    *   Most common form of probability in business and policymaking.

    *   What is the probability our product will be successful in the market?

2. *Relative frequency:* These come from histograms. For example, if 10 students out of 50 in a class received A grades, then there is a 20 percent probability (10/50) that any randomly selected student from the class received an A.

3. *Classical:* This classical definition, which is very similar to the relative frequency definition, is one on which we will focus in this chapter. It can be expressed by the following equation:

$$\frac{\text{Number of favorable outcomes (in the event)}}{\text{Number of all possible outcomes}} = \frac{\text{Probability that the}}{\text{event will occur}}$$

Using this classical definition of probability, how do we numerically compute a likelihood?

1. Define the experiment. What are you doing to create outcomes (e.g., flipping a coin)?

2. List all possible outcomes. With a coin, we'll get either heads or tails.

3. Determine probabilities of all outcomes from Step 2. If the coin is fair, the probability of a head will be 50 percent, as will the probability of tails.

4. Determine which event(s) we are interested in. Let's observe the number (or percentage) of heads that we get.

5. The sum of the probabilities of the event(s) you are interested in equals the probability that the event(s) will occur.

This process sounds easy, but it definitely gets complicated. For example, instead of flipping 1 coin, let's flip 100 coins at once. Can you list all the possible outcomes? This would take a lot of work—and a lot of time! Thus, let's introduce some language and symbols to help us succinctly describe probabilities, outcomes, and events.

Let's define outcome (or event) A, for example, to represent the outcome of getting heads when flipping a coin once. The abbreviation $P(A)$ denotes the probability that event A occurs. In a coin flip: $P(A) = 50\%$.

Note that all probabilities have three very important properties:

1. Any and every probability must be between zero and one (or 0 percent and 100 percent), inclusive.

   • A probability of zero is deterministic (i.e., the event will not happen).

   • A probability of one is also deterministic (i.e., the event will happen).

2. The sum of the probabilities of all possible outcomes equals one—always!

3. A *complement* probability of an event, A, for example, is $1 - P(A)$. That is, if $P(A)$ is 20 percent, then the complement probability of A is $1 - 20$ percent, or 80 percent. This property is often helpful if you want to find the probability of an event when all you know are the probabilities of *all other* possible events. (Note that the complement outcome or event of A is often denoted A^C.)

Simple Probability Concepts: Compound Events

There are two types of compound events.

1. Union probabilities, also called *or* probabilities

2. Intersection probabilities, also called *and* probabilities

For example, let's consider the experiment of rolling one standard six-sided die. We will define two (compound) events:

1. Event A: Rolling a 4 or higher $(4, 5, 6)$
2. Event B: Rolling an odd number $(1, 3, 5)$

Using the terms introduced earlier, we can define two compound events:

1. *Union* = (A or B) = (Rolling a 4 or higher *or* rolling an odd number)
2. *Intersection* = (A and B) = (Rolling a 4 or higher *and* rolling an odd number)

These two compound events—and thus their probabilities—are different. An easy way to think about the difference is to consider meeting a friend in New York City. You could tell your friend to meet you at 57th Street *or* 5th Avenue—but how would your friend know where you will be? Or you could agree to meet your friend at 57th Street *and* 5th Avenue. Note that the union (*or*) has a lot of possible outcomes whereas the intersection (*and*) specifies an exact place. Thus, these events are not the same. An intersection probability is likely smaller than a union probability.

Unions A union probability can be expressed by P(A or B), which expresses the probability that event A or event B (or both A and B) will occur. An easy way to show how to calculate this probability is through the use of a Venn diagram. Below, the circle on the left contains the outcomes of Event A = rolling a 4 or higher. The circle on the right comprises the outcomes from Event B = rolling an odd number. The rectangle that contains all possible outcomes is called the *sample space.*

Note that the outcome of 2, which is neither 4 or higher nor odd, is not contained in either circle but is still a possible outcome in the sample space. The outcome of 5, which is both higher than 4 and an odd number, occurs in both events.

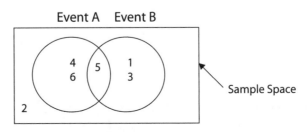

Looking at this picture, we should be able to compute the union probability:

P(4 or higher or odd number) = P(A) + P(B) – P(A and B) =

$\frac{3}{6} + \frac{3}{6} - \frac{1}{6} = \frac{5}{6}$ →*Notice that we must subtract the overlap or intersection outcome—in this case, rolling a 5—so it's not counted twice.*

In general, P (A or B) = P(A) + P(B) – P(A and B).

Marginal Probabilities   Joint Probability = Overlap

A Special Case: Unions with No Overlap

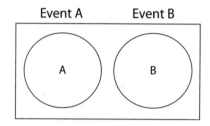

Recall that in general, P (A or B) = P(A) + P(B) – P(A and B).

In some special cases, P (A or B) = P(A) + P(B). There is no intersection (overlap), thus P(A and B) = 0. In this case, events A and B are said to be *mutually exclusive.*

When outcomes don't overlap and represent the entire sample space, we refer to these as MECE ("me-see") events, or *mutually exclusive and collectively exhaustive.* Such events are also referred to as *complementary,* because the probability of one of the events is simply one minus the probability of the other:

MECE: Mutually Exclusive and Collectively Exhaustive: **All outcomes represented in sample space with none of them overlapping**

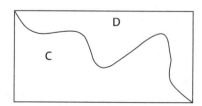

Note that unions have a general case and a special case (mutually exclusive events).

Conditional probabilities A conditional probability is written as P(B|A), or the probability of event B occurring given that (or *if*) A has already occurred. We need to define these types of probabilities before we can define joint or intersection probabilities [e.g. P(A and B)].

Assume Event A is that you have your MBA degree, and that Event B is that you get a higher salary upon graduation. We can express the conditional probability, P(B|A), as the probability of getting a higher salary if (or given that) you have an MBA degree. Pictorially, we can draw this as shown below. Note that Event A, having your MBA, has already happened. Event B, getting a higher salary, may be about to happen.

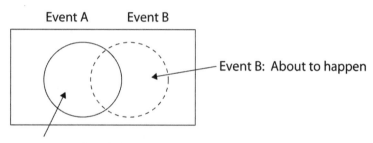

Now we must determine the probability of getting this higher salary if you have your MBA.

It should be clear that this conditional probability is not the same as the intersection probability, P(A and B) where, people have both MBAs *and* higher salaries. This is not the same as the conditional probability we seek!

Rather, we want to find the ratio of those with MBAs *and* higher salaries to those with MBAs—the intersection—but only as a fraction of those with the condition we stated; that is, only those with MBAs. Thus, the conditional probability will be the ratio of those with both MBAs and higher salaries as a proportion of those only with MBAs. Formulaically, we see that

$$P(B|A) = \frac{P(A \text{ and } B)}{P(A)} = \frac{\text{Joint Probability}}{\text{Prior Probability}}$$

Conditional probabilities have a *reduced sample space*—we care only about results based on what has already happened, nothing else!

From this formula, we can now derive a general formula for intersection probabilities. If we cross multiply, we see that $P(A \text{ and } B) = P(B|A) \times P(A)$, or the joint probability is simply the product of the conditional and prior probabilities.

Another note of caution—order matters with conditional probabilities. Order *does not* matter with unions or intersections:

$P(A \text{ or } B)\quad = P(B \text{ or } A)$

$P(A \text{ and } B) = P(B \text{ and } A)$

$P(B|A)\qquad\; \neq P(A|B)\qquad \leftarrow$ order of symbols matters!

Special Case: Events where the condition (or prior) doesn't matter What if the conditional probability—for example, the probability that you get a higher salary given that you have your MBA—were the same as just the probability of getting a higher salary? That is, what if $P(B|A) = P(B)$?

In this special case, the probability of getting a higher salary doesn't depend in any way on having an MBA. Thus, in this special case where the conditional probability is the same as the marginal probability, event B *does not depend* on event A (the prior). Said differently, having an MBA does not change the probability that you will have a higher salary upon graduation.

In this special case, events A and B are said to be *independent*. But be careful—independence (or dependence) is not the same as lack of causation (or causation). If the events are dependent, this is not to say that having an MBA *caused* you to get a higher salary upon graduation, for example.

> Dependence ≠ Causation

We can test for this property of independence in two (equivalent) ways. If events A and B are independent,

1. $P(B|A) = P(B)$, or
2. $P(A \text{ and } B) = P(B) \times P(A)$.

Either test can be used to check for independence. However, we cannot "see" independence in a Venn diagram.

Now we can compute intersection probabilities.

Intersections In general, $P(A \text{ and } B) = P(B|A) \times P(A)$. But if A and B are independent events, $P(B|A) = P(B)$, and $P(A \text{ and } B) = P(B) \times (A)$.

You'll notice that we need to be aware of conditional probabilities to find the probability of intersections. Fortunately, these are often given in problems. Look for the words *if* or *given*; these are clues to conditional statements.

A quick example will bring together all of these probability calculations. Assume we work for a company and are tracking shopping behavior for one of our products. We have men and women as customers, and our product is packaged in two different colors. We'd like to compute some simple probabilities, and we'd also like to see if there is any association—or dependence—between the shopper's gender and the color of the product's packaging. If there is no dependence, then it shouldn't matter what color packaging we use. However, if there is dependence, then we may want to target different packaging to consumers based on gender. The table below summarizes some purchase results from a recent in-store survey.

	Men	Women	Totals
Blue Packaging	20	5	25
Pink Packaging	10	30	40
Totals	30	35	65

Here we see the following probabilities:

Probability of selecting a male customer $= \frac{30}{65}$

Probability of selecting pink packaging $= \frac{40}{65}$

Probability of selecting a male *or* blue package shopper $= \frac{30+25-20}{65}$

Probability of selecting a male *and* pink package shopper $= \frac{10}{65}$

Probability of selecting a pink package shopper if male $= \frac{10}{30}$

Probability of selecting female shopper if blue package $= \frac{5}{25}$

> - Unless a probability is conditional, the denominator is always total sample space.
>
> - Only with conditionals is the denominator *smaller* than total sample space.

Are sex and package color independent? Let's test them. Does P(Pink|Male) = P(Pink)? If so, these events are *independent*.

$$\frac{10}{30} \neq \frac{40}{65}$$

Because these probabilities are not the same, we conclude that sex and package color are *dependent events* (but not necessarily causal). That is, package color is not proportionally distributed between men and women. Instead, one sex (or both) may prefer one color over another, although we cannot directly conclude that package color, alone, caused this disproportionate selection. Note, too, that we do not need to test all possible combinations to assess independence. If one event is dependent, then all events are dependent.

Try not to confuse mutually exclusive events—a special case relevant to union probabilities—with independent events—a special case relevant to intersection probabilities. They are not the same! You can "see" mutual exclusivity in a Venn diagram. You cannot see independence.

Putting It All Together: Probability Trees

A useful tool for mapping out and computing probabilities is a *probability tree*. Let's use a business example to illustrate it.

Your procurement organization has proposed new buying policies for office supplies, overnight mail, office furniture, and computers. The likelihood that a department will not adopt the policies is 30 percent. If the new policies are implemented, the likelihood of sustained cost savings for the departments that institute them is 80 percent. If the new policies are not adopted, the chance of sustained cost savings is only 40 percent.

We would like to determine the following:

- How likely is it that a department will adopt the new policies and save money?
- If the new policies are implemented, what's the likelihood that the department will save money?
- What's the likelihood that a department will save money (regardless of whether or not it implements these new purchasing policies)?
- Does policy adoption have anything to do with saving money?

A probability tree will help us map out the events and probabilities so we can answer these questions. The key is to understand what is being asked in each question in probability terms and how to get the solutions from the tree.

Probability trees help with decision making. Time moves from left to right, so the order of the events is important. Trees can only be used for MECE events; we have to show every possible outcome, and no two events can overlap.

In our problem, note that adopting (or not adopting) the new procurement policies comes first. Then a department will choose whether to enforce them—thereby saving money—or not—thus not saving any money. To start, let's map out all the possible outcomes.

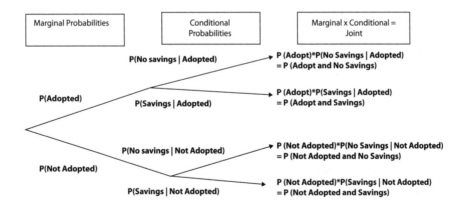

We start on the left with two possible outcomes: either a department adopts these new polices, or it does not. These are the simple *marginal* probabilities, or *priors*, since these events happen first. Then, moving to the right, a department that has adopted these new policies either will or won't end up saving money. The same is true for departments that do not adopt these new procurement policies. Thus, we have *conditional probabilities*. Whether a department saves money may or may not be dependent on whether it adopts the new policies.

Finally, at the far right, we multiply the prior branches of the tree— a marginal times a conditional—to get all possible joint probabilities. Because the events are mutually exclusive, the probabilities at each node— or "corner" in the tree where branches form to the right—add to one (100 percent). Also, because all possible outcomes are represented on the far right, all of these joint probabilities must also add to one (collectively exhaustive). Filling in the numbers from the tree, we see

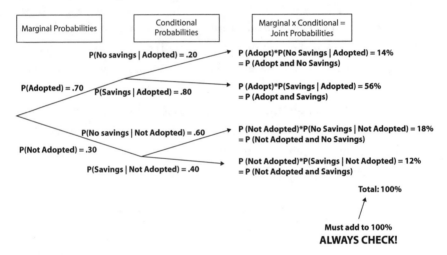

Now let's answer our earlier questions:

1. *How likely is it that a department will adopt the new policies and save money?* This is an *and* intersection probability. This probability is on the far right of the tree where P(Adopt and Savings) = 56%.

2. *If the new policies are adopted, what's the likelihood that the department will save money?* Here, note the *if* in the question. This indicates a conditional probability. In this case, we want P(Savings |Adopted), from the middle of the tree, which is 80 percent.

3. *What's the likelihood that a department will save money (regardless of whether it implements the new purchasing policies)?* This one sounds a bit tricky. All we want to know is P(Savings); that is, the *unconditional*

probability that a department will save money. Note that this probability is not on the tree. Thus, we have to be a bit clever. Take a look at the far right of the tree—where all possible outcomes are listed—and note that only two outcomes exist where a department saves money. First, a department could save money *and* adopt the new policies. Alternatively, a department could save money and *not* adopt the new policies. Adding these together—without worrying about any overlap because we have MECE events—will give us what we need. That is:

P(Savings) = P(Adopted and Savings) or P(Not Adopted and Savings)

This is a union probability, but we don't have to worry about overlap because a department cannot exist in both states (i.e., a department cannot save money and both adopt and not adopt the new policies).

Thus, we simply add these probabilities together to get: 56% + 12% = 68%.

4. *Does policy adoption have anything to do with saving money?* Finally, we are asked to consider whether policy adoption and saving money are independent events. To test this, we need to perform one of the two independence tests mentioned earlier. For example, does P(Savings|Adopt) = P(Savings)? From the tree, we can determine that the left-hand side of this equation is 80 percent. And from the previous question, we can get the right-hand side: 68 percent. Because these two probabilities are unequal, we surmise that policy adoption and savings are *dependent*. However, this does not imply causation; just because a department adopts the new policies does not mean that department will save money. On the contrary, as the tree shows, there is a nonzero probability of adopting the new policies but not saving money (14 percent).

What Does Happen versus What Should Happen: Expectation

Now that we have a tool to calculate probabilities, let's recall the mean statistic. Is there such a thing as an "average" outcome? The probability tree helps us to understand likelihoods, but can we also compute some sort of summarized statistic in terms of the financial impact of these new policies on our various departments?

Yes we can! Just as datasets have means, random variables (which hold the results of stochastic events) have *expectation* or *expected values*. We can think of the average or expected outcome as the long-term idea of what *should happen*. For example, if we flip a coin enough times, we would expect to get 50 percent heads and 50 percent tails. We won't necessarily get these percentages with only a few flips, but what should happen eventually is that we get half heads and half tails.

Like the mean, the expected value is a calculated value. Just as no person in a group has to weigh the average weight of the group, the expected value can be an impossible outcome. For example, flip a coin once. Theoretically, you should get (*expect* to get) 0.5 heads and 0.5 tails. But that's impossible; we'll either get one head or one tail.

Let's review some notation from the previous chapter. Recall the simple formula for the mean of a dataset: add up all the data values and then divide by the number of data values.

$$\mu = \frac{1}{n}\sum x_i = \sum x_i * \frac{1}{n}$$

All data — Datapoint

Probability of Selection $\Longrightarrow$ Each data point has probability 1/n of being selected

Thus, another way to think of the mean of a dataset is that it is the sum of the product of each data value with its probability of being randomly selected. In any dataset with n points, each point has equal probability $(1/n)$ of being selected. Each data point is equally likely, if you will, to be picked at random.

But is this always the case? Can different outcomes have different probabilities of being selected? Absolutely! In our example above, the probability that a department adopts the new policy and saves money is not the same as the probability of a department not adopting the policy and saving money.

Thus, we have different probabilities for different *payoffs* from the different outcomes. Using the formula above, we can define the mean or average payoff, also called the *expectation* or *expected value*.

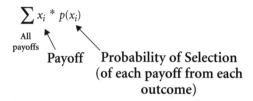

$$\sum_{\substack{\text{All} \\ \text{payoffs}}} x_i * p(x_i)$$

Payoff   Probability of Selection
(of each payoff from each
outcome)

Look closely at this revised formula for expected value—this is nothing more than a *weighted average*, where the weights are simply the different probabilities of the different payoffs (which correspond to different outcomes). That is, we simply add up the products of each and every payoff with its corresponding probability of occurrence. This process effectively weights or proportionally allocates each payoff (from each outcome) based on how likely it is to occur.

An example will help illustrate how to compute an expected value. Let's look at what our firm's CFO can do to departmental budgets depending on whether a department adopts the new policies and saves money.

- If a department adopts the new policy and saves money, then the CFO will allow the department to increase its purchasing budget by 2 percent as a reward for policy adoption and hitting savings targets.
- If a department adopts the new policy but fails to save money, the CFO will penalize the department and cut its purchasing budget by 10 percent.
- If a department fails to adopt the new policy but still manages to save money, the CFO will likely decrease the department's purchasing budget by 5 percent to encourage it to implement the policy next year.
- Finally, if a department fails to adopt the new policy and also fails to save money, the CFO will significantly cut the department's purchasing authority by 15 percent.

Question: What's the net (expected) financial impact (or *payoff*) of these new purchasing policies across all departments?

An easy way to see the expected value computation is to create a *payoff table*. A payoff table allows us to compute the expected value—or weighted average, as stated earlier—of a set of payoffs. Note in the table that we have four possible outcomes (based on the far right of the tree), the probability of each outcome, and the total payoff that each outcome generates (from the CFO's perspective). By multiplying each payoff and its probability, then summing all of these, we get the expected value.

	From Tree	Given Above	
Outcome	P(Outcome)	Payoff	P(Payoff) × Payoff
Adopted and No Savings	14%	+10%	+1.4%
Adopted and Savings	56%	−2%	−1.2%
Not Adopted and No Savings	18%	+15%	+2.7%
Not Adopted and Savings	12%	+5%	+0.6%
Total:	100% (check!)	Financial Impact:	+3.58% (sum of payoffs × their probabilities = expected value!)

From this table, we see that if the CFO implements these rewards and penalties, then the corporation should, on average across all departments, be able to save roughly 3.6 percent in its purchasing budget.

We can use this expected value to help set targets. For example, if departments actually spend about 3.6 percent more than budgeted, then these CFO controls will have made no impact. Thus, in this context, we can see the expected value as a *breakeven point*. Imagine having different customer segments—with probabilities of purchase and the margins from purchase for each segment—in a similar table. You could predict the overall (expected) margin impact of these customers, which could guide your pricing decisions and budgeting on advertisements, in-store promotions, and so on.

STATISTICS IN ACTION

Let's revisit the two-album record deal from the beginning of the chapter. Remember that there's a 70 percent likelihood that our singer's first album will be a hit, and a hit album can result in $1 million per month in profit. If her first album is a hit, then there's a 90 percent chance her second album will also be a hit. If her first album is unsuccessful, however, the likelihood that her second album is a hit is cut in half. Note that an album that does not become a hit often loses money—as much as $500,000 per month in profit. Let's use the probability tree and expected value tools to help us determine the following:

- How likely is it that both albums will become hits?
- What is the probability that just the second album will be a hit?
- Whether we can calculate how much the two-album deal is worth in terms of profit per month?

First, let's put all the probability information on a tree so we can see what's going on.

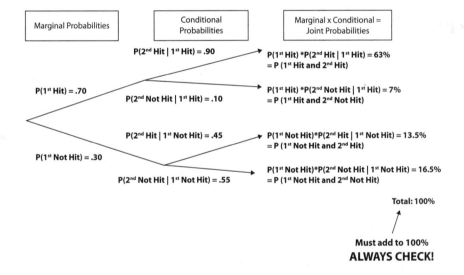

So, how likely is it that both albums will be hits? This is just P(First Hit and Second Hit), which, from the far right of the tree, is 63 percent.

Next, what's the probability of just the second album becoming a hit? We can find this unconditional probability by noting that the second album can be a hit regardless of the first album's status. Adding these two joint probabilities together gives us: 63% + 13.5% = 76.5%. Fascinating—it's actually more probable that the second album will become a hit than the first one! P(First Hit) = 70%. This is likely because even if the first album is not a hit, people will learn about the artist and may be more interested in buying a (hopefully better) second album.

Finally, how much monthly profit, on average, do we expect to make with both of these albums? This requires that we compute the expected value. Let's set up a payoff table from the record company's point of view.

		From Tree	Given in Problem	
Outcome	P(Outcome)	Payoff (per Month Profit)	P(Event) × Payoff
1st hit and 2nd hit	63%	$1 million + $1 million	$1.26 million
1st hit and 2nd not hit	7%	$1 million – $0.5 million	$0.035 million
1st not hit and 2nd hit	13.5%	–$0.5 million + $1 million	$0.0675 million
1st not hit and 2nd not hit	16.5%	–$0.5 million –$0.5 million	–$0.165 million
Total:	100% (check!)	Financial Impact:	+$1.1975 million (sum of payoffs × their probabilities = expected value!)

You'll recall that a hit album results in $1 million per month in profit, while an album that is not a hit can result in a loss of up to $500,000 (or –$0.5 million in profit) per month. Putting all the payoffs and probabilities into the payoff table shows us that we should expect to make roughly $1.2 million in profit from these two albums. Thus, we should not sign a contract with the new artist for more than this amount—or we may lose money!

TEST YOURSELF

Fed up with the proliferation of poorly made U.S. vehicles on the market, you decide you are only going to sell European small cars. Your car dealership sells five vehicles, the VW Golf, Saab 92X, BMW Z4 Roadster, Skoda Octavia, and the Lada Niva.

After 12 months in business, you discover that only 10 percent of people who walk through your doors will be buyers. Of those who buy vehicles, the breakdown of vehicle purchases is as follows:

VW Golf	15%
Saab 92X	15%
BMW Z4	20%
Skoda Octavia	10%
Lada Niva	40%

1. What is the probability that a potential customer will buy a BMW Z4? A Skoda?

2. If in June, 200 people walk through the doors of your dealership, how many will buy a Lada Niva?

   After all selling expenses are removed, you make the following profits from the sale of each vehicle type:

VW Golf	$1,000
Saab 92X	$2,000
BMW Z4	$12,000
Skoda Octavia	$1,200
Lada Niva	$400

3. What is the probability that a customer will walk through the door and provide you with at least a $1,000 profit?

4. If 400 people walk through the door in a month, what is your total expected profit?

5. Based on the figures, should you continue selling your favorite car, the Lada Niva? Why or why not?

6. You decide to stop selling BMWs due to competition from other local dealers. If the 20 percent share of BMW sales is evenly reallocated among the other vehicles (that is, VW now makes up 20 percent of your sales, Saab 92X 20 percent, Skoda 15 percent, and Lada Niva 45 percent), what is your new expected profit if 400 people walk through your doors in a month ? Are you better or worse off? Why? (Note that the behavior of your customers does not change— 10 percent of all shoppers make a purchase.)

KEY POINTS TO REMEMBER

Basic Probability Rules

- Probabilities of any outcome(s) must be between 0 and 1 (inclusive).
- The sum of probabilities of all possible outcomes must equal 1 (exactly!).

Compound Events

- Union (*or*) probabilities: The sum of the marginals less the overlap (or intersection) probability
- Special case for unions: Mutually exclusive events—no overlap! Probability simplifies to just the sum of the marginals.
- Intersection (*and*) probabilities: The product of the conditional probability and the prior probability
- Special case for intersections: Independent events. Probability simplifies because conditional probability is simply the marginal. Joint probability here is just the product of the marginals.

Probability Trees

- Easy way to map out MECE—mutually exclusive and collectively exhaustive—events. First come the marginals, then the conditionals, and finally the joints or intersections (which are just the marginals times the conditionals).
- Don't forget that all the joint probabilities (on the far right) must add to 1.

Expected Value

- Expected value is the "mean payoff." Expected value is to probability and payoff as mean (or average value) is to a dataset. It's the central tendency—or expected—payoff, which is derived by looking at the weighted average of all possible payoffs that all outcomes produce.
- A payoff table can help us determine expected values. Be sure to keep the payoffs in a specific point of view; otherwise, signs can be erroneous (+/−).

The (Not So) Normal Distribution

INTRODUCTION

In many business applications, it is helpful to know how data *behave*—that is, how data are distributed. In the first chapter, we learned that certain distributions of data have some specific properties. In a *normal distribution*, skewness is zero, kurtosis is three, and the mean, median, and mode are all equal.

Yet many students and professionals who have taken past data analysis courses seem to believe that because the Gaussian, or *bell curve*, distribution is referred to as "normal," most data are distributed that way. This is simply not true—most datasets found in business are skewed and do not follow the normal distribution. Still, a normal distribution is a useful tool to *approximate* a distribution of data.

This chapter describes the normal distribution, its properties, and how to use it to solve probability problems.

WHAT'S AHEAD

In this chapter, you'll learn:
- Properties of normally distributed data
- How to use the normal distribution, with assumptions in place, to solve probability problems

- How to measure the distances of data points from the mean in units of standard deviation
- How to use normal tables to find areas under normal distributions, then use these to solve business problems

IN THE REAL WORLD

You're in charge of financial analyst training at your investment bank. You have to make sure analysts have all the necessary skills before they are put to work on deals. Thus, you have instituted minimum passing scores on the proficiency tests that analysts in your training programs will take on subjects like financial accounting, spreadsheet skills, bond math, and valuation techniques.

For example, you have a policy that no more than 5 percent of a training class can fail a test of valuation methods. If this happens, then the entire group must be retrained (and retested) to ensure competence in valuation techniques and tools. How do you determine if your current group of analysts meets this requirement? And if they do not, what other options do you have other than the long and expensive process of retraining/retesting the entire class?

THE KEY CONCEPTS

How Data Behave: Common Myths and Perceptions

Below is a picture of a normal distribution of data as represented by a histogram. The horizontal x-axis represents the data values—for example, test scores, cases of soda sold, credit card balances—and the y-axis represents the frequency. Note that the most frequent value (the mode) is also the middle value (the median) and the average value (the mean). Many refer to this distribution as a *bell curve* because of its shape.

This distribution has no skewness—it is symmetric about the median —and it has a kurtosis equal to three. (Recall that a higher kurtosis than this indicates a more "peaked" distribution, or leptokurtic data. A lower kurtosis lower than this value—indicating a "flatter" distribution—represents a platykurtic distribution.)

The normal distribution

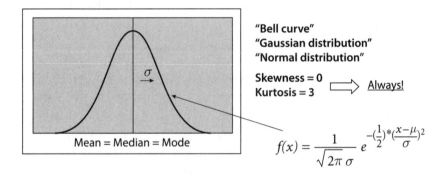

"Bell curve"
"Gaussian distribution"
"Normal distribution"

Skewness = 0
Kurtosis = 3 $\Longrightarrow$ Always!

Mean = Median = Mode

$$f(x) = \frac{1}{\sqrt{2\pi}\,\sigma}\, e^{-(\frac{1}{2})*(\frac{x-\mu}{\sigma})^2}$$

This curve, which is the *relative frequency distribution* of the data, can also be represented by the very complicated formula above. The height of the curve, represented by $f(x)$, is given by an equation with two inputs: the mean, μ, and the standard deviation, σ. Thus, if we know the mean and standard deviation of the data, then we can find out the height of the normal distribution at any data value along the x-axis. (Note that this formula also includes π, the ratio of the circumference of a circle to its diameter, as well as e, the base of the natural logarithm. Don't worry if you don't know or remember these; they're not central to our discussion.)

But what does this tell us? Recall that the height of the curve of a histogram gives us the frequency of that value in the dataset. Therefore, the total area under the normal distribution—or under any histogram—is 100 percent, or all of the data in the dataset. Also, remember that the sum of the probabilities of all possible outcomes also must equal 100 percent. Thus, we can think of this normal distribution as either a frequency distribution—of test scores, for example—or as a histogram of outcomes. The height of the curve at a particular x-value gives us the number of times (or frequency) that a specific x-value appears in the dataset. Notice that the mean (which is also the mode and median) is most likely to be picked from a dataset that is normally distributed (or approximately normal) because the curve is the tallest at this point.

The characteristics of the normal distribution are often discussed in classrooms and boardrooms. You might think it's common, for example, that

- most data are normally distributed;
- if we take a large enough random sample, our resulting data will be normally distributed;
- opinion poll results are often normally distributed; and
- 95 percent of all data points in a dataset lie within two standard deviations of the mean. That is, if we create the range defined by two standard deviations to the left of the mean to two standard deviations to the right of the mean, 95 percent of any dataset's values will lie in this range.

These are all *common myths*! And more often than not, none of these characteristics defines data that you come across in business.

As you can see from histograms and descriptive statistics, most data (or populations) are *not* normally distributed. Large random samples don't magically create normally distributed datasets. Just because you ask 1,000 people for their height does not mean the surveyed heights will be in the shape of a bell curve when plotted on a histogram. This is also true for stock prices—they're not normally distributed. Opinion polls—often binary choices such as liking/not liking a political candidate—also do not create bell-shaped data. While it's true that some nonnormal distributions have 95 percent of values within two standard deviations of the mean, this is generally not the case.

"Normal" Isn't Very Normal

Although the French mathematician, de Moivre, stated that data with a bell-shaped look appeared "normal" to him, this is one of the most common misnomers in all of statistics. Data rarely follow normal distributions, but due to misused statistical language, it becomes easy for this misconception to take hold. We will see this normal distribution throughout the remainder of this text, but in general, we will not depend on *data* being normally distributed because this is usually not the case. We need to learn how to work with normal distributions, though, to develop some more advanced concepts in the next chapter related to sampling.

For now, remember the following:

- Data sets are rarely normally distributed; most are skewed in some way or are more or less kurtotic than normal distributions.
- Large random samples do not result in or "create" bell-shaped datasets of the results/responses.
- In general, there is no guarantee of 95 percent of a dataset being within two standard deviations of the mean. Although many distributions can be created with 95 percent of the data within two standard deviations of the mean, only the normal distribution is guaranteed to have this property. Further, roughly 68 percent of the data in a normal distribution will be within one standard deviation of the mean, and approximately 99 percent of the data will lie within three standard deviations of the mean.

You must be able to prove or assume explicitly that a dataset is normally distributed before using *any* of the properties of normal distributions discussed in this chapter.

Using the Assumption of Normality to Solve Probability Problems

If we assume a dataset—or an entire population of data—is normally distributed, we can use properties of normal distributions to solve probability problems. This tool is particularly important if we want to assess topics such as expected failure rate of a manufacturing process, how often demand for a given product will exceed some target, and, in our example below, customer satisfaction ratings. But it cannot be stressed enough: If a population is not approximately normally distributed—or you have no basis for assuming this fact—then normal distributions *will not help you*! Data can follow a number of known distributions—Poisson, hypergeometric, exponential, Erlang—or no known distribution at all. Always be careful to note your assumptions when you assume a specific distribution for data.

Example: Customer satisfaction ratings Let's examine our customer satisfaction scores from the past year. We've obtained these data through surveys sent to every customer, and we received a perfect response rate; that is, every customer responded. Let's assume that this population of customer satisfaction scores is normally distributed and that we ascertain the following descriptive statistics (using a data analysis tool like Excel):

$\mu = 72$, the average customer satisfaction rating (on a continuous scale from 1 to 100)

$\sigma = 12$, standard deviation of all satisfaction scores

We must address four questions about our customer satisfaction scores:

1. What is the probability of getting a satisfaction score lower than 84?

2. How many customers gave us satisfaction scores higher than 78?

3. What percentage of customers' scores is higher than 70?

4. What is the 90th percentile of our customer satisfaction scores?

Remember rule #1: Graph the data! A picture of the problem always helps.

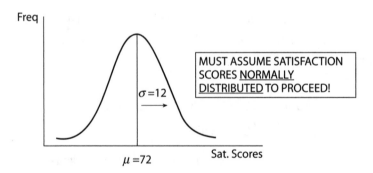

If our population of satisfaction scores is distributed as pictured above, then we can draw the solution to our first question as follows:

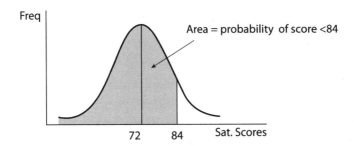

Note here that if we want the probability of getting a score less than 84, then this probability is represented as the area under the curve (or histogram) to the left of 84. (For our example, we will interpret the probability of less than 84 to be the same as the probability of less than or equal to 84.)

If you've taken calculus, then you may recognize that the way to find this area is to integrate the function that the curve represents from the far left-hand side of the curve up to the score of 84. This integral gives us the (limit of the) sum of the areas of several rectangles with height equal to the y-value of the function ($f(x)$) and with width equal to a very small change in x (or dx).

$$\text{Area} = \int_{-\infty}^{84} \frac{1}{\sqrt{2\pi(12)}}\, e^{-(\frac{1}{2})*(\frac{x-72}{12})^2}\, dx$$

$$= \text{Sum of base * height of rectangles up to } x = 84$$

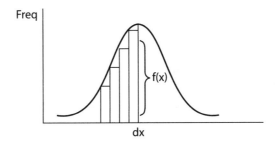

This looks complicated! But don't despair—you don't have to know calculus, and you don't have to use that formula. The good news is that we have tables to help us approximate the values of this integral. An easy and often-used way to determine unknown areas under normal curves, these tables can help us solve this and many other problems. You'll find these tables of normal areas in Appendix A.

Measuring Distance from the Mean in Units of Standard Deviation with Z-Scores and Standard Normal Distribution Tables

Do we need a table showing areas under normal curves with every possible mean and standard deviation? Do we need a particular table for this problem showing areas under a specific normal distribution with mean of 72 and standard deviation of 12? Not at all—in fact, if we have just one table with areas under one specific normal distribution with known areas, then we can translate any normal distribution problem/histogram into this distribution.

This technique is referred to as *normalizing* or *standardizing* the dataset or creating *z-scores*. As we've discovered, we cannot simply force a dataset to follow a bell-curve distribution. Thus, we're not really turning our dataset into a normal distribution by "standardizing" it—we're just translating a distribution with unknown areas into one with areas we can measure.

A Couple of Points about Standardizing a Dataset

- Standardizing a dataset doesn't make data normal. *This is why we have explicitly assumed our population of data to be normal!*

- In terms of creating z-scores—or standardized data—simply take every data point and create its equivalent z-score:

$$\text{Z-score of the value to convert} = \frac{\text{Value to convert} - \text{Mean of values to convert}}{\text{Standard deviation of values to convert}}$$

Symbolically this formula looks like:

$$Z_x = \frac{x - \mu_x}{\sigma_x}$$

But what does z-scoring or standardizing a dataset do? Let's look at the first question to find out.

Question One: What is the probability of getting a customer satisfaction score lower than 84?

Recall our picture of the problem:

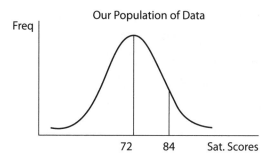

Because we don't know how to compute the area under this curve to the left of 84, we need a table to help us. But remember, we don't have a specific table with areas under normal curves with our specific mean and standard deviation. In Appendix A, however, we do have tables for a special normal distribution—one with mean of 0 and standard deviation of 1. This is the so-called *standard normal distribution*, and it is used as the benchmark distribution for computing areas under any normal distribution. The key here is to translate our distribution—with mean of 72 and standard deviation of 12—to the standard normal distribution. Then, we can compute the area we are looking for, and we're done!

The trick to the translation is the z-score formula; this is how we convert our picture of the problem, above, to one where we can actually find an area. The standard normal distribution—remember, mean is 0 and standard deviation is 1—has an x-axis in units of z-scores. This is very helpful to us.

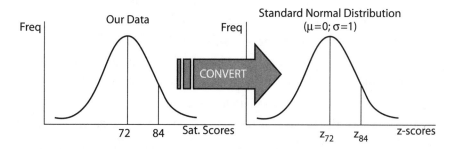

You will notice:

- The areas under the two distributions are not equal; the distribution on the left is much wider (standard deviation = 12) than the one on the right. Thus, it would take more ink to color, for example, the left-hand area than it would the right-hand area.
- However, the total areas are the same in terms of percentage (100 percent).
- And the areas are *proportionally* equal.
- If we can find the proper z-score on the right-hand chart that corresponds to the customer satisfaction score of 84 on the left, then the areas will be proportionally equal (as a fraction of 100 percent).

Let's compute the z-score for 72. Note that the z-score for the mean on the left (72) is zero—or the mean on the right. Translating 72 from one distribution to the other gives us a z-score of 0, the mean of the standard normal distribution.

Now, let's compute the z-score for a customer satisfaction score of 84.

$$Z_x = \frac{x - \mu_x}{\sigma_x}$$

$$Z_{84} = \frac{84 - 72}{12} = +1$$

But what does a z-score of 1 really mean? Very simply, *a z-score is the (unitless) number of standard deviations* that a data value is away from the mean. The positive or negative value of the z-score tells us if the value is higher or lower than the mean. In our problem, the standard deviation is 12, and 84 is 12 more than 72, so our z-score is positive 1. The fraction/formula above shows the numerator as the distance a data point is from the mean, and the denominator is just the standard deviation. Now we can use the two reference tables in Appendix A to find the area we're seeking. The first table of z-scores in the appendix shows areas under the standard normal curve from the far left tail up to z-scores with positive values (to the right of the mean). The second table of z-scores shows areas from the far left tail up to z-scores with negative values (to the left of the mean).

So how do we use these tables to find the area in question?

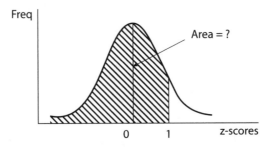

We want to measure the area from the far left to the z-score of 1. Because this is a positive z-score (to the right of the mean), we use Table A.1 to look up this area. The first column represents the first decimal place of the z-score. The remaining columns across the page represent the second decimal point of the z-score. Thus, to look up the area to the left of z-score = 1.00, we do the following.

TABLE A. Standard normal probabilities

Z	0	.01	.02	.03	.04	.05	.06	.07	.08	.09
0.0	.5000	.5040	.5080	.5120	.5160	.5199	.5239	.5279	.5319	.5359
0.1	.5398	.5438	.5478	.5317	.5587	.5596	.5636	.5675	.5714	.5753
0.2	.5793	.5832	.5871	.5910	.5948	.5987	.6026	.6064	.6103	.6141
0.3	.6179	.6217	.6255	.6293	.6331	.6368	.6406	.6443	.6480	.6517
0.4	.6554	.6591	.6628	.6664	.6700	.6736	.6772	.6808	.6844	.6879
0.5	.6915	.6950	.6983	.7019	.7054	.7088	.7123	.7157	.7190	.7224
0.6	.7257	.7291	.7324	.7357	.7389	.7422	.7454	.7486	.7519	.7549
0.7	.7580	.7611	.7642	.7673	.7704	.7734	.7764	.7794	.7823	.7852
0.8	.7881	.7910	.7939	.7967	.7995	.8023	.8051	.8078	.8106	.8133
0.9	.8159	.8186	.8212	.8238	.8264	.8289	.8315	.8340	.8365	.8389
1.0	.8413	.8438	.8461	.8485	.8308	.8531	.8554	.8577	.8599	.8621

First decimal: 1.0   Second decimal: 1.00

From the table, we see that under the standard normal distribution, the area to the left of z-score 1.00 is 0.8413, or 84.13 percent. Because this area is proportionally equal to the area highlighted in our original histogram, we now know that we have an 84.13 percent probability of getting a satisfaction score from a customer less than 84. (It is entirely coincidental in this problem that the score in the problem and the area we are seeking are both approximately 84—this will rarely be the case.)

Some Problem-Solving Tips

- Remember that 50 percent of the area (or probability) under the curve is to the left of the mean, and 50 percent is to the right (there is symmetry—no skewness).

- Look at the graph to make sure that numerical answers make sense visually. In the problem above, we would expect an area greater than 50 percent given where the score of 84 was located relative to the mean.

- Make sure the sign of the z-score makes sense; if the value you are converting is to the left of the mean, then the z-score must be negative.

- Make sure you use the correct table to compute the area.

- Most importantly: Don't forget to state your assumptions explicitly!

Let's move on to the second question.

Question Two: How many customers gave us satisfaction scores of more than 78? First, let's state our assumption: satisfaction scores are normally distributed. Now, let's draw a picture of the problem.

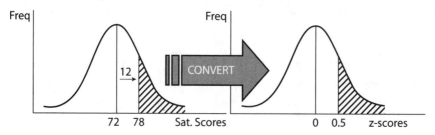

You can see that the area we want is in the right-hand tail of the distribution. Based on our tables, we already know that we will *not* be able to read this area directly off the table (yet). Note that the satisfaction score of 78 translates to a z-score of 0.5; that is, 78 is 0.5 standard deviations to the right of the mean.

$$Z_{78} = \frac{78-72}{12} = .5 \quad \leftarrow \textbf{Half of a standard deviation to the right of the mean}$$

Using the positive z-score table, we see that the area up to a z-score of 0.5 is:

$$Z_{78} = 0.5 \rightarrow \text{Area from left up to z-score} = 0.5 \text{ is } 0.6915$$

But this is the area up to 78. We need the area greater than (to the right of) 78 or a z-score of 0.5. A little graphical arithmetic may help here. Because the total area under the curve is 1 (or 100 percent), we can deduce this right-tail area by subtraction.

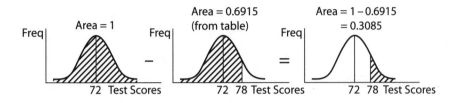

Thus, the number of customers—in percentage terms—who gave us satisfaction ratings higher than 78 equals 30.85 percent. If we knew our total number of customers, we could answer this question with a specific number (but again, only under the assumption that scores follow a normal distribution).

Question Three: What proportion of the customers gave us scores higher than 70? First, we state our assumption: scores are normally distributed. Next, we draw a picture of the problem.

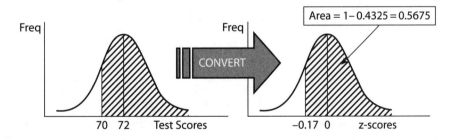

$$Z_{70} = \frac{70-72}{12} = -0.17$$

The z-score is negative because it is to the left of the mean on the standard normal curve. On the negative z-table, Table A.2, find the area to the left of −0.17, which is equal to 0.4325. Next, subtract that area from 1 to get the area to the right of a score of 20 (or to the right of z-score equal to −0.17): 0.5675, or 56.75 percent.

Assuming that these satisfaction scores are normally distributed, 56.75 percent of the population gave us satisfaction scores greater than 70.

Question Four: What is the 90th percentile of our customer satisfaction scores? First, our explicit assumption: scores are normally distributed. Now in this problem, instead of being asked for a probability, we are asked for an actual satisfaction score: the 90th percentile of scores. This means that 90 percent of scores are below it and 10 percent of scores are above it. As usual, drawing a picture of this problem will help.

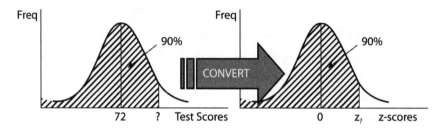

In this problem, we know the area (90 percent), the mean, and the standard deviation. What we do not know is the value—or satisfaction score—that gives us this area. To solve for this, we set up the same conversion process to z-scores, but we solve for a different quantity or value we wish to convert. We start with the z-score formula.

$$Z_? = \frac{? - 72}{12}$$

It looks like we have two unknowns—the z-score and the value to convert. But we know the area needed to create the z-score, which is equal to 0.9. So look for 0.9 inside the positive z-score table (Table A) because the 90th percentile will be to the right of the mean (which equals the median or 50th percentile). We're working with our table "from the inside out," looking for an area first and then to the corresponding column to find the z-score.

TABLE A. Standard normal probabilities

z	0	.01	.02	.03	.04	.05	.06	.07	.08	.09
0.0	.5000	.5040	.5080	.5120	.5160	.5199	.5239	.5279	.5319	.5359
0.1	.5398	.5438	.5478	.5317	.5587	.5596	.5636	.5675	.5714	.5753
0.2	.5793	.5832	.5871	.5910	.5948	.5987	.6026	.6064	.6103	.6141
0.3	.6179	.6217	.6255	.6293	.6331	.6368	.6406	.6443	.6480	.6517
0.4	.6554	.6591	.6628	.6664	.6700	.6736	.6772	.6808	.6844	.6879
0.5	.6915	.6950	.6983	.7019	.7054	.7088	.7123	.7157	.7190	.7224
0.6	.7257	.7291	.7324	.7357	.7389	.7422	.7454	.7486	.7519	.7549
0.7	.7580	.7611	.7642	.7673	.7704	.7734	.7764	.7794	.7823	.7852
0.8	.7881	.7910	.7939	.7967	.7995	.8023	.8051	.8078	.8106	.8133
0.9	.8159	.8186	.8212	.8238	.8264	.8289	.8315	.8340	.8365	.8389
1.0	.8413	.8438	.8461	.8485	.8308	.8531	.8554	.8577	.8599	.8621
1.1	.8643	.8665	.8686	.8708	.8729	.8749	.8770	.8790	.8810	.8830
1.2	.8849	.8869	.8888	.8907	.8925	.8944	.8962	.8980	(.8997)	.9015

Closest to .90

The value closest to 0.9 is 0.8997. Backing out to the row and column corresponding to this value gives us a z-score of 1.28.

Thus, the z-score we seek is: $z_?=1.28$. Using this in the equation, above, gives us an equation with only one unknown. We can solve for this unknown—the value we would have converted to get a z-score of 1.28—by simply cross multiplying.

$$1.28 = \frac{?-72}{12}$$
$$12*1.28 = ?-72 \Rightarrow ? = 87.36$$

Our mystery satisfaction score—the one that defines the 90th percentile of all scores—is 87.36. Again, this assumes normality and a one-to-one correspondence between customers and satisfaction scores.

Thus, we can use properties of normal distributions and areas under the standard normal curve to help us solve probability and percentage problems. However, we must be ever cognizant of the assumption required to use these tools in the first place—that the population of data is normally (or bell-curve) distributed. If scores are not distributed in this way, then the analyses we've performed above will not be correct.

STATISTICS IN ACTION

Example: Training test scores We return to our training/proficiency test scores and minimum acceptable scores scenario from the beginning of the chapter. Let's assume that our latest training class scored an average of 82 on their valuation techniques proficiency test, with a standard deviation of 15 points. As training director, you want no fewer than 5 percent of your analysts failing (or scoring below 60). Have you achieved this goal?

Let's assume that test scores are normally distributed. A picture of the problem will help.

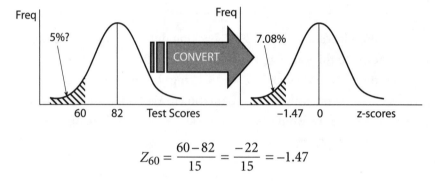

$$Z_{60} = \frac{60-82}{15} = \frac{-22}{15} = -1.47$$

Area under standard normal curve at $-1.47 = 0.0708 \rightarrow 7.08\%$ of the class has failed.

We are not in compliance with our policy—too many analysts are failing the proficiency exam! If this is the case, what can be done? For example, in the future, what average score should we strive for—assuming σ unchanged—to make sure we comply with our policy?

In this problem, we want to find the mean of test scores that we should try to achieve to comply with our policy. First, let's draw a picture of the problem.

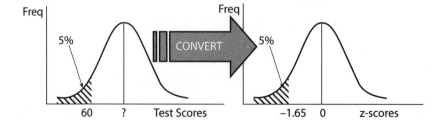

Using the z-score tables to look up 5 percent area in the left-hand tail gives us:

$Z_{50} = -1.65$ (this is the z-score with approximately 5 percent area in the left tail). Now, using this in our z-score formula:

$$-1.65 = \frac{60-?}{15} \Rightarrow (-1.65*15) = 60-? \Rightarrow = 60 + (1.65*15) = 84.75$$

Thus, we should strive for an average test score of at least 84.75 to ensure that no more than 5 percent of the analyst class fails the test.

TEST YOURSELF

Recently, a survey was conducted among subway commuters to Manhattan during June, July, and August. Thousands of people were interviewed at the Grand Central, Fulton Street, and Penn Station subway stations, such that we can consider this dataset a population. The average commuting time for this population of commuters was 49 minutes, with a standard deviation of 6 minutes. Assuming a bell-curve distribution...

1. What percentage of commuters commutes for less than 37 minutes?

2. What is the 95th percentile of commuting times?

3. What is the commuting time necessary to be at the 65th percentile?

4. What is the 90th percentile of average commuting times?

5. Is there anything about the way the survey was conducted that could bias the results?

KEY POINTS TO REMEMBER

- Although the bell curve distribution may be called *normal*, it is rare to find data from a population distributed in such a way.

- Thus, it is very important to be able to prove or to assume, in writing, that a dataset is from a normally distributed population to use the tools and techniques from this chapter.

- In terms of techniques, we can use areas under normal curves to solve probability problems (in percentage terms).

- The technique of *standardizing* a dataset—which does *not* make the data normally distributed, necessarily—allows us to convert any normal distribution into a standard normal distribution.

- The standard normal distribution is in units of standard deviations, or z-scores. We know areas under standard normal distributions from tables (see Appendix A).

- Using these areas, we can solve probability and data problems as long as data are assumed to be normally distributed.

- However, if data are not normally distributed, none of the tools of this chapter is applicable.

PART II

ESTIMATING POPULATION BEHAVIOR USING ONLY A SAMPLE OF DATA

Large Random Samples

INTRODUCTION

Thus far, we've talked about populations of data—that is, situations where we have all the data available. Yet from a practical perspective, we can rarely measure entire populations. Sure, you may have data on all of your customers, but do you have data on all possible customers? Probably not.

Therefore, we need to develop approaches to analyze data when all we have are parts or *samples* of populations. In fact, we will specifically limit our discussions to samples that have been selected *randomly* and that are *representative* of the population.

For now, let's consider a simple scenario. We have a random and representative sample of data from a population. We can find the sample mean, $\bar{x}$, and the sample standard deviation, s. Recall that in this situation, we *no longer know the population mean and standard deviation* (μ and σ). But can we use our sample mean $\bar{x}$ to *infer* or *estimate* the population mean μ? If so, then we'll have a valuable tool in our data analysis arsenal: the ability to use sample data to infer population behavior.

In the previous chapter, we assumed population behavior was normal. We were somewhat uncomfortable with this assumption (because it happens so rarely), so if we can use a sample of data to infer how a population "looks," we won't have to make such assumptions. Now we no longer care—and we will never know—how the population is distributed. We will consider estimating μ with $\bar{x}$, where μ is the unknown population mean and

$\bar{x}$ is the sample mean of a single (random and representative) sample from a population of data.

But do we pay a price by doing so? Is something lost when we use only a sample of data to estimate the behavior of the entire population from which it was sampled?

WHAT'S AHEAD

In this chapter, you'll learn:

- How (and when) to use a sample mean to estimate a population mean; that is, how to use a sample of data to infer or estimate population behavior (on average)

- Properties of sample averages of data, including the distributions of all possible sample averages and their mean and standard deviations

- The central limit theorem—including required assumptions—and how it helps us understand behaviors of averages

- Differences between standard deviation (of data) and standard error (of averages)

- The prices we pay for sampling, or using a sample of data to infer population-level behaviors

IN THE REAL WORLD

You're in charge of strategic planning for your company, and your boss—the president—would like to understand customer profitability better. But you're in a retail business, and you have a huge number of customers and purchase transactions. The president needs an answer in about an hour before an investor relations meeting. What can you do? Can you simply look at a sample of customers, determine the average profitability, and use this to help answer the president's question?

THE KEY CONCEPTS

How Can We Use a Slice of a Pie to Estimate What the Whole Pie Looks Like?

We have only an hour to give the boss a good estimate for the profitability of all our customers. How can we look only at a sample of data (profitabilities) and use these to estimate the overall (population of customers) profitability? The answer is by using *statistical inference*.

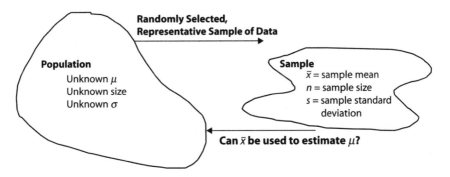

We take a random and representative sample of data from the population, look at the sample statistics, and ask if the sample mean can be used to estimate the population mean. This assumes, of course, that the population mean is a good statistic to use because the population is not too skewed such that the mean could be "pulled" higher or lower based on some outliers. Note that we could also perform inferential analysis with the median—or any other descriptive statistic—but we will limit our analyses here (and in subsequent chapters) to the mean.

What Is a Random Sample? What Is a Representative Sample?

A sample is considered to be *random* if every item in the population from which the sample is drawn is equally likely to be picked. For instance, if every customer in our company database is equally likely to be selected for our sample, then our sample will be random.

In addition, a sample is said to be *representative* if it is "big enough." We'll make this definition more precise later, but in general, a sample size of greater than 30 (customers, parts, receipts, students, scores, etc.) is considered to be representative of the population.

Often you hear the term *biased random sample*. This simply is impossible! If a sample is truly random, the sample hasn't been biased in any way. Also, note that *representative* does not mean the same thing as *statistically valid*. A representative sample is also not necessarily *weighted*. A random sample of 100 people may have more women than men, proportionally, whereas the population being sampled may have more men than women. This does not imply the sample is biased—remember, it's random! A representative sample, for our purposes, is simply a "large enough" sample.

So How Can Samples Tell Us Anything about the Population?

The answer to this question is central to this chapter and to a first course in statistics, in general. Remember that in most real-world populations

- we don't know anything about the population distribution;
- we don't know any statistics or even what the picture (histogram) of the population resembles;
- we will have a single large random sample of data from this population, and this sample will have its own mean and standard deviation; and
- we will assume the average of the population will not be substantially skewed/affected by outliers.

Consider a population of data with population mean of μ_x and standard deviation of σ_x. Note that we have used x subscripts on the parameters to indicate that they are the mean and standard deviation of the population *data values*. Remember, we no longer know—nor can we assume—the shape or properties of this distribution. We want to estimate this unknown population average by using a single random and representative sample of data.

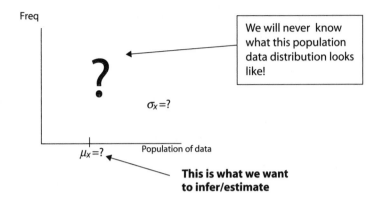

Now we want to try something that is somewhat theoretical but critical to our inference framework. Let's start by taking a single random and representative sample of size $n = 100$ data points. First, let's draw the histogram of this sample data, and second, let's compute the mean and standard deviation.

Then we'll put back or "replace" all the data from our sample into the population. This is referred to as *sampling with replacement*. We do this to avoid changing the population in any way after we've taken our sample.

Now, once we've replaced these sample data points into the population, let's simply repeat the sampling process. Take a second sample of size $n = 100$ and draw its histogram and compute its sample mean and standard deviation. The histogram, mean, and standard deviation of this second sample could be the same as those of the first sample, but they could also be very different. Replace the sample data.

Finally, let's just continue this process—sample 100 random data points, draw the histogram, compute the mean and standard deviation, and replace the sample data—an infinite number of times. We will have an infinite collection of histograms, sample means, and sample standard deviations (all from samples of size 100).

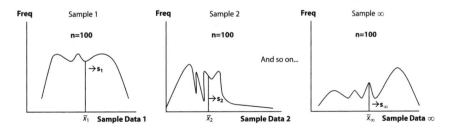

Think of this exercise as a fishing trip. Randomly catch 100 fish, find the mean and standard deviations of the weights of your fish, draw a histogram of their weights, and then throw the fish back into the lake. Keep doing this over and over again. (Wouldn't it be nice to have a fishing trip that never ends?) Some fish may be caught several times, and some may not. If you perform this sampling exercise an infinite number of times, however, you will eventually get every fish in the lake represented in one or more samples.

In the real world, we only get to take *one* sample, not an infinite number. Thus, this framework is helpful only in a theoretical sense—yet the results will help us later on in this chapter.

Now, let's collect all the *means* (not data points) from this infinite list of samples (the same as collecting all the average weights of all your catches of 100 fish). Draw a histogram of all these *means*. Because you performed this sampling exercise an infinite number of times, you will be drawing a histogram of every possible sample mean that you could ever get. Thus, you are now graphing the distribution of all possible sample means. This distribution is called the *sampling distribution of the mean.*

But what is the shape of this distribution of all possible sample means? Does the shape depend on the shape of the population of data? We hope not because then we'll never know what the population of data looks like! Let's think about this intuitively for a moment. It's relatively unlikely that many of the means will be small. Why? To get a small average with a large random sample of data, we would have to randomly select all of the *small data points and/or small outliers.* This is equivalent to going fishing and randomly catching the 100 smallest fish in the lake. It's possible but highly unlikely. Likewise, it's also improbable that we will get a really high average (or randomly catch the 100 largest fish in the lake). Thus, we would expect the histogram of all possible averages to have few high or low averages.

So if we don't get many high or low averages out of our infinite collection, we are more likely to get averages that comprise fish of all different weights. But how does this look on a histogram? Without many high or low averages, we get the following distribution of all possible sample means obtained from representative (large), random samples of the same size, the *sampling distribution of the mean.*

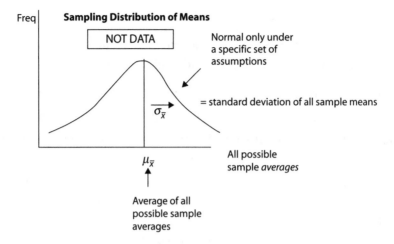

We get approximately a *normal distribution*! If we collect all possible sample averages created from random and representative samples of the same size—while sampling with replacement—this infinite collection of averages would form roughly a normal distribution when plotted on a histogram.

Also, note the symbol changes on the histogram. Because we are dealing with a distribution of *averages*—not data points—we label the mean of all possible means as $\mu_{\bar{x}}$ and the standard deviation of all possible samples means as $\sigma_{\bar{x}}$. This will help us distinguish histograms of *averages* from histograms of *data* moving forward.

Recall from the previous chapter that if we know a distribution is normal—and we know the mean and standard deviation—we can use z-scores and tables to find areas under the normal curve. But what are the "average of all averages" and the "standard deviation of all averages" in the histogram above? If we don't know what the population of data looks like, how can we know what the population of all possible averages looks like?

The Big, Fancy Central Limit Theorem for Sample Means

The *central limit theorem* (or CLT) is one of the key theorems in a first course in statistics. This theorem shows how a distribution of all possible sample means should appear and also how to derive the mean and standard deviation of all these means.

The central limit theorem states that if

- an infinite number of samples of the same size are taken randomly from an unknown population of data (with replacement), and

- the samples are "representative" (meaning large enough or with $n > 30$),

then the sampling distribution of $\bar{x}$ (that is, the distribution of all possible sample means) will be approximately normally distributed with mean *equal to* the mean of all possible sample averages (which equals the mean of the population) and with standard deviation *equal to* the standard deviation of the population of data divided by the square root of the sample size.

The standard deviation of the distribution of all possible sample means is referred to as the *standard error of the mean*. Thus, standard deviation is a property of the *data* while standard error is a property of *averages*. They are not the same thing! Pictorially, the CLT gives us the following.

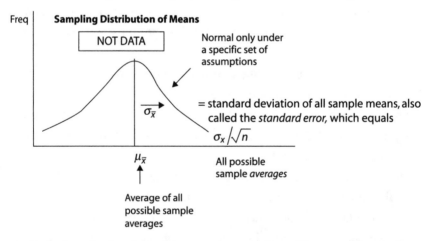

Let's decode the theorem one step at a time. If we could sample an infinite number of times (with replacement), all the averages we would get would form approximately a normal distribution *regardless of the shape of the population of data from which the samples were taken*. But be careful—if we do not have samples that are both randomly taken and representative, the CLT *does not apply* because we cannot guarantee that the distribution of averages will be normal. (Don't forget that the CLT tells us that all possible *sample averages* are normally distributed, not the population of data).

Something still seems odd, however. The average of all averages should be the average of all the data. This makes sense—but what should we use as the mean value in this sampling distribution of all possible sample means? We'll never know the population (of data) mean—that's what we're trying to estimate! Also, the standard error of the means is the standard deviation of the population of data divided by the square root of the sample size. But because we'll never know the standard deviation of the population of data, how can we determine the standard error?

The answer: Do the only practical thing we can do—take a large random sample (n) from the population. From this single sample, we will get a sample mean, $\bar{x}$, and a sample standard deviation, s. Of course, we will know the size of the random and large sample n. Using these three pieces of data, we can make some assumptions about how all possible averages might be distributed, in terms of their mean (or average of all averages) and standard deviation (or standard error, because we're talking about means).

But where does our sample mean belong? Did we get a high or low average from our single sample? We'll never know. Because this is the best estimate for our population mean, let's put it where the population mean (of the data) belongs—in our formula; it's the mean of all means, or $\mu_{\bar{x}}$.

Similarly, we can use the standard deviation from our single sample to approximate the population (of data) standard deviation. That will help us determine the standard error of all these averages in the following way: $\sigma_{\bar{x}} \approx s/\sqrt{n}$. Because we don't know the population data mean and standard deviation, we have to use a single (random and representative) sample of data—and its mean and standard deviation—to help us assume the mean of all means and the standard error of these means. A picture will help here.

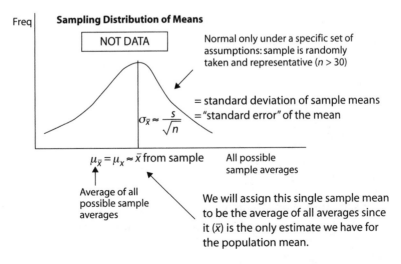

To summarize, if we take a random and representative sample from a population of data, the CLT guarantees that the distribution of all possible means will be normally distributed *regardless* of the shape of the population of data from which the sample came. We will let our single-sample mean serve as the mean of all possible means, and we will use the sample standard deviation to help us estimate the standard error of the distribution of all possible means.

But a few questions still remain: Are the mean and standard deviation from our single sample of data actually correct? Does our sample mean really belong in the middle (as an estimate of the mean of all possible means and thus of the population of data mean)? Or did we randomly get a high or low average such that we risk drawing the histogram of all possible averages incorrectly? Is the standard deviation of our sample close to the standard deviation of the population?

We will never actually know these answers precisely—and that's OK; we know that when we sample, we have to make inferences! We will develop ways to get some sense of an answer to the first question, though. Think about it this way: If you go fishing and catch 100 random fish, do you really think the average of this sample of fish—say six pounds—is really, exactly the average weight of all the fish in the lake? Probably not. But can we be more precise about whether six pounds is close to the real population mean? Later we'll discover that we can resample and find out how close or not we actually are.

To review, for our single sample of data (assuming the sample was taken randomly and has a size of over 30), we have the following:

- $\bar{x}$ is the sample mean, which we will assume is the same as the mean of the population of data (and of averages), or $\mu_{\bar{x}} = \mu_x = \bar{x}$.

- n is the sample size, or number of data points in a random sample from the population.

- s is the sample standard deviation.

- $\sigma_{\bar{x}}$ is the standard deviation of sampling distribution, or the standard deviation of all possible sample means. This is also referred to as the *standard error of the mean.*

Note something curious, here, as well. The standard error—estimated by $\sigma_{\bar{x}} \approx \frac{s}{\sqrt{n}}$—is mathematically less than the standard deviation (of the population of data). Why is this? Again, let's appeal to our intuition. Which is more spread out: weights of fish or all possible averages of samples of fish? Or which do you think varies more: your day-to-day weight or your average weight when averaged monthly (using approximately 31 days of weights to create an average)? Averages move around or "wobble" much less than data points. Our monthly average weight won't change nearly as much as our day-to-day weights. Thus, mathematically:

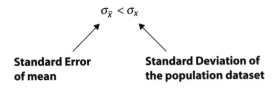

$$\sigma_{\bar{x}} < \sigma_x$$

Standard Error of mean　　　**Standard Deviation of the population dataset**

Standard error is less because averages are not as spread out as data—but how much less? By a factor of $1/\sqrt{n}$.

Rule #2 of Statistics: You Always Pay a Price for Sampling, Guessing, or Estimating!

Rule #1 of statistics was: Always graph the data!

The second rule is: *You always pay a price for sampling, guessing, or estimating.*

If we use these imprecise and hypothetical methods, the price is as follows:

- We can no longer talk about or describe *individual/data* behavior, because we do not know and cannot assume how the population of data is distributed. Instead, if the CLT is satisfied, we can only describe *average* behavior.

- We can no longer estimate μ (the population data mean) using a single number (or *point estimate*). We need a range of possible numbers (or an *interval estimate*) because the single sample mean ($\bar{x}$) is likely not exactly the population mean (μ).

The first price is significant. We can no longer talk about the probability that a test score is greater than some value, as we did in Chapter 3, when we could assume how the population of data was distributed. In fact, the only known behavior now—if the CLT holds true—is the behavior of all possible *averages*. We'll never know the shape of the population if all we can do is sample from it.

The second price is also pretty hefty—and one that many forget. Just because a large random sample of our fish gives you an average weight of six pounds, for example, this does *not* imply that the actual, true population mean (of all data over all time, for instance) is exactly six pounds. Thus, taking into account this uncertainty, we should answer such questions as "What do you think is the average weight of all fish in the pond?" with a range of possible averages, not just one average from a single sample of data.

Standard Error versus Standard Deviation—What's the Difference?

When the sample is random and representative, the sample standard deviation is a good approximation of the population standard deviation. But as we know, the standard deviation of the sample data does not equal the standard error of the distribution of averages. In fact, the standard error is smaller—we can determine how much smaller by adjusting the sample standard deviation. We divide the standard deviation of our sample by the square root of the sample size, n, to determine the standard error of all possible sample means.

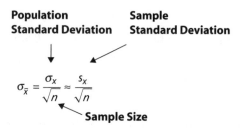

$$\sigma_{\bar{x}} = \frac{\sigma_x}{\sqrt{n}} \approx \frac{s_x}{\sqrt{n}}$$

Note that the larger the sample size, the closer the standard deviation of the sample, s_x, gets to the standard deviation of the population of data, σ_x, and the smaller $\sigma_{\bar{x}}$ becomes. This makes sense, because the more data you sample, the less variable or volatile your estimates of the overall population average will be. Just as in sports, the more you do something—like hit a baseball or catch a football—the less variable your hitting or catching becomes. You become a more accurate (less variable) player in terms of your batting *average*, for example.

You'll also notice something surprising: the spread or volatility of the averages *does not* depend on the size of the population. Thus, if a population of fish is 10,000 or 1,000,000 fish, a random sample of size 100 fish will give us the same standard error (or volatility) of the mean. Neither the size nor the shape (on a histogram) of the population matters when we sample. A few examples will help here.

STATISTICS IN ACTION
Example: River Water Pollution

A random sample of 36 vials of river water provides the following statistics when looking at the level of the carcinogen DDT in the river:

$\bar{x}_{\text{DDT concentration}}$ = 100 parts per million (ppm) = sample mean

$s_{\text{DDT concentration}}$ = 30 ppm = sample standard deviation

n = sample size = 36 (we get this from the problem statement as well as the fact that this sample of 36 vials of water was collected randomly)

1. How likely is it to retest this river a year later and get an average DDT concentration lower than 90 ppm (assuming s doesn't change)? Here we are being asked for the probability of getting an *average* concentration of fewer than 90 ppm a year from now, assuming we take the same size sample and that the standard deviation of DDT concentrations is roughly the same next year as it is this year. This requires us to know how all possible *average concentrations* of DDT are distributed, not the DDT concentrations themselves! Thus, we have to look at how our sample was taken. From these statistics, we can draw a picture of the problem (always a good idea with probability problems).

Note that we've put the mean (100 ppm) from our single, random, and large sample in the middle as though it were the mean of all means and

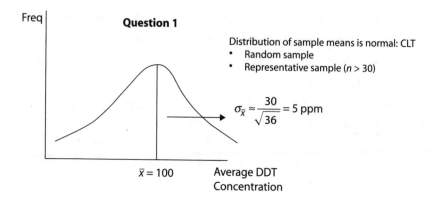

thus the mean of the population data (or the true average pollution level of the entire river). Similarly, we've used the sample standard deviation (30 ppm) and the sample size (36) to compute the standard error of all possible averages. Finally, because the central limit theorem applies—we used a large random sample of data—we know all possible averages are approximately *normally distributed.*

Again, our 100 ppm average may be in the right place on the histogram—or it may not. We're putting it in the best place we can because it's our only estimate for the population mean at this point.

Recall that our question asked about the likelihood of getting an average concentration lower than 90 ppm. Well, because we know how average concentrations are distributed as well as the mean (100 ppm) and standard error (5 ppm) of all possible averages, we should be able to solve this problem using z-scores and our normal tables.

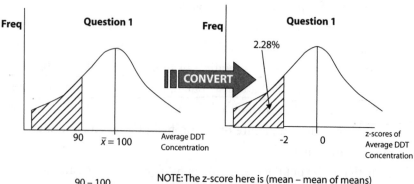

Here, z-scores are computed in the same way with one exception: because we are talking about *averages*, we divide by the standard deviation of all the *averages*, or *standard error*. Do not divide by standard deviation unless you are trying to solve a *data* problem (and have assumed the population of data is normal for some reason).

From our z-tables, we can determine that the area to the left of $z = -2$ is 2.28 percent. Therefore, it is rather unlikely that we will resample in a year and obtain a mean DDT concentration lower than 90 ppm.

2. How likely is it that DDT concentrations are less than 150 ppm? We simply cannot answer this question. Look carefully; this question asks us for the probability that concentration levels—*not average levels*—do not exceed 150 ppm. The answer requires us to know how all concentration levels are distributed. Because we know nothing about how the population of all DDT concentrations is distributed—nor are we comfortable making any assumptions about this distribution—we cannot determine an answer to this question. Many would go ahead and assume the concentrations are normal or just solve this as though it were an average problem. But neither of these solutions is correct!

Recall Rule #2 of statistics: We always pay a price for guessing or sampling. In this case, because we've sampled, we can only talk about *average behavior and probabilities*, not the behavior of the population of data (DDT levels).

3. What is the 90th percentile of average DDT levels? We are asked about averages, so we can answer this question because we have taken a large, random sample of data and the CLT applies. Recall that the 90th percentile of average DDT levels will be the average level where 90 percent of all possible average levels will be below this average and 10 percent of all possible averages will be above it. A picture of the problem always helps.

A z-score of 1.28 will give us the 90 percent of the areas to the left, so $z_? = 1.28$. Cross multiplying allows us to solve for the 90th percentile of average DDT concentrations.

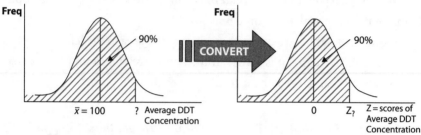

Distribution of sample means are normal: CLT
- Random sample
- Representative sample ($n > 30$)

$\sigma_{\bar{x}} \approx \dfrac{30}{\sqrt{36}} = 5 =$ Standard error of the mean DDT concentration levels

$Z_? = \dfrac{?-100}{5}$ NOTE: We are dividing by the standard *error*, not standard deviation, since we are dealing with averages here.

$$1.28 = \frac{?-100}{5}$$

$$5*1.28 = ?-100 \Rightarrow ? = 106.4 \text{ ppm}$$

Thus, an average DDT level of 106.4 ppm defines the 90th percentile of all average DDT concentrations.

TEST YOURSELF

A survey was recently conducted with MBA statistics students, and a random sample of data was collected regarding average hours per week devoted to an MBA course in data analysis. A total of 36 students responded, and the sample variance was 36 hours squared. (Recall that *hours squared* is the units of variance). The sample mean was 8 hours.

1. What is the likelihood that students spent, on average, fewer than nine hours per week studying for their statistics course last term? Make all necessary assumptions.

2. What may be some factors that would cast doubt on the quality of the sample?

3. Past experience shows that those students who spent fewer than two hours per week on statistics generally do not perform well in the class. Given this precedent, what proportion of students did not perform well in their data analysis classes last semester?

KEY POINTS TO REMEMBER

In this chapter, we have developed a way to use random, large samples to help us determine how averages "behave." This is important because we cannot know distributions or behaviors of populations of data in general. We pay a price for sampling, and one of these prices is that we can only talk about average behavior, not population (or data) behavior. But even this limit is only possible if the two criteria of the central limit theorem are met: if our sample is taken randomly and it is representative (or large), with a sample size exceeding 30.

Some key points to remember include the following:

- We don't necessarily know anything about the population data distribution any longer. We don't know how it's distributed, its shape, or even its mean and standard deviation.

- To infer the population mean, we have to take a large, random sample of data from the population.

- We assume that the average is the most appropriate statistic (point estimate) to use to summarize the population of data.

- When we take a large, random sample, the CLT tells us that all possible sample means will be approximately normally distributed regardless of the shape or characteristics of the population of data from which the sample was taken. Note that a large sample is not necessarily a statistically valid sample (and vice versa).

- We use our sample mean to estimate the mean of the population, and we use the sample standard deviation to help compute the standard error of all possible means.

- The central limit theorem tells us *nothing* about the population of data distribution! The CLT only applies to distributions of *averages*.

- When analyzing business situations/problems, be sure to identify clearly whether you are solving a *data* problem or an *average* problem. If a data problem, you must know how the data are distributed (at a population level) to solve the problem. If you do not, you cannot solve such a problem. However, if you have a large random sample, you can use this sample—and its mean and standard deviation—along with the CLT to define how all possible sample *averages* will behave or be distributed.

- Don't forget Rule #2 of statistics: we always pay a price for guessing, estimating, or sampling. In fact we pay two. First, we can only talk about averages, not data. Second—and this is the topic of the next chapter—we need to use a range of possible means to estimate the population mean, not just a single sample mean (which likely is not exactly the population mean, anyway).

Using a (Large) Sample Mean to Estimate an Unknown Population Mean

INTRODUCTION

In the previous chapter, we developed the notion of *sampling* a population to determine how averages are distributed. The central limit theorem (CLT) helped us to label the distribution of all possible sample averages, and we learned an important rule: once you sample, you can no longer talk about data distributions/behaviors. Only average behavior or distributions can be studied (and only then if the CLT criteria are met). This was the first "price" that we pay when sampling. But what about the second price?

When we sample, it is unlikely that the mean of our sample is equal to the true mean of the population of data (which we know nothing about). Thus, instead of using just the sample mean to estimate the population mean, we need a *range* of possible means that is likely to contain the population mean.

Back to our fishing example from Chapter 4: If we go fishing and randomly catch 100 fish that weigh, on average, six pounds, then it's unlikely that the weights of all fish in the lake average to precisely six pounds (though it is possible, we'll never know for sure). So instead of simply saying that the average weight of all fish in the lake is six pounds, it's better to provide a range—say between four pounds and eight pounds—with some degree of confidence to estimate the average weight of all fish in the lake (the population average). This range could be larger—and thus more likely to contain the actual mean weight of all fish in the lake—or it could be narrower and be less likely to contain the true population mean.

In this chapter, we will develop a tool—called *confidence intervals*—to help us create these ranges of possible means, also referred to as *interval estimates*, for the population mean.

WHAT'S AHEAD

In this chapter, you'll learn:

- How to create interval estimates for a population mean using a single sample of data

- How to interpret these interval estimates or confidence intervals from a practical perspective

- How to compare sample means using confidence intervals

- How to determine whether two means are statistically equal or statistically significantly different

- How to control and interpret possible errors made when using a single sample mean to construct a confidence interval (that is then used to estimate the population mean)

IN THE REAL WORLD

In the previous chapter, the president of your company challenged you to create some measure of profitability for your customer base in only an hour. Here's the bad news: you only have 30 minutes left. The good news is that you took a large random sample of your customers and determined the average profitability and the standard deviation of profitability from this sample. Now you know how averages are distributed, but you're not satisfied to give the president only a one-number answer for average customer profitability. He may not have much confidence in your estimate because you'd have to explain random sampling, the CLT, and all kinds of other statistical stuff to him involving a laundry list of Greek letters.

So what do you do? Perhaps instead of a number—like $1,000—you could provide the president with a range that likely contains the true (but unknown) population average customer profitability. But how wide should you make this interval? Is the width completely arbitrary? If not, what are some standard widths of these interval estimates? Does the width depend on anything like sample size or the variability of the sample data? Only 29 minutes left!

THE KEY CONCEPTS

Using a Range of Numbers Instead of a Single Number to Estimate the Population Average

We can now address the second price of sampling and add to Rule #2 of statistics:

> **Rule # 2 of Statistics:**
>   **We always pay a price for sampling/estimating.**
>   1. We can no longer talk about data behavior or probabilities; we can only talk about average behavior or probabilities.
>   2. A single-number estimate (or "point estimate") $\bar{x}$ is not good enough to estimate the population mean, μ. We need a range of averages—an "interval estimate"—to show a range of possible means that might contain the population mean.

In the previous chapter, we effectively addressed the first price. We learned what kinds of problems we can solve with samples—and under what assumptions—as well as some constraints we have to worry about (like getting a large sample size or a random sample). Yet if a sample mean by itself isn't good enough to use to estimate the population mean, then what is? Perhaps a range of possible means that could contain the real population mean would suffice. Still, there a chance that our interval estimate will not capture the population mean—how do we compute and manage/reduce that chance?

Let's return to the example we used in the previous chapter. We had 36 randomly selected vials of river water with the following statistics related to DDT concentrations.

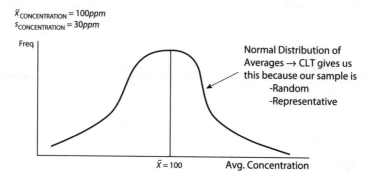

Our goal is quite simple: We want to use $\bar{x}$ from our single sample of river water to estimate the true population mean DDT concentration, μ. Remember, we have no idea what the population of concentrations (data points) looks like, so we are trying to use this sample—and its statistics—to estimate the population (data) mean.

To create such an interval estimate, consider the following graph:

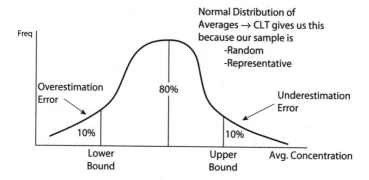

We have arbitrarily defined an interval estimate around our sample mean such that 80 percent of the area under the curve is within this interval. This interval should capture or represent 80 percent of all possible sample means. Another way to think about it is that we have an 80 percent probability that the true population mean is inside—or captured by—this interval estimate.

As such, if the true population mean were outside the interval to the left, then our interval is completely greater than (or to the right of) the true population mean—we've *overestimated* the population mean with this interval. Conversely, if the true population mean were in the right tail— greater than the interval—then we have *underestimated* the true population mean with our interval estimate. (Note that the sum of overestimate and underestimate error in this case is called *total estimation error*. The total estimation error is often referred to as *alpha*, or α.)

Constructing an Interval Estimate for a Population Mean (Using a Single Sample of Data)

But how do we construct an interval estimate? Well, if the CLT applies— and it does in this case—then we should be able to find the upper and lower bounds of the interval by using the areas under the curve and our z-tables. First, we have to convert this picture into a graph with z-scores.

We start by noting that this interval, which is symmetric about the mean, can be expressed as the mean plus or minus a distance. The distance along the x-axis can be measured in units of standard error, or z-scores. Thus, the interval estimate we wish to create is:

$\bar{x}$ plus or minus some number of standard errors based on area defined by the interval

$= 100 \pm$ (a z-score) $\times$ (standard error)

$= 100 \pm z_{\alpha/2\_in\_one\_tail} \times$ (standard error)

$= 100 \pm z_{\alpha/2\_in\_one\_tail} \times$ (5 ppm)

The z-score we need to use is defined by half of alpha—the total estimation error—in one tail. Total estimation error here is 20 percent (or alpha), so half of this is 10 percent. We can use this area, along with our z-tables, to find the z-score with this much area in one tail.

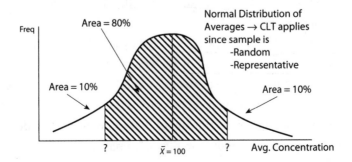

To determine this interval, let's look up what z-score would give us 10 percent in the left tail. We can easily get this from our z-table as follows.

z	0	.01	.02	.03	.04	.05	.06	.07	.08	.09
−1.3	.0968	.0951	.0934	.0918	.0901	.0885	.0869	.0853	.0838	.0823
−1.2	.1151	.1131	.1112	.1093	.1075	.1056	.1038	.1020	.1003	.0985
−1.1	.1357	.1335	.1314	.1292	.1271	.1251	.1230	.1210	.1190	.1170
−1.0	.1587	.1562	.1539	.1515	.1492	.1469	.1446	.1423	.1401	.1379

Closest to 10%

Thus, the z-score with 10 percent defined in the left tail is -1.28.

If we draw what this interval would look like in terms of z-scores, we see that the bounds of the interval estimate are 1.28 standard errors away from the sample mean.

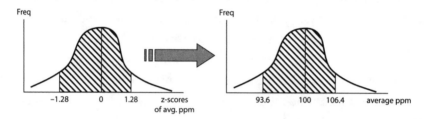

Thus, our interval estimate—or an *80 percent confidence interval for the population mean DDT concentration*—is given by:

$$100 \pm 1.28 \times 5 = [93.6, 106.4]$$

But what does this interval represent?

How to Interpret Confidence Intervals

To be clear, a confidence interval is not a "certainty interval." Remember that the interval is based on our sample mean, which is an estimate of the population mean. If we happened to sample outliers, we could have a skewed sample. And that could lead to overestimating or underestimating the true population average.

A confidence interval can be interpreted as a probability statement regarding the true population mean. If we were to use the formula above to create many different confidence intervals (with the same confidence level) by sampling over and over again, 80 percent of these intervals should contain the true population mean. The higher the confidence, the wider the interval used to capture the population mean. A smaller confidence level—or higher alpha value, which represents the total estimate error—results in a narrower interval.

Let's consider the standard error component of the confidence interval. A larger sample size decreases the standard error. A smaller sample size increases it. Thus, for the same confidence level, a larger sample size will create a narrower confidence interval. The more data that we sample, the more precise (narrower) our interval estimate should be.

But what if 80 percent of all the different intervals we create (via sampling) end up *not* containing the true population mean? Is our approach wrong? Or are our initial sample means, which we used as the center of the various interval estimates, in the wrong place, possibly due to sampled outliers?

Using Confidence Intervals to Assess Statistical Equality

As mentioned above, two key factors drive the size (width) of a confidence interval:

1. Sample size

    → Increase n and the interval gets smaller.

    → Standard error decreases as sample size grows.

2. Confidence level

    → Confidence level is based on the allowable estimation error (α).

    → Confidence level = $(1 - \alpha)$.

When it comes to using confidence intervals to assess *statistical equality* (as opposed to *statistically significant difference*), we must understand some properties that may seem confusing at first.

- Any (future sampled) average (or confidence interval) that resides inside (or overlaps) our initial confidence interval is statistically *equal* to the sample mean used to create the interval.

- Any (future sampled) average (or confidence interval) that resides outside (or does not overlap) our established confidence interval is statistically *different* than the sample mean used to create it.

- Thus, numbers may be different, but as averages, different numbers can be statistically equal due to sampling and because we use *intervals* to estimate means, not just single numbers. Although 1 may not equal 3 as numbers, as averages, if they are in overlapping confidence intervals, they are statistically equal to each other.

- The total estimation error (alpha) defines what it means to be equal versus statistically significantly different when it comes to averages because alpha effectively defines the boundaries of a confidence interval.

An example will help illustrate these points. Assume we sample the river for DDT levels again a year later (with the same sample size and standard deviation). Now assume that in the second sample, the average pollution level increases 4 percent (from 100 ppm to 104 ppm).

The fundamental question here is: Did the pollution level significantly increase on average, or is this 4 percent increase within an acceptable range of sampling error and not indicative of increase pollution (of DDT) at the population level?

Let's review the statistics and the confidence interval we created earlier:

$$n = 36 = \text{sample size}$$
$$s = 30 \text{ ppm} = \text{sample standard deviation}$$
$$\bar{x}_{old} = 100 \text{ ppm} = \text{mean of first (old) sample}$$
$$\bar{x}_{new} = 104 \text{ ppm} = \text{mean of second (new) sample}$$

The 80 percent confidence interval used to estimate the true population mean (from the "old" sample): [93.6 ppm, 106.4 ppm].

Did we see a statistically significant increase? No, we did not. Note that a sample mean of 104 ppm is inside the 80 percent confidence interval that we created above. Based on random sampling of the population, an average of 104 ppm is statistically equivalent to an average of 100 ppm. Thus, the only thing that caused this difference is sampling error, *not a significant increase in the average pollution level of the river*. Even though the numbers are numerically different, they are not pollution levels. They are *average pollution levels* from random samples, and as such, they are statistically equal.

This is an important lesson. All too often, observers, politicians, or the press will note that an average increases or decreases—average compensation, average stock price, average age, average weight—and proclaim that real differences are being seen. But if differences in average weight, for example, are an effect of random sampling and trends in diet or exercise, then we really cannot say a meaningful, *statistically significant difference* has been discovered.

Back to our pollution example, if we had observed a new sample mean of 108 ppm, then we might be able to claim that this new sample mean is *statistically significantly higher* than the prior mean. It may be beyond random chance (sampling differences/errors) to observe a sample mean this high. We only allowed a 10 percent chance for this to happen—at an 80 percent confidence level. With a sample mean of 108 ppm, we might conclude that the river is significantly more polluted with DDT, an average, than before.

However, we have to look at the variability—and the confidence interval—around the second sample mean (108 ppm). If two intervals overlap, there is still no difference in means! Thus, when comparing confidence intervals (using the same alpha, sample size, and standard deviation), overlap means we cannot prove a significant difference between two means. However, if two intervals *do not* overlap, then we can conclude that the two means are *statistically significantly different*.

Limitations of Confidence Intervals in Decision Making

In our pollution example, we allowed ourselves a 10 percent chance to get a mean higher than 106.4—thus, it's statistically possible to get a mean this high. Yet is it possible that our first mean (100 ppm) may have been too low due outliers in the sample? Or could it be that our second sample mean (108 ppm) suffered from high outlier concentrations such that it was skewed high? These possibilities challenge our conclusion. *outleirs*

To make this comparison, we had to have samples of the same size and standard deviation so the standard errors of the means remained unchanged. Practically, this can never be guaranteed. If pollution levels have been higher on average, we may have naturally seen more variability in the pollution levels. Also, we may not be able to create equal random sample sizes at different times (due to cost, for example). We'll have to sort this out in the next chapter. But for now, we have at least four possible reasons why the second mean (108 ppm) is significantly higher than the first mean (100 ppm).

1. The first sample underestimated the average pollution level (perhaps due to low outliers).

2. The second sample overestimated the average pollution level (perhaps due to high outliers).

3. Randomness happens! We allowed a probability, 10 percent, for this type of average to be observed—purely randomly—so it's possible (but not that probable) to sample and get a mean this high.

4. There really is higher pollution, on average, in the river (for example, at 108 ppm on average).

It is worth noting again that confidence interval comparisons are best made when the intervals are created with the same sample size and standard deviation. (Otherwise, a large difference in variability between the two datasets could cause us to perceive a difference—or not—in the two means.) Because sampling twice with the same standard deviations is unlikely, our ability to use confidence intervals to assess true significant differences is limited (at least for now). In the next two chapters, we'll discover a more practical tool to help us decide whether two means are statistically significantly different.

Playing Games with Confidence Intervals

Depending on your confidence level and your sample size, you can play some games with these interval estimates, which can lead to bad decision making. For example, if you led the company responsible for putting DDT into the river water, and a second sample shows an average of 108 ppm (with the confidence interval around it not overlapping the confidence interval around 100 ppm, from before), the Environmental Protection Agency (EPA) may attempt to fine you because you have "significantly" increased the average DDT level in the river.

But a clever trick or two can make the problem go away. First, just decrease the total error (alpha), which is the same as increasing the confidence level. Assume the confidence level is 95 percent. If a 95 percent confidence interval given the original mean of 100 ppm is created, the new average of 108 ppm will now be *inside* the interval and *not* statistically higher than the average of 100 ppm.

We could also simply sample less. A smaller sample size (n) will increase the standard error for the confidence interval, and this, in turn, will expand the width of confidence interval. Smaller samples lead to broader intervals and lower possibilities of seeing statistically significant differences. This reminds us of an old statistics adage: If you don't want to see a difference, don't look very hard!

To combat this sort of trickery, many scientists, courts, and statisticians have agreed on a minimally acceptable confidence level to show significant differences: 95 percent confidence. Under the central limit theorem, sample means are distributed approximately normally, so we know that about 95 percent of all possible sample means will be within approximately two standard errors of the mean (or 1.96 from the z-table). Thus, many consider a mean outside the bounds of two standard errors of the mean to be an outlier or significantly different mean. In a 95 percent confidence interval, we allow a total estimation error of 5 percent, or 2.5 percent in each tail. If we see an average that lies in either tail, we consider that mean to be significantly different from the mean that we used to build the interval in the first place.

Thus, it's often best to use a confidence level of 95 percent (or even 99 percent in some academic or technical applications) when creating confidence intervals for means.

STATISTICS IN ACTION

Below is a table of some randomly selected credit card balances from our credit card portfolio of customers. Can we quickly create a 95 percent confidence interval for the average outstanding balance?

$210	220	230	240	270	300	300	320	320	320
340	370	370	380	400	410	450	450	470	470
490	500	500	510	510	540	570	580	580	610
610	620	640	640	650	660	690	750	760	790

We can compute the following (using any data analysis tool or Microsoft Excel, for example):

- $\bar{x}$ (the mean of the sample) = $476
- s (the standard deviation of the sample) = $160.49
- n (the size of the sample) = 40
- α (error allowance, or 1 – confidence level needed) = 1 – 95% = 5% (or 0.05)

We then use the confidence interval equation to get

$$\bar{x} \pm z_{\alpha/2} \left(\frac{\sigma}{\sqrt{n}} \right)$$

$$= 476 \pm z_{0.05/2} \left(\frac{160.49}{\sqrt{40}} \right)$$

$$= 476 \pm z_{0.025}(25.37)$$

$$= 476 \pm 1.96(25.37)$$

$$= \$476 \pm 49.73$$

Therefore, the 95 percent confidence interval for the average outstanding balance is $426.27 to $525.73. (Note that we've assumed that outstanding balances were sampled randomly. The central limit theorem helps us create an estimation interval for the mean regardless of the shape of the population distribution.)

You often see another good example of confidence intervals in action during election season: poll results. For example, a poll is conducted, and 51 percent of those surveyed said they would vote for Candidate A, while only 47 percent of those surveyed said they would vote for Candidate B. (Clearly, 2 percent were either undecided or wished to vote for another candidate.)

So numerically, it would appear that Candidate A has the lead and is winning in the polls. Yet the TV news anchor says that this race is a "statistical dead heat"? Why?

The answer lies in a little number that is often shown—and still more often misunderstood—in the lower corner of the televised poll results: the *margin of error*. Margin of error is nothing more than the half-width of the confidence interval around these polling percentages (often based on a 95 percent confidence requirement). To be clear, the margin of error *is not* the alpha error. It's simply the half-width, or *bound*, of the confidence interval.

With a margin of error of 5 percent in the poll above, we see that Candidate A's percentage of voters could range from 46 percent to 56 percent. Similarly, Candidate B's percentage of voters could range from 42 percent to 52 percent. Because they overlap, Candidate A's percentage—51 percent—is inside the confidence interval of Candidate B's percentage.

Thus, these two candidates are in a statistical dead heat; there is no clear leader. But if Candidate A had a percentage of voters outside Candidate B's interval, and the two intervals did not overlap, then we could claim there was a significant difference—Candidate A was getting a significantly larger share of voters (and thus is likely to win).

Therefore, we've seen confidence intervals—in the form here as percentages of a binary selection—many times before. Now we know what that "margin of error" is all about. It's just half the width of the confidence interval!

How to Determine the Sample Size (n) for a Given Confidence Level and Bound (B)

To compute the sample size that is *statistically valid* to create a confidence interval with width $2B$—where B is the desired half-width of the confidence interval—we need to know: s (an estimate, based on a prior sample, of the population standard deviation), n (the size of the sample), B (the bound), and α (the maximum total estimation error you will allow). Then use the following equation:

$$n = \frac{(z_{\alpha/2})^2 s^2}{B^2}$$

Always round n up to the nearest whole number. This will provide you with the minimum sample size (or number of responses, for example) required to create an interval with $1 - \alpha$ confidence with width $2B$ (the distance between the upper and lower bounds). Note that a statistically valid sample size may be nonrepresentative (less than 30). Also, a large, representative sample does not necessarily imply that it is large enough to create a "valid" confidence interval of a specific width with a specific confidence level.

Further, this formula is based on the central limit theorem being applied. If the sample size you get back is less than 30, then we need to use a different technique (and some extra assumptions) to validate this sample size. (More on this in the next chapter.) Let's work through an example.

A manufacturer produces gumballs that have a mean diameter of 10 mm with a standard deviation (estimated from prior sampling) of approximately 0.75 mm. Due to aging machinery, the plant produces gumballs as big as 12 mm and as small as 9 mm. The manufacturer wishes to estimate the mean diameter to within 0.05 mm of its true (population) value with 99 percent confidence. What sample size should be used to waste this mean estimate!?

The solution:

$\alpha = 1\% = 0.01$

$z_{0.01/2} = z_{0.005} = 2.575$

$s = 0.75$

$B = 0.05$ (that is, the manufacturer wishes to estimate the population mean gumball diameter to within 0.05 mm—that is plus or minus 0.05 mm—of its actual value)

$$n = \frac{(z_{\alpha/2})^2 s^2}{B^2} = \frac{(2.575)^2 0.75^2}{0.05^2} = 1{,}491.89$$

So the manufacturer would need to sample 1,492 gumballs to be 99 percent confident it has estimated the gumball diameter to within 0.05 mm of its true (population) mean value.

Notice how big the sample size would need to be if the manufacturer only wanted to estimate within 0.5 mm of the true population mean.

$$n = \frac{(z_{\alpha/2})^2 s^2}{B^2} = \frac{(2.575)^2 0.75^2}{0.5^2} = 14.92$$

Only 15 gumballs are needed to have a valid sample. But this is not a representative sample, so the central limit theorem would not apply, and we would have to use a different technique or formula (with some additional assumptions) to determine the valid sample size.

Assuming that the gumballs were sampled randomly, in the second case, we would need a way to handle this small sample of gumballs—without the assistance of the CLT—to help us create a confidence interval for the mean diameter estimate. Specifically, the calculation of the sample size that produced this small sample size is invalid. This formula comes from our large-sample definition of a confidence interval (via the central limit theorem). With such a small (nonrepresentative) sample, we cannot use this formula!

TEST YOURSELF

A study of hours spent in training (per year) at a company was conducted with 49 participants. The mean number of hours spent in training was reported to be 89.25 hours. The standard deviation was 13.44 hours.

1. Calculate a 95 percent confidence interval for the average time spent in training per year at this firm.

2. Perform the same calculation again, but use a total estimation error allowance of 10 percent.

3. If the minimum average number of training hours that our HR organization strives for is 80 hours per year, how many people did not get this much training?

4. How likely is it that we will resample this population—assuming the sample size and standard deviation of hours do not change—and get a mean number of training hours below 85 hours?

KEY POINTS TO REMEMBER

To form a confidence interval for a population mean using a large random sample (so the CLT applies), we need to know the following:

- $\bar{x}$ (the mean of the sample)
- σ (the standard deviation of the population) Note: This can be approximated by using the standard deviation of the sample s if σ is unknown, which it usually is.
- n (the size of the sample)
- a (the total estimation error allowance or tolerance)

  We then use the following formula:

  $\bar{x} \pm z_{\alpha/2}\left(\frac{\sigma_x}{\sqrt{n}}\right)$ (which is equivalent to $\bar{x} \pm z_{\alpha/2}\,\sigma_{\bar{x}}$), where $a \div 2$ is the amount of error under just one tail of the distribution of averages.

  As mentioned above, if σ is unknown, then the interval can be approximated by

  $$\bar{x} \pm z_{\alpha/2}\left(\frac{s}{\sqrt{n}}\right) \text{ (where s is the sample standard deviation)}$$

  A confidence interval can be interpreted and used as follows:

- If we were to resample repeatedly and create many more confidence intervals, 80 percent of the intervals should contain the true value of the population mean.
- Confidence intervals that overlap do not give us enough evidence that the two means (used to create them) are statistically significantly different.
- However, if two confidence intervals (using the same alpha, of course) do not overlap, then there is a statistically significant difference between the two means.

  A 95 percent confidence interval—or two standard errors on either side of the mean—is commonly used in scientific, business, survey, and academic applications.

Small Samples: What Happens When What You Have Just Isn't Enough?

INTRODUCTION

Thus far, we have focused on sampling when the central limit theorem (CLT) applies because we have random and representative samples. But in business, situations often arise when we simply do not have representative samples. For example, we may survey 40 customers, but only 15 are male and 25 are female. If we want to understand male and female customer average profitability, for example, both of these samples are small. Thus, the CLT will not apply—even if these samples are random.

Often we cannot avoid small samples due to cost. It's simply too expensive to conduct an experiment—like a test-marketing campaign—in more than 30 places. Therefore, we need some tools that allow us to work with small samples.

WHAT'S AHEAD

In this chapter, you'll learn:
- What techniques can be used to understand average behavior when random samples from populations are small (30 or fewer)

- What key assumptions are required to use these "small-sample" techniques
- Alternative ways—beyond the scope of this text—that you may hear about or see that are better suited for small-sample inferences

IN THE REAL WORLD

You work for a retailer of consumer electronics—televisions, portable music players, DVD players, etc. Your company has 20 stores. You've been asked to study the effects of a recent marketing/advertising campaign that was conducted in the areas around ten randomly selected stores.

You have data from each of the stores before and after the advertisements ran in the ten markets. Based on this sample, can you determine if the average sales across all stores increased after the campaign occurred?

THE KEY CONCEPTS

The t-Distribution of Averages

If we have a random but small sample—defined as a sample size of 30 or fewer items—the CLT no longer applies. Thus, we cannot know how the distribution of all possible sample averages will look (or the mean and standard error of this distribution). What can we do? And what's the problem with small samples, anyway? *Outliers more obvious*

As we've learned, the problem with small samples is that the average can be even more heavily influenced by outliers. A large outlier in a sample of 1,000 items is less noticeable, but in a sample of only 10 items, it will skew the average much more.

In general, it's just not clear what the sampling distribution of small sample means looks like. When we have small samples, how can we accommodate this increased possibility of an outlier skewing our sample average?

The answer requires us to make a huge assumption. If we can assume that the population from which we select a small random sample is *normally distributed*, then we can know the behavior of all possible sample averages. But you'll recall that very few data distributions are normally distributed, so this analysis is based on a rather bold assumption.

If this makes you feel uncomfortable, it should. We should always question our assumptions about the unknown—in this case, a population of data from which a small random sample has been taken. However, it is important to note here, when these "samll-sample" techniques can be used, because there are many examples and cases where analysts *did not* take such assumptions into account and simply proceeded with small sample inferences using large sample (CLT-based) techniques. Failing to make—and validate—such assumptions could lead to erroneous confidence intervals and poor or incorrect inferences about population means. Be careful!

If we can assume the population of data that has been sampled with sample size, n, is normally distributed—that large lake of fish and their weights, for example—then the distribution of all possible averages that could be sampled will assume a *t-distribution* with ($n - 1$) *degrees of freedom*. Simply put, if the population is normal, small sample averages follow a distribution that is almost bell curved. The difference is that the small sample average distribution will have fatter tails—thus, leptokurtic—given that more outlier averages could occur (because an outlier will have a much larger effect on any given small sample average). Here's a picture of the t-distribution compared with the normal distribution.

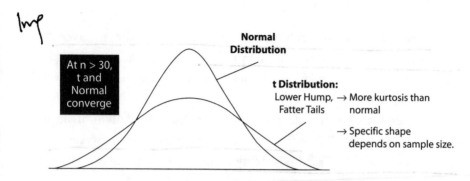

ASSUME POPULATION NORMAL IF N ≤ 30

- You can only use t-distribution for averages if population data are explicitly assumed normal!

- It's a big assumption. Statisticians usually use other tools to deal with small samples that don't depend on such assumptions.

Because outliers can more drastically affect the mean in small samples, the sample size becomes a factor in calculations of probabilities or areas under the t-distribution. The actual shape—and the area distribution—under the t-distribution will change depending on the sample size. This change is represented by the *degrees of freedom* of the t-distribution, which is simply the sample size minus one (n – 1). Thus, if we have a sample of size 12, the degrees of freedom will be 11. We can then use the degrees of freedom to calculate the area under the t-distribution.

What If the Sample I've Taken Isn't Random?

Unfortunately, if a sample isn't random, then there's nothing we can do to estimate the population mean (using the simple tools in this text). Even if we have a large sample of data, if it was not taken randomly, the CLT doesn't apply, and we won't be able to infer the behavior of all possible sample averages.

So be careful when performing calculations. If you have a nonrandom sample—data on customers that were not randomly sampled, for example—don't use normal or t-distributions to help you understand average behaviors!

In this chapter, we are only talking about situations where we have small samples. These samples still have to be taken randomly, and other assumptions have to be in place to use the t-distribution.

How Do I Create a Confidence Interval Estimate Using the t-Distribution?

Let's look back at a problem from Chapter 5 and make one small change. We had taken a large sample of vials of river water and analyzed the average concentration of a pollutant:

$$n = 36 = \text{sample size}$$
$$s = 30 \text{ ppm} = \text{sample standard deviation}$$
$$\bar{x} = 100 \text{ ppm} = \text{sample mean}$$

Also, recall that we created an 80 percent confidence interval estimate for the true population mean concentration:

$$[93.6 \text{ ppm} , 106.4 \text{ ppm}]$$

Now, let's assume that due to the high costs and time required to do such sampling, we could only afford to take a sample size of nine vials of river water. Let's create a similar confidence interval (80 percent confidence, or alpha error of 20 percent) using this small sample. Although 95 percent confidence is more common, we will use the 80 percent level from the previous chapter to compare the large-sample and small-sample intervals. The 80 percent confidence interval, in this case, will be given by

$$100 \pm (\text{t-score with } \alpha/2 \text{ in one tail}) \times (\text{standard error})$$

Like the z-scores we used earlier, the t-score will come from the t-table in Appendix A. This t-score depends on not only the confidence level but also the degrees of freedom. Here, the degrees of freedom are $9 - 1 = 8$, or the sample size less one.

✙ *But we can only use this technique if we explicitly assume that the population of concentration levels is normally distributed.* This is a critical point. If we have our suspicions about this assumption, then we had best use a different approach.

But with this assumption in place, we can proceed. First, let's look at the t-table in Appendix A. Looking up information on this table is done differently than the z-tables. Here, we have to know the upper tail probability—in this case 10 percent because each tail has 10 percent of the area in it with an 80 percent confidence interval. To find the proper t-score, simply find the intersection of the degrees of freedom (8, in this case) and the upper tail probability of 10 percent.

Look up t-statistic in the table

t distribution critical values

						Upper tail probability p						
df	.25	.20	.15	.10	.05	.025	.02	.01	.005	.0025	.001	.0005
1	1.000	1.376	1.963	3.078	6.314	12.71	15.89	31.82	63.66	127.3	318.3	636.6
2	0.816	1.061	1.386	1.886	2.920	4.303	4.849	6.965	9.925	14.09	22.33	31.60
3	0.765	0.978	1.250	1.638	2.353	3.182	3.482					
4	0.741	0.941	1.190	1.533	2.132	2.776	2.999					
5	0.727	0.920	1.156	1.476	2.015	2.571	2.757					
6	0.718	0.906	1.134	1.440	1.943	2.447	2.612					
7	0.711	0.896	1.119	1.415	1.895	2.365	2.517					
8	0.706	0.889	1.108	1.397	1.860	2.306	2.449					
9	0.703	0.883	1.100	1.383	1.833	2.262	2.398	2.821	3.250	3.690	4.297	4.781
10	0.700	0.879	1.093	1.372	1.812	2.228	2.359	2.764	3.169	3.581	4.144	4.587
11	0.697	0.876	1.088	1.363	1.796	2.201	2.328	2.718	3.106	3.497	4.025	4.437
				1.000	1.000	1.000	2.170	2.303	2.681	3.055	3.428	3.930	4.318

Upper tail probability: 10%
Degrees of freedom: 8

We see that the proper t-score to use to create our confidence interval is 1.397. Next, we need to compute the standard error of this t-distribution.

Calculate Standard Error:

$$\sigma_{\bar{x}} = \frac{30}{\sqrt{9}} = 10 \text{ ppm}$$

Now we can construct our 80 percent confidence interval with this small sample:

$$100 \pm 1.397 \times 10 = 100 \pm 13.97 = [86.03 , 113.97]$$

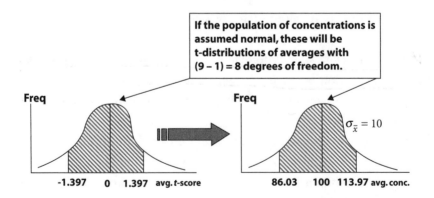

If the population of concentrations is assumed normal, these will be t-distributions of averages with (9 – 1) = 8 degrees of freedom.

You'll notice that this confidence interval is larger than the one we created for the larger sample ($n = 36$). There are two reasons. First, the standard error is larger due to the smaller sample size. This will widen the bounds of the interval. Second, the t-statistic used to create this interval is greater than the z-score used to create the large-sample interval. With its "fatter" tails, the t-distribution takes into account more possible averages that we could get with 80 percent confidence, given that outliers will have bigger impacts on these sample means.

It's worth mentioning again that this approach is only valid if we assume the population that we took the sample from is normally distributed. Simply using a t-distribution because the sample size is less than 30 is incorrect.

Why Must We Assume the Population of Sampled Data Is Normal to Use the t-Distribution?

Simply put, with small samples, to get a distribution of sample means that looks nearly bell shaped (or t-distributed, in this case), we need to sample from a population that was bell shaped to start. Imagine we randomly select a small sample from a population of data that is heavily skewed right, for example. In this case, it's unclear what all possible sample averages will look like because the "look" will depend on where in the distribution we sample from. With a highly skewed distribution, one outlier could greatly skew the a sample mean (or many of them), and this could cause our distribution of all possible averages to be just about anything.

Yet if we sample from a normal distribution, we are assured that the distribution of all possible averages will be t-distributed, *not normally distributed*. Note that the standard error and confidence intervals are calculated just as when we use z-scores—all that changes is the distribution of averages. The t-distribution has larger tails—to accommodate outlier effects—and also depends on the sample size (minus one) to help us determine its shape (and thus areas under it). Without assuming a normal population, we simply won't know what the distribution of all possible averages will look like with any specificity.

But What If Assuming Population Normality Makes No Sense (or Is Just Plain Wrong)?

In this case, we must use more advanced tools—*nonparametric methods*—to assess average behavior. Such methods are called *nonparametric* because they do not depend on the parameters of the data—like the mean and standard deviation—which can be heavily influenced by outliers in a small sample.

The Wilcoxon rank-and-sum method and the Mann-Whitney U-statistic are examples of tests/tools that may be more appropriate with small sample situations. We do not cover these methods in this text, but a more advanced statistics book can provide you with information on these topics.

So Why Is n > 30 Considered to Be a "Large" Sample?

Why do we keep using this seemingly arbitrary sample size as the threshold for representative samples? The answer is found on both the z-table and t-table. You'll notice that the t-table only increases incrementally until degrees of freedom equal 30 (or sample size of n = 31). There is a practical reason for this.

Look at the z-statistic and t-statistic for a 95 percent confidence interval using a sample size of 31 (or degrees of freedom equal to 30). The z-score for this interval is 1.96, and the t-score for a 95 percent confidence interval estimate is 2.042. Note that both of these round to approximately 2. Thus, at sample sizes greater than 30, we can say that the normal distribution and the t-distribution converge. For large samples, we no longer care about degrees of freedom, and for all intents and purposes, the two distributions are identical. In fact, if you compare a t-distribution for 999 degrees of freedom (or n = 1,000) and a normal distribution, you will see very little difference. Yet if the sample size is 30 or fewer, there is enough difference between the two curves—and thus between the areas underneath them—that we use the t-distribution. Again, we must also be clear to assume the population is normal because for small sample sizes, we no longer get the predictable "normal" shape to the distribution of all possible sample means.

STATISTICS IN ACTION

Below you'll find some of the outstanding credit card balance data from Chapter 5.

$210	220	230	240	270	300	300	320	320	320
340	370	370	380	400	410	450	450	470	470

Now, let's create the same confidence interval estimate for the population average outstanding balance using this small sample of data:

- $\bar{x}$ (the mean of the sample) = $342
- s (the standard deviation of the sample) = $83.51
- n (the size of the sample) = 20 (watch out—SMALL SAMPLE!)
- α (error allowance, or 1 − confidence level needed) = 1 − 95% = 5% (or 0.05)

Before we use the t-distribution to help us with this interval estimate, we must remember to assume that the population of all credit card outstanding balances is normal. Now we can use the confidence interval equation to get

$$\bar{x} \pm t_{\alpha/2}\left(\frac{s}{\sqrt{n}}\right)$$

$$= 342 \pm t_{0.05/2,19\ DOF}\left(\frac{83.51}{\sqrt{20}}\right)$$

$$= 342 \pm t_{0.025,19}(18.67)$$

$$= 342 \pm 2.093(18.67)$$

$$= \$342 \pm \$39.09$$

Therefore, the 95 percent confidence interval for the average outstanding balance is $302.91 to $381.10.

We assume that outstanding balances were sampled randomly and the population of outstanding balances is normally distributed. Note that the CLT does not apply or help us here!

TEST YOURSELF

Return to the "Test Yourself" section of Chapter 5 and rework problems 1, 2, and 4, but this time use a sample size of only 19 participants. Be sure to clearly state any assumptions required to solve these problems.

KEY POINTS TO REMEMBER

This chapter has outlined the key assumptions, tools, and techniques to use when creating interval estimates for population means using small random samples.

- The t-distribution of sample averages: We learned how to use the t-table, how to calculate degrees of freedom, and how to find areas under t-distributions.

- To use a t-distribution, we must assume the population of data that was sampled randomly is normally distributed. Without this assumption, we will not know how all possible sample averages are distributed.

- Don't just use the t-distribution when you have small samples. Don't forget the key assumption that needs to be in place! If you don't believe this assumption can be upheld, then don't use these tools. Instead, talk to a statistician or professional data analyst about using a more appropriate nonparametric technique—like Wilcoxon—to deal with these small sample issues/inferences.

PART III

MAKING DECISIONS AND INFERENCES USING ONE OR TWO SAMPLES

Hypothesis Testing with One Sample: Comparing a Sample Mean to a (Historical) Population Mean

INTRODUCTION

In Chapter 5, we used confidence intervals to establish significant differences (or lack thereof) between two means. Recall that we can use two confidence intervals around two different sample means to compare population means, but this is best done when sample sizes and standard deviations of the samples are equal. (Of course, the confidence levels of the two intervals must also be identical.)

This is a big constraint. Most often, we wish to compare a sample mean—and by inference, a population mean—to either another sample mean or to a historical or commonly believed population mean. We'll learn how to compare two sample means in the next chapter, but to get there, we need to learn how to compare a single sample mean (and again, by extension, a population mean) to a perceived historical (population) mean or *benchmark*. We want to see if the world has changed significantly from what we have always believed. We can do this by taking a single random sample and comparing this sample mean to our prior beliefs. We first discuss how to do such a comparison with a large sample, then cover how to handle a small sample situation.

For example, if our suppliers have historically given us an average of 15 percent discount on all of our purchases, can we use a random sample of data to see if their current average discount is significantly higher or lower? What about just a different average discount? Note here that we can be very directive in our query; that is, we can ask if the new average is only higher than, only lower than, or just different from our historical or prior average.

WHAT'S AHEAD

In this chapter, you'll learn:
- How to compare a sample mean to a historically accepted (population) mean
- How to use *hypothesis tests* to make decisions regarding whether the mean of a population has not changed
- How to execute a hypothesis test and how to interpret the results
- How to understand the differences between one-tailed and two-tailed tests (and what this means about our total estimation error, alpha)

- How to articulate possible inferential errors (and their causes) that could occur with our hypothesis testing and therefore lead us to incorrect decisions/ inferences (so-called *Type I* and *Type II* errors)
- How to handle hypothesis tests of one mean when small samples are involved

IN THE REAL WORLD

It is commonly believed—either from historical analyses of all of our customer data or through conventional wisdom—that our customers spend, on average, $25 per visit to our store. This has been the case for some time, and management has asked us to try to improve this per-visit average spending.

We've put together some marketing and promotional events to try to draw customers into the store and to get them to spend more, on average, each time they visit. To see if our marketing and promotional activity worked, we looked at a random sample of 49 customer receipts after the new campaigns have been in effect for one week and noted that the average per-visit spending is up to $28 with a standard deviation of $14.

Has our marketing and promotional activity significantly increased our average per-visit sales? How can we tell? Even if the sample leads us to this conclusion, are there possible errors that we could have made with our inference?

What if we could only afford to sample 16 customers, not 49 as we planned?

THE KEY CONCEPTS

A Framework for Using Sample Data to Make Decisions

In hypothesis testing, we are interested in making an inference or decision about the population mean (μ)—for instance, asking if it has changed—based on a sample of data. We are less interested in estimating μ, which requires confidence intervals, than in testing a prior belief about the value of μ.

For example, we know that if our main assembly line operates continuously with no maintenance shutdown for more than 30 hours per week on average, then we run the risk of the line's suffering serious breakdowns due to such long average run times and lack of proper preventative maintenance.

Using a random sample of shift run times, we want to determine whether this benchmark of 30 hours, on average, of continuous use is being exceeded by our main assembly line. As with the single-sample tests of means we will discuss, we will be testing a single random sample of data against a commonly held or historical belief about the population mean.

Let's start by defining the two hypotheses that are required to perform hypothesis testing of means:

1. *Null hypothesis* (symbolized by H_0 or "*H naught*"): This hypothesis states the status quo or current belief about the population mean. In the above example, the null hypothesis is that our assembly line operates as it should; that is, with average run times of 30 hours or less.

2. *Alternative hypothesis* (symbolized by H_A): This hypothesis, often called the *research hypothesis*, states what alternative or new belief may be true given the sample of data we have collected. In our example above, we are researching or sampling assembly line run times to see if average run times *exceed* 30 hours.

Another way to think about these hypotheses is what happens when a suspect in a crime is arrested. Despite any evidence, when the police arrest a suspect, the default or initial belief is that the suspect is *not guilty*. This is our null hypothesis. Now, based on a review of the evidence (or data), a judge and a jury may find the suspect guilty—the alternative hypothesis. In this case, the judge and jury have decided to *reject the null hypothesis,* based on the evidence, in favor of the new belief that the suspect actually committed the crime.

Of course, another outcome is possible. After examining the evidence, the judge and jury could decide that the data presented was not compelling in terms of the suspect's guilt. In this case, they would not reject the null but would instead *reserve judgment* or not change their default belief of innocence.

Let's consider another example, this time from the United Nations' Millennium Project. Countries outside of the G8 (the group of the eight most economically powerful nations) typically have an average per capita gross domestic product (GDP) of $1,250. Now the United Nations has claimed that its Millennium Project has substantially improved the average per capita GDP for these countries. In fact, a random sample of 49 non-G8 countries revealed an average per capita GDP of $1,400 with a standard deviation of $700.

Did the Millennium Project increase average GDP/capita for non-G8 countries? Is a $1,400 average GDP/capita higher than the historical mean of $1,250? That may seem obvious—$1,400 is numerically greater than $1,250—but wait! These are not numbers; they are *averages*, and as we recall from confidence intervals, different averages (via their intervals) can be statistically indistinguishable or significantly different from each other. Thus, from a statistical perspective, we are asking if $1,400 as an average is statistically significantly greater than $1,250. This is what we would like to use the large and random sample of data to prove.

How much greater than $1,250 does our sample mean have to be before we will say it is statistically significantly higher than $1,250? Does the sample mean need to be $1,300 or higher? $1,500 or higher? How much greater average GDP/capita do we need to see from a random sample to claim that our null hypothesis is no longer valid?

In this case, let's arbitrarily allow for a 10 percent probability that we will randomly sample and get a mean GDP/capita that is significantly higher than $1,250. How do we set up these two hypotheses and then test whether our new mean (from our sample) is statistically higher than $1,250 as the population mean?

Using a (Large) Sample of Data to Help Us Decide

We can describe our null and alternative hypotheses as the following:

- H_0: Millennium Project did not increase average GDP/capita.

- H_A: Millennium Project did increase average GDP/capita.

But because we are dealing with beliefs about population means, let's restate these more mathematically like this:

- $H_0: \mu_{\text{non-G8 countries}} \leq 1,250$
- $H_A: \mu_{\text{non-G8 countries}} > 1,250$

Here, we see that our current belief about the true mean GDP/capita is $1,250 (or less). Our alternative belief is that the average is higher. Let's use our sample of data to determine whether we should continue to believe that the mean is $1,250 or reject this thinking in favor of the view that the Millennium Project significantly increased the average (population) GDP/capita. A picture of the problem always helps.

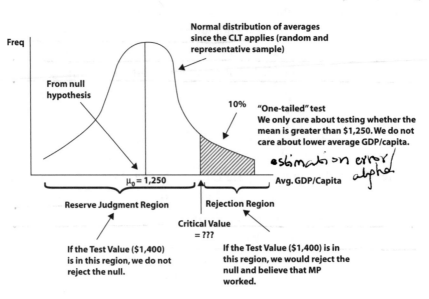

Note a few key observations from this picture:

- We have used the central limit theorem to describe the distribution of all possible average GDP/capita because we have taken a large random sample from the population.

- We have assigned the mean of all possible means to be our *default* or *null hypothesis belief*. This is because it is the default belief about the population mean before we consider our sample data.

- This picture is different from the approach we used when creating confidence intervals, where we placed the sample mean in the middle. Recall that we are not trying to estimate the population mean; instead, we wish only to see if our prior belief about it is still true given a sample of data.

- Also, this picture differs from the confidence interval framework because we are only concerned with the one tail highlighted—the right tail.

This is because we are testing whether our new mean ($1,400) is greater than $1,250. We do not care if our sample mean is less than $1,250, so we don't assign a probability to it.

- The total shaded area, 10 percent in this case, is still referred to as *estimation error*, or *alpha*. Note, though, that instead of 5 percent being in the left tail and 5 percent in the right, all the alpha is all in the right tail (per the last point).

- Standard error is calculated in the same way as before.

- Two key values will be placed on this chart as we solve the problem: the *critical value* and the *test value*. The test value is the mean from our sample data ($1,400). The critical value, which is defined by the 10 percent area in the right tail in this case, marks the possible sample mean such that if our test value were smaller, then we would not reject the null hypothesis. Yet if our test value is greater than the critical value, then this evidence compels us to believe the alternative hypothesis—that the Millennium Project has statistically significantly increased average GDP/capita—and reject our null hypothesis.

Thus the two critical pieces of information that we need to determine are this critical value and whether our test value (from our sample) lies in the *acceptance (of H_0) region* or in the *rejection region*.

To determine the critical value, let's find the z-score that corresponds to 10 percent of the area in the right tail. The z-score tables give us this value as 1.28; that is, the critical value is 1.28 standard errors to the right of the mean. Now, using this z-score, we can determine the critical value.

$$z_{cv} = \frac{cv - 1,250}{100} \longleftarrow$$

$$1.28 = \frac{cv - 1,250}{100}$$

$$cv = 1,250 + 100*1.28$$

$$cv = 1,250 + 128 = 1,378$$

Standard error!! Not standard deviation!!

$$\frac{700}{\sqrt{49}} = 100$$

Adding this information to our picture gives us:

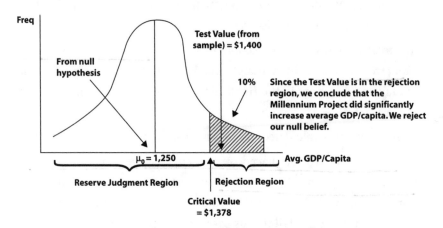

Thus, the critical value is $1,378. This means that any sample mean below $1,378 will not compel us to change our mind and believe our population mean is now higher than $1,250 (our null hypothesis). However, if we get a sample mean above $1,378, we will conclude that the population mean is now statistically significantly greater than $1,250.

In this case, because our test value of $1,400 is *greater* than $1,378, we *reject the null hypothesis* and believe that the Millennium Project did, in fact, significantly raise average GDP/capita.

Decisions Always Come with Possible Errors

Is it possible that we have reached this conclusion in error? For example, in our judge and jury scenario, it is possible that we can reject the null hypothesis—that is, believe a suspect is guilty based on the evidence—when the suspect really didn't commit the crime. We could put an innocent suspect in jail, or *reject the null when we should not have*. Note that our picture shows us this as a probability of 10 percent—the size of the rejection region. Thus, this error possibility/probability is called a *Type I error* or α (alpha).

In the Millennium Project example, such a Type I error would mean we think the project has significantly raised the average GDP/capita, but in fact, a large outlier or two may have skewed the mean higher (or some other effect occurred with our sampling). In this case, our skewed sample results, *not the Millennium Project*, would have caused us to reject the null hypothesis.

(2) error

Another error is also possible, however. Imagine if we had not rejected the null when we should have in our Millennium Project example. It is still possible that the project actually increased the average GDP/capita but a few small outliers skewed our sample mean lower. In this case, when we do not reject the null and the alternative hypothesis is true, we run the Type II risk of committing a *Type II error* or β (beta). The value of the Type II error, which we will not compute here, can be calculated by redrawing our picture above. However, we will focus our analyses only on managing or minimizing Type I or *sampling error* because this is the one we can control based on our alpha tolerance/threshold.

To review:

- α =Type I error: Rejected H_0 when we shouldn't have ("jail the innocent").
- β = Type II error: Did not reject H_0 when we should have ("free the guilty").

Answer

In our Millennium Project example, we rejected the null hypothesis—believing that the project significantly increased average GDP/capita for non-G8 countries—but we have a 10 percent chance of a Type I error (or alpha). This means that some high GDP/capita outliers in our sample could have caused us to believe the average GDP/capita ($1,400) was higher than $1,250, not the Millennium Project and its effects.

2 tailed

Two-tailed test example Let's change the wording of our initial problem slightly. Let's assume that Millennium Project officials claim that the project simply created a *different* average GDP/capita level (not necessarily a higher average). This is an example of a two-tailed hypothesis test in which we will now reject the null if we observe a significantly *higher or lower* average GDP/capita. Our hypotheses now look like this:

$$H_0: \mu_{\text{non-G8 countries}} = \$1,250$$
$$H_A: \mu_{\text{non-G8 countries}} \neq \$1,250$$

Thus, our sample mean either is equal to $1,250 (the null hypothesis) or *statistically significantly different* from $1,250 (our alternative hypothesis). In this case, with a Type I error allowance of 10 percent, we have to allow for the higher and lower possibilities by *splitting the alpha*.

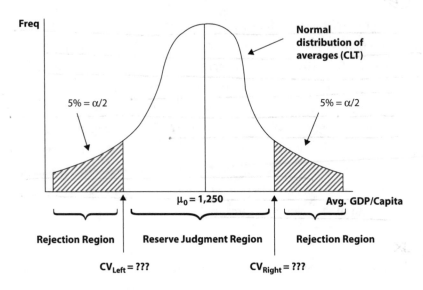

Now we have *two* critical values. Given our test value of $1,400, we only need to determine the right-hand critical value because it is impossible for $1,400 to be in the left tail. This is one of the values of two-tailed tests. If we do not know whether our sample results will be greater or less than our default mean, then a two-tailed test gives us more flexibility. Also, given that the alpha is now split—5 percent in each tail—we will need *more compelling evidence* from our sample to reject the null hypothesis (because the tails are smaller and the critical values are thus further away from the null mean of $1,250).

To determine the critical values, we use the same procedure as before with a 5 percent area in each tail. The Type I error tolerance is still 10 percent—this has not changed. Now, half of alpha is in each tail instead of only one tail.

$$z_{cv} = \frac{cv - 1,250}{100}$$

$$1.65 = \frac{cv - 1,250}{100}$$

$$cv = 1,250 + 1.65*100$$

$$cv_{Right} = 1,250 + 165 = 1,415$$

$$cv_{Left} = 1,250 - 165 = 1,085$$

Redrawing our picture, we get the following:

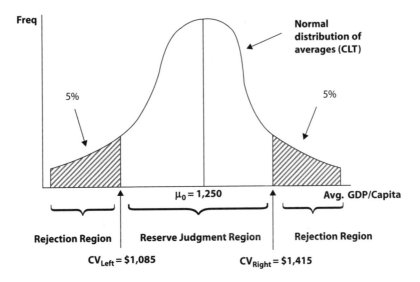

Because our test value of $1,400 is not in either tail, we *fail to reject* H_0. Thus, in this case, it appears that the Millennium Project did not create a statistically significantly *different* average GDP/capita.

How can this be? In the last example, the mean GDP/capita was statistically *greater*. So how can it not be significantly *different*? We have made this two-tailed test harder to pass because the rejection regions are smaller (only 5 percent each). This is another reason why many tests are two-tailed. We require more compelling evidence if we are to reject the null. (We could also just change alpha for the one-tailed test.) Note, though, that the problem statement—and, in fact, the alternative hypothesis—will always clue us in on whether a test is one-tailed or two-tailed. If we wish to assess just *difference*, it will be a two-tailed test. However, if we test a specific difference—greater than or less than—we use a one-tailed test.

In this case, because we reserved judgment with our null hypothesis, we now run the risk of thinking the Millennium Project did not create a statistically different average GDP/capita, when, in fact, it did. Thus, we have the possibility of a Type II error due to low outliers in the sample (which may have skewed the $1,400 average too low). The Millennium Project may have worked, but our sample didn't show a difference.

You probably noticed that a two-tailed hypothesis test looks very familiar—it's our old friend, the confidence interval, but with the null mean in the middle, not the sample mean.

What about Small Samples?

Chapter 6 discussed how to use random but nonrepresentative (or small) samples to create confidence intervals. We can use the same techniques and assumptions to test hypotheses. Let's use the same initial problem (one-tailed test) but now with a sample size of only $n = 16$ countries.

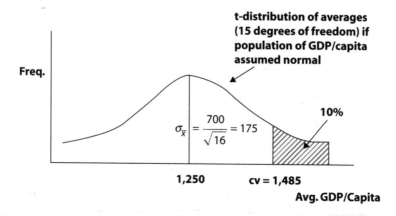

Our hypotheses, default mean ($1,250), and Type I error tolerance, remain unchanged. However, the standard error changes—because the sample size is now smaller—and we must assume the population of all GDP/ capitas is normally distributed. By doing so, we can use a t-distribution with $(n - 1) = 15$ degrees of freedom to describe all possible small-sample averages from this population.

$$H_0: \mu_{\text{non G8 countries}} \leq 1,250$$
$$H_A: \mu_{\text{non G8 countries}} > 1,250$$

$$t_{cv} = \frac{cv - 1,250}{175}$$

Degrees of freedom $= 15 = (n - 1)$
Upper-tail probability $= 10\%$

Therefore:

$$1.341 = \frac{cv - 1,250}{175}$$

$$cv = 1,250 + 235 = 1,485$$

Thus, our critical value is now $1,485, and our test value is still $1,400. When we had a larger sample, we rejected the null hypothesis, but here the test value is less than the critical value. Therefore, we cannot reject the null hypothesis and must conclude that the Millennium Project *did not* create a higher average GDP/capita for non-G8 countries. However, this conclusion depends on our assumption of population (dates) normality. We may also have committed a Type II error due to low sample outliers. The Millennium Project may have worked, but our small sample did not compel us to reject it.

An Easier Way to Evaluate Hypothesis Tests: p-Values

In all of the previous examples, we had to find critical values to determine the result (and possible error) of our hypothesis tests. These results have depended on a predetermined (and often arbitrary) Type I (or alpha) error tolerance.

A more flexible way exists to help us quickly—and with less math and fewer arbitrary assumptions—determine the results of hypothesis tests: p-values or probability values. A *p-value* is simply the area in the tail (or tails depending on type of test) based on the *test value* from our sample of data. After the hypothesis test, we can compare this p-value to the Type I error allowance to determine if the null hypothesis should be accepted or rejected. A picture will help.

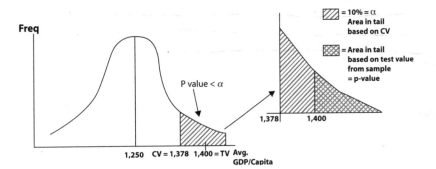

Recall that the null hypothesis was that the Millennium Project created an average GDP/capita of $1,250 or less while the alternative hypothesis was that the Millennium Project created an average GDP/capita greater than $1,250. Above, we see two areas under the right tail:

1. Area in the tail based on the *critical* value, or *alpha* (10% = Type I error)

2. Area in the tail based on the *test* value, or the *p-value of the test*

Pictorially, the p-value must be less than alpha because the test value is in the tail (rejection region). Thus, if we knew this p-value, we would immediately know that it is less than 10 percent and we would therefore reject the null hypothesis (with the possibility, of course of a 10 percent Type I error). Let's compute the p-value of this test. Again, note that the computation of the p-value *does not* depend on alpha or a critical value. It's just the area in the tail(s) based on the test value from our sample.

$$z_{Test\ Value} = \frac{1{,}400 - 1{,}250}{100} = 1.5$$

Now, using the z-table, we find that the area in the tail and to the right of the test value is 6.7 percent. What does a 6.7 percent p-value mean? It means, in probabilistic terms, that under the assumption of the null hypothesis, there is only a 6.7 percent probability of sampling the population and getting a mean higher than $1,400. Because we allowed up to a 10 percent probability of getting a sample mean higher than $1,400, we know a sample mean of $1,400 would allow us to *reject the null hypothesis*.

This p-value is very helpful because it does not depend on alpha (although our conclusion does, of course). If the p-value is less than alpha—whatever we choose alpha to be—we end up *rejecting* the null. However, if the p-value is greater than or equal to alpha, we end up *reserving judgment* and not rejecting the null hypothesis. In summary:

- p-value < α → reject H_0 (with possible Type I error).
- p-value > α → reserve judgment on H_0 (with possible Type II error).

For example, knowing the p-value above (6.7 percent) allows us to say the following:

- At an alpha of 10 percent, we would reject the null (with possible Type I error).
- At an alpha of only 5 percent, however, we would reserve judgment (with possible Type II error) and *not* reject the null hypothesis.

Thus, knowing the p-value of a hypothesis test allows us more flexibly to determine the result of the test—without requiring calculation of a critical value and without knowing the Type I error tolerance in advance of our test.

Still, it is important to note a few things that the p-value is not:

- The p-value is *not* the probability that H_0 is false.
- The p-value is *not* the probability that H_A is true.
- Do not compare p-values from one test to p-values from other tests with, for example, different sample sizes.

Now let's discuss how to find the p-value of a two-tailed test.

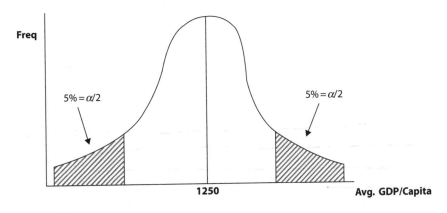

It's important to note that alpha is still the same—10 percent. If we compared the p-value of the one-tailed test (6.7 percent) to this alpha of 10 percent, we would *reject* the null hypothesis—but this conclusion is wrong. Looking back at how we solved the two-tailed problem with critical values, we see that we ended up *reserving judgment* for the null and not rejecting it. How could this be?

The answer lies in the splitting of the alpha. Because there are two possible rejection regions in a two-tailed test, we need to *double* the area found with the one-tailed p-value. In the two-tailed case, the value of 6.7 percent is only half of the p-value of this test (the right-tailed piece). Therefore, for a two-tailed test, we double this area and get the total p-value of the two-tailed test as 13.4 percent.

Comparing this two-tailed p-value (13.4 percent) to the total alpha (still 10 percent), we see that the p-value for the two-tailed test is *greater* than the alpha. This implies that we do not reject the null (with the possibility of a Type II error, of course). Now our results are consistent.

Always compare *total* alpha to the *total* p-value. The p-value depends on the number of tails tested; two tails mean twice the area under one tail to get the total p-value.

Most software programs—including STATA, SAS, SPSS, Minitab, and even Microsoft Excel—report both the one- and two-tailed p-values for hypothesis tests. This is because the software doesn't know your hypotheses, so the software returns both p-values so you can decide. You will always note that for tests of means, the two-tailed p-value is simply twice the one-tailed p-value.

But What Type I Error Tolerance (Alpha) Makes Sense?

A common concern at this point is which alpha (Type I error) tolerance is best? If the alpha is large, clearly it will be easy to reject null hypotheses. But if alpha is too small, it will be very difficult to reject the null.

The most common alpha level to use in most research and business contexts is 5 percent. If we use a 5 percent Type I tolerance in a two-tailed test, we create a 95 percent confidence interval, or an interval created by two standard errors on either side of the hypothesized (null) mean.

Still, in many manufacturing and auditing contexts, *six sigma* tolerance is required; that is, six standard errors on either side of the mean. You'll notice that our tables do not extend that far, and the area beyond six standard errors of the mean is very, very small. But when large numbers of parts or data are being created, transmitted, or quality checked, such precise tolerances become important given the costs of Type I errors!

Still, in this text—and in many examples of hypothesis testing you will encounter—alpha levels of 5 percent or 1 percent are common.

A Recipe for Hypothesis Testing of Means (Single Sample) imp

To review, note the following "recipe" for conducting hypothesis tests of single-sample means:

Step 1 Ask yourself what you are testing: what will be accepted only if the data provide convincing evidence of its truth? This is the alternative (research) hypothesis (H_A).

Step 2 The null hypothesis (H_0) is the opposite—the hypothesis that will be accepted unless the data provide convincing evidence that it is false.

Step 3 How many observations are we examining? What is your n? If the sample size is larger than 30, then we know the results are approximately normal due to the central limit theorem and use z-scores and the z-table for our tests. If $n \leq 30$, then we must assume the population data are normally distributed and use the t-scores and the t-table for our tests.

Step 4 Ask yourself: Is this a one-tail or two-tail test? If your H_A asks for an answer greater or less than some value, then it is a one-tailed test. When your H_A asks for an answer that does not equal a specific value, then you are looking at a two-tailed test. In a one-sided test, you are looking at the area under the right or left tail. In a two-sided test, you are looking at the area under both tails.

Step 5 You are given or decide upon a Type I error tolerance α. This is the area under the tail or tails that you must use to find the critical value(s). If your test statistic falls in this region, you *reject* the null hypothesis (H_0). To find the t-score or z-score that marks this boundary, draw a diagram and use the tables to find the t or z that corresponds to the area. (Remember: Degrees of Freedom $= n - 1$ when looking up your t-statistic.)

Step 6 Once you know the critical value(s), simply compare the test value (from the sample) to the critical value(s).

Step 7 If the test statistic falls in the rejection region(s), then you *reject* the null hypothesis (H_0) and accept the alternative hypothesis (H_A). This can lead to a Type I error, however, due possibly to sample outliers, not a fundamental change in the population mean.

If the test statistic does not fall in the rejection region(s), then you fail to reject the null hypothesis (H_0) (also called *reserving judgment* on the null hypothesis). Note that we do not say we accept H_0 but simply that we fail to reject it. This can lead to a Type II error, however, not resulting from a fundamental change in the population mean.

If we reject the null hypothesis (H_0) and accept the alternative hypothesis (H_A), then we have α probability of being wrong (Type I error). But if we don't reject the null when we should have, then we have a Type II error or β probability of making an incorrect inference or decision. We will not cover how to compute a Type II error in this text.

STATISTICS IN ACTION

A car manufacturer claims that under typical urban driving conditions, the car will travel 20 miles per gallon of gasoline on average. One owner of this car notes the mileages while driving in the city on nine different occasions. Given her data, she claims that her car does not get the same gas mileage that the manufacturer states. She finds that the results, in miles per gallon (mpg), for the different tanks were as follows: 15.6, 18.6, 18.3, 20.1, 21.5, 18.4, 19.1, 20.4, and 19.0. Test the driver's claim by carrying out a test at the level of significance α equals 0.05. What assumptions must be made to perform this test?

We must assume that the distribution of measurements from which the sample was taken is approximately normal (given the small sample) and that the nine measurements were taken randomly. Now we can perform the test. The null and alternative hypotheses are as follows:

- H_0: $\mu = 20$ (The automobile gets 20 miles to the gallon.)
- H_A: $\mu \neq 20$ (The automobile does not get 20 miles to the gallon as claimed.)

From the data above, we can compute: $\bar{x} = 19$ and $s = 1.6583$.

Using 8 degrees of freedom $(9 - 1)$, the rejection regions for a level of significance of 0.05 will be above $20 + 2.306 \times (1.6583 \div 3) = 21.27$ mpg and below $20 - 2.306 \times (1.6583 \div 3) = 18.73$ mpg. Our test value, from our small random sample, is 19. Is 19 mpg in the rejection region or not? *Conclusion / answer*

In this case, because our test value of 19 mpg is not in either tail—it's inside the acceptance region and not in either rejection region—we *do not* reject the null. We cannot refute the claim of the manufacturer. Statistically, on average, the driver is getting the claimed gas mileage performance on average. However, we run the risk of making a Type II error because outliers in the small sample may have caused this conclusion, not a difference in actual average gas mileage. Also, the huge assumption of normality of population gas mileages is a significant limitation of our analysis unless we can know (or can prove) this assumption.

TEST YOURSELF

The Non-Profit Times conducted a random sample of 126 U.S. nonprofit companies at the beginning of 2005. The results reported that the average salary of an executive director of a nonprofit was $92,411 per year with a sample standard deviation of $25,326. A research team from a competing newspaper, which was skeptical of these results, conducted a survey of its own with the same size sample of companies and obtained a mean salary of $87,566 for executive directors (with approximately the same standard deviation as the *Non-Profit Times*'s sample).

1. Set up the appropriate null and alternative hypotheses for testing whether the original sample overestimated the average executive director annual salary.

2. Now test the competing newspaper's view that the original sample overestimated the average executive director annual salary. Use an estimation (total) error of 5 percent.

KEY POINTS TO REMEMBER

This chapter outlined a technique for using samples to help us make inferences and decisions about our (past) beliefs regarding population average behavior. Specifically, we learned how to do the following:

- Set up the null and alternative hypotheses.

- Determine the acceptance and rejection regions, both graphically and mathematically.

- Assess the results of a hypothesis test by either comparing test values to critical values or comparing p-values of these tests to presumed Type I error levels.

- Specify sampling errors that could have caused our inferential results (as opposed to real changes in the population mean): Type I error (alpha, or rejecting the null when it should not have been rejected) and Type II error (beta, or not rejecting the null when it should have been rejected).

- Handle both large-sample and small-sample hypothesis tests by using the same assumptions and distributions (z-tables or t- tables) from our study of confidence intervals.

Hypothesis Testing with Two Samples: Comparing One Sample Mean to Another

INTRODUCTION

The tools and frameworks that we learned in the last chapter helped us compare a single sample mean to our belief about the real population mean. This is a useful tool, but it is fairly limited in its application. We rarely know population means, and any beliefs we have about them usually come from samples anyway.

Thus, we need a way to compare the mean of one sample to the mean of another. By comparing two sample means, we will be able to perform many valuable analyses. For example, we can compare average customer satisfaction levels before and after implementing a new policy. We can compare the average profitability of one customer segment to the average profitability of another (or to the average profitability of a competitor's segment of customers). We can also do *with/without* testing—we can see if average productivity or quality levels for our assembly lines vary whether we implement a new maintenance program. Still, the organization and size of our sample data are important, and we will develop different tools and techniques depending on these qualities.

Though this chapter focuses on how to perform two-sample tests without using a computer, you'll find a lot of convenient software to help you once you understand the process—Microsoft Excel and statistics packages like STATA and SPSS are especially useful. Appendix B contains tutorials on how to perform such tests—as well as descriptive statistics and regression analyses—using Microsoft Excel.

WHAT'S AHEAD

In this chapter, you'll learn:
- How to compare two sample means and make inferences about whether the two populations' means are equal
- How to determine whether data are organized as paired or unpaired
- How to perform a hypothesis test of *mean differences* for paired samples

- How to perform a hypothesis test of *difference of means* for unpaired (also referred to as independent) samples
- What impacts small samples have on these hypothesis-testing techniques—and the assumptions required to use them
- How to interpret possible inferential errors in terms of Type I and Type II errors

IN THE REAL WORLD

As chief marketing officer, you would like to know if your latest advertising campaign increased average sales of your product. What about average number of daily hits to your company's Web site? Is there a way to see if these averages are really different after the ad campaign or just random "noise" in our samples? With one campaign, we looked at sales before and after the ad. After other ad campaigns, however, we compared our average sales to a competitor's in randomly selected retail locations. Is there a difference between these two kinds of tests? And how do we handle small samples, because sometimes we cannot afford—or simply don't have enough stores—to sample more than 30 locations?

This analysis requires us to compare two sample means. But the way we compare sample means depends on the way we collect and organize the data. Thus, before we talk about testing hypotheses of two sample means, we need to examine how different ways of organizing data can lead to different hypothesis-testing techniques.

THE KEY CONCEPTS

Data Organization: Paired versus Independent (or Unpaired) Samples

Let's focus on the two most common ways data are collected to compare two means. First, let's consider *paired data* or *paired samples*. When data are paired, a third variable, called a *pairing variable*, is used to pair two data points or observations. For example, consider a study where we randomly sample customers and look at their sales before and after a major advertising campaign.

Paired Data/Random Samples		
Random Customer ID	Pre-Ad Sales	Post-Ad Sales
00105	$200	$220
02784	150	140
05483	75	100
10458	120	120
...	...	...

Here, we did not randomly sample some customers before the ad ran and randomly sample other customers after the ad. This wouldn't make sense given what we are trying to understand. We want to look at the same customers—before and after the ad campaign—and see if the campaign made a difference in their sales. After the ad, some sales are higher, but some are lower or unchanged. So did customers buy significantly more, on average, after the ad ran? How can we test this? We'll answer this momentarily.

So if the table above shows paired data, what do unpaired data look like? Consider a similar example but with a different sampling/data collection technique.

Independent (Unpaired) Random Samples			
Our Random Customer ID	Our Monthly Sales	Competitor's Random Customer ID	Competitor's Monthly Sales
00105	$200	50119	$220
02784	150	51338	140
05483	75	55783	100
10458	120	58932	120
...	...	...	...

In this case, we randomly sampled *twice*—one random sample is of our customers, and the other is a random sample of a competitor's customers. In this case, there is no connection or *pairing variable* that creates any link between our customer and a competitor's customer. In fact, we may have 60 of our customers collected but only 40 of our competitor's customers. This is fine—and sometimes preferred! If we have a 60 percent market share and our competitor has the other 40 percent, we probably want to *proportionally sample* our customers in this way to avoid overstating or understating either our or our competitor's customer sales.

In this case, the data are *unpaired* or *independent samples*. Just as in probability, *independence* means that the collection of one sample has nothing to do with how we randomly collected another sample. Here, we are comparing two different sample means—the average monthly sales to our customers with the average monthly sales of our competitor. But how do we test unpaired data differently from paired data?

Paired Data: Testing the "Mean Difference" between Two (Large or Small) Samples

We're in luck—we actually already know how to do a paired test! When data are paired, the comparison test actually reduces or simplifies to a single-sample test, which we discussed in the previous chapter. To perform a paired test, we need to create a fourth column and simply subtract the pre-ad sales from the post-ad sales for each customer.

Paired Data/Random Samples			
Random Customer ID	Pre-Ad Sales	Post-Ad Sales	Post-Ad Sales Minus Pre-Ad Sales
00105	$200	$220	$20
02784	150	140	–10
05483	75	100	25
10458	120	120	0
...	...	...	...

We can take the far-right column and find descriptive statistics. These differences will have a mean—a *mean difference*—and a standard deviation. Consider the mean difference for a moment. If the mean difference is significantly greater than zero, this must imply the post-ad sales are significantly higher than the pre-ad sales. If the mean difference is zero or close to zero, however, then there really isn't any significant difference between the pre-ad and post-ad sales. This sounds like a hypothesis test:

- H_0: The mean difference (post-ad sales minus pre-ad sales) is less or equal to zero (that is, the advertising campaign did not create a significant difference in average customer sales).

- H_A: The mean difference is greater than zero (that is, the advertising campaign did work by creating significantly more sales post-ad versus pre-ad).

If we write these mathematically, we denote the sample mean difference—that is, the average of the column of differences, above—as $\bar{x}_\Delta$, and we will use this as an estimate of the real population mean difference, μ_Δ. (Here, the subscript Δ denotes *change in* or *difference*.) Similarly, we will denote the standard deviation from the sample of differences to be s_Δ, and we will use this statistic to approximate the population standard deviation of these differences, σ_Δ. Thus, our hypotheses become

$$H_0: \mu_\Delta \leq 0$$
$$H_A: \mu_\Delta > 0$$

A few notes about this paired test:

- The null hypothesis states our default belief—that the ad campaign either had no effect or had a negative effect on average sales. That way, we can use the data to try to prove that our ad did strictly *increase* average sales.

- Although we are testing for a difference of zero in this example, any difference can be tested. For instance, we can use paired tests to see if the increase we achieved from this ad campaign was at least $10, on average, per month. The number on the right-hand side of the hypothesis statements, then, is just the threshold for the test and can be any number/average you wish to test.

- Because these hypotheses are stated like single-sample tests—that is, we're testing a mean difference, not two different sample means—we can use the frameworks and tools from Chapter 7 to help us.

But these hypotheses bring a question to mind. We know how *averages* are distributed when we sample—based on the central limit theorem (CLT) if the samples are random and representative—but how are *average differences* distributed? Does the CLT apply to mean differences, or is another distribution required?

Let's work out an example to help us determine the answer. Assume that when we run descriptive statistics on the column of differences, we get the following results (again the subscript Δ means "difference"):

- $\bar{x}_\Delta = \$3$ = mean difference from sample data (post-ad minus pre-ad monthly average sales)

- $s_\Delta = \$15$ = standard deviation of differences from sample

- $n_\Delta = 36$ = number of differences (or pairs) of data in sample

We are still sampling averages (just average differences, not averages of data), so all possible averages will still follow an approximately normal distribution because we have a large, random sample of these differences. Assuming an alpha (Type I error allowance) of 5 percent, we get the following picture:

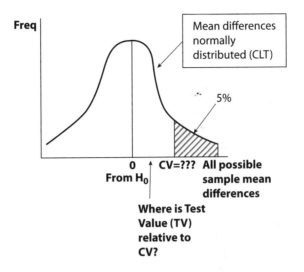

Let's compute the critical value and see where the test value—the mean difference of $3 from our sample—lies. First we need the standard error of this distribution. Then, using the standard error of these mean differences, we can compute the critical value. Here, the critical value turns out to be $4.10.

$$\sigma_{\mu_\Delta} = ? = \frac{s_\Delta}{\sqrt{n_\Delta}} = \frac{15}{\sqrt{36}} = 2.5$$

$$z_{CV} = \frac{CV - 0}{2.5} = 1.645$$

$$CV = 2.5 * 1.645 = 4.1$$

$$TV = \bar{x}_\Delta = 3$$

Because our test value ($3) is not in the rejection region, we conclude that this average increase of $3 is *not statistically significant.* The ad campaign was unsuccessful because it did not create a difference of at least $4.10.   two conclusion

Thus, we do not reject the null, but we do run the risk of a Type II (beta) error because small outliers in the *differences* (not the actual sampled sales values) could have pulled our test value lower than the critical value, not a poor customer sales result.

This was pretty simple. We apply the same tools that we used in Chapter 7 to differences between our paired datasets. But do we handle small samples the same way as before? Yes! Let's rework this problem with a small sample size:

$n_\Delta = 16$, which implies the degrees of freedom are $= n_\Delta - 1 = 15$

Note that even though this is a two-sample test, a paired test reduces to a single-sample test (of mean differences), and the degrees of freedom are still sample size − 1.

What assumptions do we need to make to use a t-distribution with this small sample of mean differences? Just as before, only one is required: if we can assume the population of differences (that is, the population of all possible post-ad sales minus pre-ad sales) is normally distributed, then the distribution of all possible sampled mean differences will be t-distributed with $(n - 1)$ degrees of freedom, where n is the number of pairs. Pictorially, we get the following:

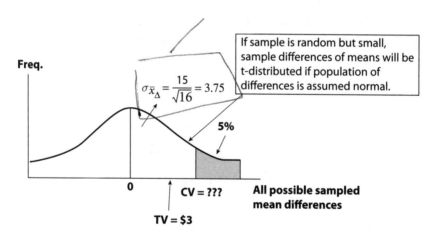

Note the change in standard error given the new sample size. With an alpha of 5 percent, we can use the t-table with 15 degrees of freedom to find the t-statistic for the critical value (1.75). Solving for the critical value yields

$$t_{cv} = \frac{CV - 0}{3.75} \rightarrow 1.75 = \frac{CV}{3.75} \rightarrow CV = \$6.56$$

Again, we fail to reject the null hypothesis. Even with this small sample, we do not show that the ad campaign worked (with the possibility of a Type II error, again, as before).

Independent or Unpaired Data: Testing the "Difference of Means" for Two (Large or Small) Samples

Now let's develop techniques for testing two independent (or unpaired) means. Recall the table where we collected random samples of 49 of our customers and 36 of our competitor's customers.

Independent (Unpaired) Random Samples			
Our Random Customer ID	Our Monthly Sales	Competitor's Random Customer ID	Competitor's Monthly Sales
00105	$200	50119	$200
02784	150	51338	205
05483	75	55783	250
10458	120	58932	100
...	...	...	...

From these two independent samples, we can obtain descriptive statistics such as mean, standard deviation, and sample size.

$\bar{x}_{ours} = \$150$ $\bar{x}_{competitor} = \$200$

$s_{ours} = \$140$ Sample sizes are not necessarily equal. $s_{competitor} = \$180$

$n_{ours} = 49$ $n_{competitor} = 36$

At first glance, it would appear that our competitor's customers have more average monthly sales than ours ($200 versus $150). However, our competitor's customer sales are more variable (standard deviation of $180 versus $140). We need to know if this $50 difference in means is significant. Are our competitor's average monthly sales statistically higher than ours? If so, we may want to develop a strategy to compete more effectively. If not, perhaps we should not yet spend money focusing on this single competitor.

Let's develop some tools to help us answer these questions by starting with the hypotheses. Note here we have two independent means, and we want to see if our competitor's average monthly sales are higher than ours. We will formulate the null hypothesis with the assumption that there is *either a zero or negative difference* between our average monthly sales and those of our competitor. This will make the alternative hypothesis that the competition has significantly *higher* average monthly sales than we do. In shorthand, we have

$$H_0: \mu_{\text{competitor}} \leq \mu_{\text{ours}}$$
$$H_A: \mu_{\text{competitor}} > \mu_{\text{ours}}$$

But we don't have a constant or threshold on the right-hand side of these equations as we have had on others. No problem—just rearrange these equations algebraically to get

$$H_0: \mu_{\text{competitor}} - \mu_{\text{ours}} \leq 0$$
$$H_A: \mu_{\text{competitor}} - \mu_{\text{ours}} > 0$$

Again, the constant on the right-hand side can be any arbitrary threshold, but in this case, we want to determine whether our competitor has significantly higher average monthly sales than ours regardless of how large they are. A common application of these tests, incidentally, is to put a percentage on the right-hand side and use these tests to validate advertised claims such as "Our prices are 20 percent lower (on average) than our competitor's prices." A test of unpaired or independent means is a test of the *difference of means* (unlike a paired test, which is for *mean difference*).

Now we are faced with the same question as before: How are all possible differences of means distributed? We aren't looking at a distribution of averages as we have before; we are looking at a distribution of *differences*.

Note that each independent sampling distribution of means—that is, the distribution of all possible average sales for our customers and the distribution of all possible average sales for our competitor's customers—would be roughly normal by the CLT, if each sample is random and large enough. Each would have its own mean and standard error.

So what happens if we literally subtract one distribution from the other? If we subtract our sampling distribution of average sales from our competitor's sampling distribution of average sales, what results? The answer is good news for us: another normal distribution!

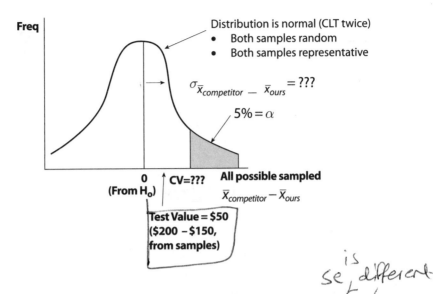

But how do we determine the critical value? We know the test value is $50—derived from our samples by subtracting $150 from $200—but to find the critical value, we need to know the standard error of this distribution. What is it? Is it the standard error of our competitor's averages minus the standard error of ours ($30–$20)? This may seem intuitive, but it's not so. To compute the standard error for the difference of means, we have to take into account the standard errors of both distributions (samples sizes and standard deviations). To do so, we define the standard error of the difference of means to be

$$\sigma_{\bar{x}_{competitor} - \bar{x}_{ours}} = \sqrt{\frac{\sigma^2_{competitor}}{n_{competitor}} + \frac{\sigma^2_{ours}}{n_{ours}}} \approx \sqrt{\frac{s^2_{competitor}}{n_{competitor}} + \frac{s^2_{ours}}{n_{ours}}}$$

To get the standard error of the difference of means, we add the *variances* of the two independent sampling distributions and then take the square root of the entire quantity. Note that because we never know population standard deviations, we use the sample standard deviations to approximate them.

Using this standard error formula for large-sample difference of means, we can compute the standard error of the distribution above.

$$\sigma_{\bar{x}_{competitor} - \bar{x}_{ours}} = \sqrt{\frac{s^2_{competitor}}{n_{competitor}} + \frac{s^2_{ours}}{n_{ours}}} = \sqrt{\frac{180^2}{36} + \frac{140^2}{49}}$$

$$= \sqrt{900 + 400} = \sqrt{1300} = 36.06$$

Now we can find the critical value (CV).

$$z_{CV} = \frac{CV - 0}{36.06} \Rightarrow CV = 36.06 * z_{CV}$$

From the standard normal table, we see that the z-score with 5 percent in the tail is 1.645. Thus,

$$CV = 36.06 \times 1.645 = \$59.32$$

Recall that our test value—the difference of means between our two samples—was $50. Because our test value is not in the rejection region, we must reserve judgment and not reject the null hypothesis. That is, our average sales are no different from our competitor's average sales. Of course, we run the risk of a Type II error because low differences of means could have caused this result, and the competitor could still be significantly outperforming us in terms of average monthly sales.

What happens when we have small unpaired samples with no assumptions about the populations from which they came? Do these same techniques apply? The answer is *no*! We cannot do anything until we make *two* critical assumptions regarding the populations from which our two independent (small) samples were taken:

1. *Both* populations sampled must be assumed to be normally distributed.

2. The variances (or standard deviations) of the two populations must be assumed to be *equal* (even if the sample ones are not).

Thus, if *one or both* independent samples are small, and the two assumptions above are in place, we *pool the variance* between the two samples to guarantee that the distribution of the differences of small sample means will be t-distributed with degrees of freedom equal to the sum of the two sample sizes minus two $(n_{competitor} + n_{ours} - 2)$. This is equivalent to just the sums of the degrees of freedom of each small-sample means distribution when considered separately $(n_{competitor} - 1) + (n_{ours} - 1)$.

So why make these assumptions? Assuming normality for both populations is expected given our treatment of earlier small samples. But why

equal spread/variance

the extra requirement that the populations from which the random samples are drawn have equal spread or variance? This is to ensure that if we see a difference in the means, it's because the means are actually different! If we didn't have the equal variance assumption, one population could be much more spread out—and could have more outliers—than the other. In this case, we could randomly sample—even from normal distributions—and still believe that one mean is significantly higher than the other. But this could be because one distribution is more variable than the other, not because the means are necessarily statistically different.

Let's rework the last problem, and this time, we'll just change the sample sizes as follows:

$$\bar{x}_{ours} = \$150 \qquad \bar{x}_{competitor} = \$200$$
$$s_{ours} = \$140 \qquad s_{competitor} = \$180$$
$$n_{ours} = 16 \qquad n_{competitor} = 9$$

assumption

Now we have two small samples. If we assume both populations of sales are normally distributed and have equal variance (or standard deviation), then we know the sampling distribution of all possible differences of means will be t-distributed with $(16 + 9 - 2) = 23$ degrees of freedom.

formula for std error

But the formula for standard error changes with small, independent, and random samples. We have to "pool" the variance to use a t-distribution for the distribution of the differences of (small sample) means. The formula below is a bit complicated, which is why a software application is particularly useful to perform these calculations. (Also, software tools allow you to specify whether data are independent or paired and whether equal variances are assumed for small samples. See Appendix B for hypothesis-testing tutorials using Microsoft Excel.)

Standard error of small sample difference of means is

$$\sqrt{S_p^2 \left(\frac{1}{n_{competitor}} + \frac{1}{n_{ours}} \right)}$$

where S_p^2 is the pooled variance of the two samples. This pooled variance term is given by:

$$S_p^2 = \frac{\left(n_{competitor} - 1\right) S^2_{competitor} + \left(n_{ours} - 1\right) S^2_{ours}}{n_{competitor} + n_{ours} - 2}$$

Pretty complicated, huh? Note the degrees of freedom for this test in the denominator of the pooled variance term. If we compute this standard error using the small-sample statistics, above, we will get

$$\text{Standard error} = \sqrt{S_p^2 \left(\frac{1}{9} + \frac{1}{16} \right)}, \text{ where}$$

$$S_p^2 = \frac{[(9-1)\$180^2] + [(16-1)\$140^2]}{9+16-2}.$$

$$= \sqrt{(131,478.26)*(0.174)} = \$151.25$$

Solving for the critical value (CV), we get

$$t_{CV} = \frac{CV - 0}{151.25} \Rightarrow CV = 151.25 * t_{CV}$$

Here, the t-score with 5 percent in the right tail and 23 degrees of freedom is 1.714.

Thus, the critical value is 151.25 × 1.714 = $259.25, well to the right of our test value, $50. Again we fail to reject the null with the possibility of a Type II error.

Is There a Preferred Way of Organizing Two-Sample Data/Tests?

So which is better: paired data or independent samples? In short, there isn't one test that is better. In many situations, the test depends on how the data were collected as well as on what type of comparison you want to make. As we've seen, before/after tests are usually paired, while with/without tests are usually independent. While there is no "best" way to test two samples, just make sure you run through your checklist for two-sample tests.

- How are the data organized: paired or independent?
- Do you have large or small samples? (Remember, if one sample is small, treat it like a small sample problem.)
- If you have small samples, what assumptions are required to perform the appropriate test of means?
- Are you doing a one-tailed or two-tailed test? Look at the problem statement and/or your hypotheses.

- Draw a picture of the problem!
- What standard error formula is needed? Remember, independent, small-sample tests, with the assumptions of population normality (of both populations) and of equal variances of the populations, use the pooled variance in the calculation of standard error. This calculation is different from the independent, large-sample standard error.
- Paired tests, however, reduce to single-sample tests, and the standard error calculation is the same whether small or large samples are involved.
- Regardless of the outcome of your test, what possible error could you have made (Type I or Type II)? Why? What could have caused the error?

Here's a quick table that can help you spot what type of test—and what assumptions are required—when you face two-sample comparisons.

Two-Sample Hypothesis Testing: Test and Assumptions

	Small Sample(s) (Either or Both ≤ 30)	Large Sample(s) (Both > 30)
Paired Random Samples	• Test to use : Paired test of means with t-distribution and $(n-1)$ degrees of freedom • ASSUMPTIONS: – Population of mean differences normally distributed	• Test to use : Paired test of means with normal distribution • REQUIREMENTS: – Central limit theorem applies (random and representative paired samples)
Unpaired or **Independent** Random Samples	• Test to use : Two-sample test of difference of means with t-distribution and (n_1+n_2-2) degrees of freedom • ASSUMPTIONS: – Both populations of data normally distributed – Both population (data) variances equal (even if sample ones are not)	• Test to use : Two-sample test of difference of means with normal distribution • REQUIREMENTS: – Central limit theorem applies to both sampling distributions (both samples random and representative)

STATISTICS IN ACTION

Let's look at some problems utilizing these various two-sample tests and inference tools.

[handwritten: 2 eqs. men vs women salan. Unpaired large]

[handwritten marginal: ①]

First, we want to test to see if the salaries of men and women at our company are equal (with a Type I error allowance of 5 percent). Let μ_{men} be the mean of men's salaries and μ_{women} be the mean of women's salaries. We want to try to prove that the average salaries are not the same. Because the men and women haven't been paired in any way, we can see that this is a test of the difference of means. Further, because we are looking here for just a difference, we will perform a two-tailed test. We will set up the hypotheses as follows:

$$H_0: (\mu_{men} - \mu_{women}) = 0$$
$$H_A: (\mu_{men} - \mu_{women}) \neq 0$$

We are now ready to take our samples and test our hypotheses. Below are the results of our sampling.

	Men	Women
Sample Mean	$20,000	$24,000
Sample Standard Deviation	$2,500	$3,600
Sample Size	100	225

[handwritten: assumption]

Assumptions: Both samples are large and random, so the CLT applies to both and, thus, the distribution of the difference of means will be approximately normal.

Our test statistic is −$4,000 (given by $20,000 − $24,000). But is this significantly different from zero? Let's find the left-hand critical value. Note that we will use the sample standard deviations to estimate the population standard deviations in the standard error formula.

$$z_{LeftCV} = \frac{LeftCV - 0}{\sqrt{\frac{\sigma^2_{men}}{n_{men}} + \frac{\sigma^2_{women}}{n_{women}}}} \Rightarrow LeftCV = z_{LeftCV} * \sqrt{\frac{2,500^2}{100} + \frac{3,600^2}{225}}$$

$$= z_{LeftCV} * \$346.55$$

[handwritten: conclusion]

The z-score that gives us 2.5 percent in the left tail is −1.96. Using this z-score in the formula above gives us a left-hand critical value of −1.96 × $346.55 = −$679.24.

Because our test value (−$4,000) is to the left of this critical value, our test value is in the left-hand rejection region. Thus, we can reject the null hypothesis and claim that men's and women's average salaries are not only

[handwritten: paired/small]

unequal but also that women earn statistically significantly *more* than men, on average. Still, we risk a possible Type I error by reaching this conclusion when, in fact, average salaries are (statistically) equal. This could have been caused by high outlying female salaries, low outlying male salaries, or both.

Let's do one with small samples. Suppose you are interested in the effects of interracial contact on racial attitudes. You have a fairly reliable test of racial attitudes in which high scores indicate positive attitudes. You administer the test to a biracial group of fourteen 12-year-old girls. The girls do not know one another, but they have all signed up for a week-long community day camp. The campers spend the next week taking nature walks, playing ball, eating lunch, and doing other activities. At the end of the week, the girls are again given the test. Thus the data consists of 14 pairs of before-and-after scores. The null hypothesis is that the mean of the population of "after" scores is equal to the mean of the population of "before" scores, or that a week of interracial contact has had no effect on racial attitudes. A Type I error tolerance of 10 percent is allowed.

Here are the results of the surveys.

Student	Test Scores		
	Before	After	Difference
1	34	38	−4
2	22	19	3
3	25	36	−11
4	31	40	−9
5	27	36	−9
6	32	31	1
7	38	43	−5
8	37	36	1
9	30	30	0
10	26	31	−5
11	16	34	−18
12	24	31	−7
13	26	36	−10
14	29	37	−8

Mean	−5.785714
Std Dev	5.740257
Count	14

Assumption

This is a small-sample paired-data test. Thus, we need to assume the population of differences is normally distributed to proceed. Because this is a paired test, we will have $(n - 1) = 13$ degrees of freedom. This is also a two-tailed test because the null hypothesis is that the mean difference (before – after) is zero. That means the alternative will be that the mean difference is not zero.

We note that the test value from the sample is negative (–5.786). Let's compare this to the left-hand critical value. Based on 13 degrees of freedom and 5 percent in the left tail, the t-score is –1.77. Thus, the critical value is given by

$$t_{LeftCV} = -1.77 = \frac{CV - 0}{\frac{5.74}{\sqrt{14}}} = \frac{CV}{1.53}$$

So the left-hand critical value is 1.53×-1.77, or –2.71. Because our test value (–5.78) is to the left of this critical value, we reject the null hypothesis and conclude that interracial contact created a different average racial attitude.

But did the scores get higher or lower after the campers were together for a week? A quick look at the table shows that most scores were higher postcontact. Said another way, when we subtract the "after" score from the "before" score, we get a lot of negative numbers. This indicates that racial attitudes improved postcontact and did so significantly.

Because –3.77 falls in the rejection zone, we reject the null hypothesis and accept the alternative hypothesis that interracial contact does have an effect on racial attitudes. However, we risk a Type I error here due to possible low outlier mean differences in our small sample.

TEST YOURSELF

1. The table below shows results from a survey in which 20 adults were asked how many minutes they watched a particular television program. Specifically, respondents were asked this question before your product was placed in the TV show they were watching and then again after your product was placed in the show.

Before Placement	After Placement	Before Placement	After Placement
28	30	25	26
32	30	27	28
15	18	25	29
25	27	31	33
24	26	30	32
23	18	31	27
30	28	16	27
11	15	30	31
34	32	29	30
30	32	27	29

Set up a hypothesis test, preferably in a software tool, to determine whether the average number of minutes watched increased significantly after your product was placed in the TV show. Use a Type I error tolerance of 10 percent.

2. Now let's look at a similar analysis where we compare the average minutes watched after product placement between male and female TV viewers.

Males—After Placement	Females—After Placement	Males—After Placement	Females—After Placement
28	30	25	26
32	30	27	28
15	18	25	29
25	27	31	33
24	26	30	32
23	38	31	27
30	28	16	27
11	35	30	31
34	32	29	30
30	32	27	29
25	27	31	33

(Continued)

(Continued)

Males—After Placement	Females—After Placement	Males—After Placement	Females—After Placement
24	26	30	32
23	18	31	27
30	28	16	
11	35	30	
32	30	27	
15	38	25	
25	27	31	
23	27	31	
30	27	16	
11	31	30	
34	30	29	
30	29	27	

Perform a hypothesis test to determine if average minutes watched post-placement was different between male and female viewers. Use an alpha of 1 percent.

KEY POINTS TO REMEMBER

In this chapter, we have developed tools and techniques to compare two sample means in situations where samples are paired or independent and either large or small.

- Data organization is critical; determine whether data are paired or unpaired (independent).

- Determine whether samples are small or large. If samples are small, then recall the required assumptions:

  - *Paired data:* Assume population of differences is normal.

  - *Unpaired data:* Assume populations of data sampled are normal and that these populations have equal variances.

- If samples are small, remember that the calculation of standard error is the same for paired small samples and paired large samples. Degrees of freedom are $n - 1$.

- The standard error for small independent samples (with the two required small-sample assumptions in place) utilizes the pooled variance formula. The degrees of freedom are first sample size + second sample size − 2.

- One-tail or two-tail tests can be performed with paired or unpaired data.

- Use of software tools for two-sample tests is preferred because software programs take into account small sample formula changes, report one-tailed and two-tailed p-values, and so on.

- There's no best way to organize data (paired versus unpaired). The way the data are collected and the type of results that are being tested will determine how the data are organized and what test is most appropriate.

IV
PART

UNDERSTANDING AND MEASURING RELATIONSHIPS BETWEEN AND AMONG VARIABLES

9

CHAPTER

Measuring and Modeling Relationships between Two Continuous Variables

INTRODUCTION

Thus far, all of the statistical analysis we have performed has been *univariate analysis*, or one dataset or variable at a time. For example, we looked at how test scores might be distributed, how average customer profitability might be distributed (with small and large samples), and how to use an interval of means to estimate the population mean. We also compared a mean to an historical benchmark, and we compared a mean from one sample to the mean of another.

Now we will apply the same frameworks that we've used with univariate data—or a single column of data in a spreadsheet, for example—to two variables at a time, or *bivariate data analysis*. We now look at the statistics of the relationship between two variables, including how to summarize the relationship, graph it, determine whether the relationship is statistically significant, and build interval estimates using the relationship. We'll develop many of the tools and analyses that we used with one-variable problems for two variables (and eventually for more than two). We will restrict our analyses to continuous or measurement (numerical) variables—not other types, such as categorical variables (e.g., gender, race, ethnicity)—and we will focus exclusively on *linear* relationships between two variables.

WHAT'S AHEAD

In this chapter, you'll learn how to:

- Describe relationships between two continuous variables (mathematically and graphically)
- Recognize the difference between *predictions* and *forecasts*
- Measure the strength of a the relationship between two variables
- Build a simple linear model of the relationship

- Apply and test assumptions required for simple linear regression modeling
- Measure the significance and "fit" of the regression model
- Use a regression model to make predictions
- Measure input variable (slope) significance
- Perform regression diagnostics by looking at *residuals*, or unexplained prediction errors

IN THE REAL WORLD

Your firm makes textbooks. Lots and lots of textbooks. But as CFO, you want to get a better handle on the costs of producing these textbooks. The total cost of manufacturing a textbook, at a simple level, is

$$\text{Total Cost} = \text{Fixed Cost} + \text{Variable Cost}$$

Variable cost is

$$\text{Variable Cost} = \text{Marginal Cost} \times \text{Quantity Produced}$$

Putting these together, we see that

$$\text{Total Cost} = \text{Fixed Cost} + \text{Marginal Cost} \times \text{Quantity Produced}$$

This cost model has the form of a straight line, or $y = b + mx$, where y is the total cost, b is fixed cost regardless of quantity produced, m is the marginal cost (or cost of manufacturing just one unit/book), and x is the quantity of books produced.

The fixed cost can also be interpreted as the y-intercept of the line, and the marginal cost, m, can be interpreted as the slope of the line that best fits the relationship between quantity and total cost (also called the *regression line*).

So how do we create this model if all we have are quantities and total costs of past batches of books produced? Can we use this equation to predict the total cost of 20 textbooks? How about 200 textbooks?

How do we build, interpret, and improve this model? What assumptions are required to build the model? Because statistical software must be used to create these models, how do we interpret the output from such tools (like Excel, SPSS, and STATA)? The answers to these questions, which appear as a practice problem, are discussed in this chapter.

THE KEY CONCEPTS

Describing Relationships between Two Continuous Variables

As in univariate analysis, we can describe *bivariate* data with numbers and pictures. Further, we can use sample models to estimate population models, and we can use characteristics of these relationships/models to make decisions regarding statistical significance and predictions. As we have throughout this text, we will look only at *continuous variables*, variables that can be measured in intervals or numerically/quantitatively (like height, weight, income, and years of education). We will not create relationships between *categorical* or *coded* variables (such as gender, ethnicity, product line, letter grade, and so on). Thus, we need numerical or "number" variables to use the tools we discuss in this chapter. We are trying to understand relationships between variables, not *causation*. Variables may be related—such as a stock market index and the temperature outside the stock exchange—but this does not necessarily imply a *causal* linkage between the variables.

Bivariate data are *paired* data, where the pair describes two features or attributes. For example, we could collect the heights and weights of different people, or we could collect their salaries and years of education. Our goal in this chapter is to describe a relationship, if one exists, between these two variables. For example, is there a relationship between height and weight? Between salaries and years of education? Does the relationship change if we look at different genders, age ranges, or ethnicities? These are questions we will answer, but first we need to *describe* and *measure* a relationship between two variables. We start by looking at the data graphically using a *scatterplot*. Below is a graph of the gross national product (GNP) per capita of various countries along with their HIV infection rates.

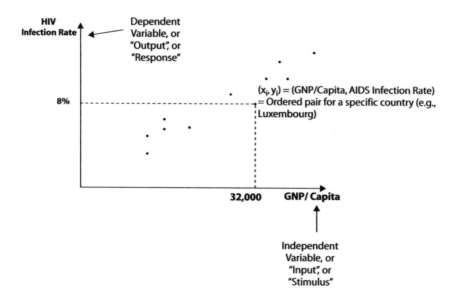

We see that the x-axis is the independent or *input variable* axis, representing GNP per capita, and the y-axis is the dependent or *output variable* axis, representing HIV infection rate. Each country in the sample plotted here is represented by one dot in the scatterplot. Above, the point or ordered pair connected by the dotted lines (x_i, y_i) represents Luxembourg's GNP/capita (32,000) and HIV infection rate (8 percent) (these are made-up numbers just for purposes of this example). This is called an *ordered pair* because the data listed for this country are in the order of GNP/capita first, followed by HIV infection rate. The order does matter; here we are using GNP/capita to *predict* or to *estimate* the HIV infection rate across all of these countries. The model we would like to build—using a straight line—will be our shorthand for this relationship.

The key to regression and relationship analyses is an initial scatterplot. Always look at a picture of the relationship first. Recall Rule #1 of statistics: *Graph the data!* We can learn a great deal about the relationship between GNP/capita and HIV infection rates just by just looking at a picture.

Because we will only be modeling relationships with straight lines—so-called *linear regression*—we need to see if the relationship even lends itself to a linear approximation or linear model. Below are some examples of scatterplots where the relationship between the variables is somewhat linear (modeled by a line) but where a line isn't necessarily the best model to use to describe the relationship.

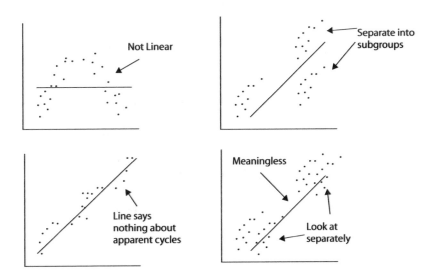

While a line can pass through the data in these cases, a linear model to describe the relationship may not be the best tool to use. We could have nonlinear data (upper left), data that cycles (lower left), data in different groupings in the same dataset (upper right), or data in two ranges with no "middle" (lower right).

But how can we quantify a (linear) relationship? How can we know if it's a "good" or "poor" linear relationship? If we have a good linear model, how can we use it to make predictions?

This brings us to Rule #3 of statistics.

Rule #3 of Statistics: Predictions Are Not Forecasts!

In this chapter and the next, we will build *predictive* models, not *forecasting* models. This distinction is important. If we aren't careful, we may try to use the tools of this chapter to build a linear model based on the passage of time, using time on the x-axis. While this may be appropriate, we must be aware of precautions about so-called *time-series data* in regression models. As we will see later, some assumptions are required to build good linear models, and time-series data may violate some of these assumptions.

Thus, we will focus on building models that help us make predictions based on past *outcomes* (such as past levels of GNP/capita), not past *time* (such as last year's GNP/capita). This means we will not be building models with time as an input (or x-axis) variable.

Measuring the Strength of the Relationship

Now, let's develop a way to quantify how "linear" a relationship between two variables is. We recall a couple of formulas from the first chapter:

$$\frac{1}{n}\sum(x_i - \mu_x)^2 = \sigma_x^2 = \text{Population variance of GNP/Capita}$$

$$\frac{1}{n}\sum(y_i - \mu_y)^2 = \sigma_y^2 = \text{Population variance of HIV infection rate}$$

Now, look at the following expression, which references each of the variance terms above.

$$\frac{1}{n}\sum(x_i - \mu_x)(y_i - \mu_y) = \sigma_{xy}$$

This is the formula for the *covariance* of x and y, or in our example above, how closely the GNP/capita and HIV infection rate linearly "track" or "trend" with each other. A few notes about covariance, which is sometimes denoted $Cov(x,y)$:

- Covariance is one measure of how much two variables vary linearly with each other.

- Covariance is more *positive* when a pair of values differ from their respective means in the same direction.

- Covariance is more *negative* when a pair of values differ from their respective means in opposite directions.

Note that covariance has both a population and sample representations. Note below that the term involving x (the input variable) is in dollars, and the HIV infection rate, or the term involving y (the output variable), is measured in percentages.

$$\sigma_{xy} = \frac{1}{n}\sum (x_i - \mu_x)(y_i - \mu_y)$$

$$S_{xy} = \frac{1}{n-1}\sum (x_i - \bar{x})(y_i - \bar{y})$$

$$\$ \qquad\qquad \%$$

As you can see, the units of covariance of our two variables are the product of the units of the two variables (in this case $\$$ and $\%$, because GNP/capita is measured in dollars, and HIV infection rate is measured in percentages).

So is there anything wrong with covariance as a measure of the strength of the linear relationship? Consider the following example:

Set A of countries: Covariance of GNP/capita and HIV infection rate
= 100 $\$\%$

Set B of countries: Covariance of GNP/capita and HIV infection rate
= 10 $\$\%$

Why is the covariance for Set A so much higher than the covariance for Set B? Is it because the countries in Set A have more volatility in GNP/capita, or is it because Set A's countries have more outliers in HIV infection rate? Could it be both? Because covariance has the units of both variables, we cannot tell which variable is contributing to a higher covariance. Furthermore, these units—$\$\%$—don't really make sense, practically speaking. Can you imagine a quantity measured (simultaneously) by these two units? Just as we did with variance of a dataset, where variance is in units of the data squared, is there some way to adjust covariance so that it becomes a more meaningful quantity?

Take a look at the following expression. Here, we've divided the covariance by the product of the standard deviations of each variable.

$$\frac{\sigma_{xy}}{\sigma_x \sigma_y} = \frac{Covariance\ of\ GNP/Capita\ and\ HIV\ Infection\ Rate}{Standard\ Deviation\ of\ GNP/Capita * Standard\ Deviation\ of\ HIV\ Infection\ Rate}$$

This ratio, which has no units because they cancel out, is called the *correlation* of GNP/capita and HIV infection rate. Because we are using population parameters, this ratio is given the Greek letter *rho* (ρ).

$$\rho = \frac{\sigma_{xy}}{\sigma_x \sigma_y}$$

If we create the sample statistic version of correlation, we get

$$r = \frac{S_{xy}}{S_x S_y}$$

The correlation between two variables can range between -1 to +1. Correlation has the same sign (+ or −) as the slope of the regression line that best fits the data, but correlation *is not* the slope of the regression line. Instead, it gives us direction (via its sign) and magnitude (via its quantity) of the strength of the linear relationship between the variables. Let's look at some examples.

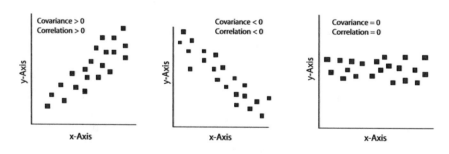

As x increases, y increases.	As x increases, y decreases.	As x increases, y is unchanged.
"Positive linear relationship"	"Negative linear relationship"	"No linear relationship"
Correlation > 0	Correlation < 0	Correlation = 0
Slope of regression line > 0	Slope of regression line < 0	Slope of regression line = 0

If two variables are "perfectly correlated" with correlation equal to 1 or −1, then all data points will fit perfectly on the regression line regardless of its slope. A correlation of 1 will provide a perfect fit between regression line and points with a positive slope. Alternatively, a correlation of −1 will give us all the points on the regression line, but the regression line will have a negative slope.

An example will help. Let's try to build a model to predict a country's GNP/capita. We are looking at GNP/capita on the y-axis. If we have several other macroeconomic variables to choose from, which single (independent) variable is best correlated with GNP/capita? Here are some variables (along with their variable names) we can choose from:

- Population (*pop*)
- Urban population (*urbpop*)
- Population growth (*popgrow*)
- Birth rate (*birth_rt*)
- Infant mortality (*inf_mort*)
- Life expectancy (*life_exp*)

To figure out which variable is best correlated with GNP/capita (*gnp_pcap*), we need to build a *correlation matrix*. All statistical tools, including Microsoft Excel, will generate these. See the tutorials in Appendix B for assistance with creating correlation matrices and linear regression models using Excel. Below is some output from a statistical tool.

	gnp_pcap	pop	urbpop	popgrow	birth_rt	inf_mort	life_exp
gnp_pcap	1.0000						
pop	-0.0340	1.0000					
urbpop	0.6143	-0.0878	1.0000				
popgrow	-0.4062	-0.0420	-0.5102	1.0000			
birth_rt	-0.5993	-0.0852	-0.7286	0.7473	1.0000		
inf_mort	-0.5496	0.0019	-0.7172	0.5545	0.8746	1.0000	
life_exp	0.5918	0.0212	0.7307	-0.5356	-0.8685	-0.9595	1.0000

Note that the first column has all the variables listed. All variables are also listed across the top row. In the intersections are the correlations. Notice that a variable is perfectly correlated to itself; this is why we see *1.0000* across the diagonal. Also, note that half of the table appears to be missing. This is not an error; we only need to see half of this table because the correlation of *gnp_pcap* and *birth_rt*, for example, is −0.5993, the exact same as the correlation of *birth_rt* and *gnp_pcap*. Because order doesn't matter, we do see all the possible correlations in the table above.

If we wish to build a linear relationship model to predict GNP/capita, which single independent (or input) variable would we pick? We want the variable that is best correlated with GNP/capita. Look at the column in the correlation matrix under *gnp_pcap*. In descending order of correlation, we get the following:

> Highest correlation: Urban population
> Second highest: Birthrate
> Third highest: Life expectancy

These results may surprise you. Perhaps you thought life expectancy was the second-best correlated variable with GNP/capita.

As you can see, when it comes to picking the best correlation, the *sign does not matter*. We only care about getting the best *absolute* correlation regardless of whether this correlation is negative or positive. Thus, life expectancy is the third-highest behind the (negative) correlation given by birthrate.

Now that we've determined that urban population is the variable that is best correlated with GNP/capita, let's take a look at how to model this relationship and assess its significance in a statistical way.

Building a Simple Linear Model of the Relationship

Now we discuss how to build a simple linear model or "shorthand" to represent the relationship between two variables. Just as we used the mean (or median or mode) to represent the central tendency of a dataset, we can create lines or linear regression models to represent the central tendency of the relationship between two variables. (Another way to think of a regression line is the expected value of an output given a specific, or fixed, input value.)

To start, we must graph the data. Below is a combination graph that shows both the scatterplot between GNP/capita and urban population, as well as the best-fit or *regression* line through all the data points.

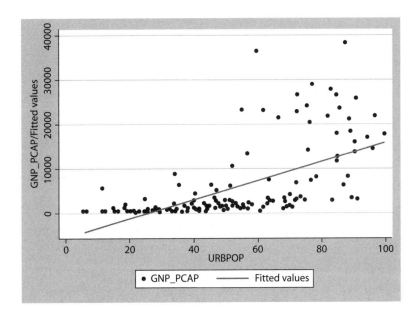

A few notes about this chart:

- The independent/input variable (*urbpop*) is on the x-axis. The dependent/output variable (*gnp_pcap*) is on the y-axis.

- The straight line is the regression line and represents the best-fit model through all points.

- The dots represent the actual values in the data set.

- Does the regression line appear like a good fit? At this point, you can visually determine if the line seems like a good fit vis-à-vis the actual values.

- If a linear model does not seem to make sense, you may want to try building a regression model using a new or different variable (or trying to model this relationship with a nonlinear function, which is beyond the scope of this text).

Now, let's look more closely at this model and its relationship to the scatterplot. In fact, let's just look at one point and observe how well the line (or regression model) estimates the GNP/capita for a specific value of urban population.

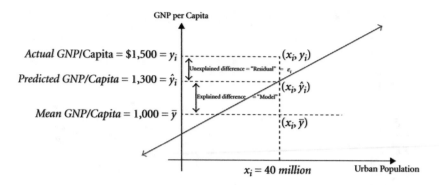

Three features stand out. First, the point (40 million, $1,500) is the actual GNP/capita for a country with 40 million in urban population (for example, Luxembourg). But note that the regression line, at 40 million of urban population, *underestimates* the actual GNP/capita of Luxembourg. The regression line gives a *predicted GNP/capita* of only $1,300. (This predicted value is often called "y-hat" given the little "hat" symbol over the y. This "hat" always indicates a predicted value from a model.)

Thus, we have a difference or *residual* between the actual GNP/capita ($1,500) and the predicted GNP/capita ($1,300). This difference in values, $y_i - \hat{y}_i$, is called a *residual* or *error term* and is denoted by the symbol ε_i.

However, the predicted value of $1,300 of GNP/capita is higher than the average GNP/capita ($1,000) across all countries in the scatterplot. This is just the difference between Luxembourg's predicted GNP/capita and the average across all countries in the dataset used to build this linear predictive model.

This brings up a question: Why are both Luxembourg's predicted and actual GNP/capita values greater than the overall average GNP/capita?

This question requires two answers, and each answer points to a different reason why Luxembourg has higher-than-average GNP/capita.

1. *Because the regression model says so.* Our regression line/model is upward sloping. As urban population increases, GNP/capita should increase. Thus, the reason our regression prediction ($1,300) is larger than average ($1,000) is due to the positive correlation between GNP/capita and urban population. This $300 difference is the *explained difference* because it is explained by the input variable (urban population) and the model we have built.

Still, there is another reason that Luxembourg's actual GNP/capita is higher than average: because the regression model (or urban population) explains only $300 of the $500 difference between Luxembourg's actual GNP/capita and the average of all countries in the dataset.

2. This remaining $200 difference between the predicted value and the actual value is the *unexplained difference*. Our model—based solely on urban population—doesn't explain this extra difference (higher than predicted GNP/capita). It could be due to other (unmodeled) factors such as worker education, industrial base, and the like.

Thus, we now have two sources of difference or *variance* that describe why Luxembourg's GNP/capita is higher than average. Part of the reason (difference) is due to urban population. This relationship comes from the model we built. The other part of the reason (difference) is due to factors not included in our model or unexplained/unmodeled effects (including just plain randomness or random errors).

Let's put some mathematics behind our model. Just as in univariate statistics, we will have a population *parameter* and a sample *statistic* in our study of linear regression. If we look at the population—all countries of the world over all time with all historical GNP/capita values and urban population values—we can determine any actual GNP/capita using an equation of a line as follows:

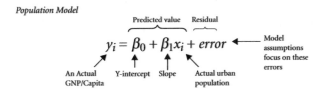

Here, we see that an actual value for GNP/capita ($1,500) is the sum of a predicted value (from the regression line, or $1,300) plus a residual ($200). The y-intercept and slope of the regression line are given by the two parameters, β_0 *and* β_1, respectively. Yet because we will rarely, if ever, have entire populations of data, we need to take a random sample and estimate the slope and intercept terms

Sample Model

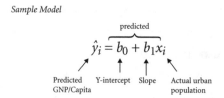

In the sample model, we focus solely on using the sample statistics (y-intercept = b_0, and slope = b_1) to estimate or to infer the population parameters of the regression line—the y-intercept (β_0) and the slope (β_1)—but not the error term. This is because we will never know the true population error (because we won't know the true population GNP/capita value for any country). Thus, our sample will help us to build predicted values that we can then use to infer actual population values for GNP/capita.

You'll notice that this process is similar to how we treated means. We took a sample, found a sample mean ($\bar{x}$), and then used it to estimate (with confidence intervals) or infer (with hypothesis tests) what the population mean (μ) might be. We are doing precisely the same thing here—using a sample model slope and intercept to estimate the population slope and intercept parameters—but our focus is on a predicted output value (GNP/capita) based on an input (urban population) and the linear relationship between these two variables.

Recall that in our study of means, we had to have some special conditions in place—such as the central limit theorem with random and representative samples to make inferences. The same is true with linear regression—assumptions are required for this type of modeling.

Assumptions Required for Simple Linear Regression Modeling

The assumptions required to perform simple linear regression focus on the error terms or residuals—the differences between the actual GNP/capita values and the predicted ones we get from the regression model. If we look at the scatterplot of data and determine that a linear relationship likely makes sense, then we must have the following four assumptions in place for the residuals at the population level.

Population Model Assumptions for Residuals

1. *Average of residuals* = 0: This means that our population regression line, on average, will generate no positive or negative error. If this is not the case, then the regression line (or model) may systematically underestimate or overestimate the true values of GNP/capita, for example.

2. *Variance (or standard deviation) of residuals is constant regardless of the value of the input variable*: This means that the GNP/capita errors are equally distributed around the population regression line regardless of the value of urban population. Thus, our model is no better or worse at estimating the GNP/capita for high-urban-population countries than it is for low-urban-population countries.

3. *All residuals are independent*: This means that any error made in estimating one country's GNP/capita has nothing to do with any error made in estimating another country's GNP/capita. Remember the concept of independence from probability? Here it is again!

4. *All residuals are normally distributed*: This is a big assumption! Here, for every urban population value, the errors in GNP/capita are assumed to be bell-curve distributed.

Putting all of these assumptions together, we see that our population regression model is based on the assumptions that any errors or residuals (differences between actual and predicted GNP/capita values) have a mean of zero, are equally spread around the regression line, are independent, and are normally distributed. Graphically, this means the following:

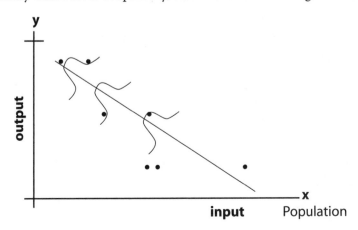

Although we cannot check these assumptions—because we will not likely have a population of data—we can look at our sample scatterplot to see if any of these assumptions might be violated.

For example, recall the scatterplot from our GNP/capita and urban population model.

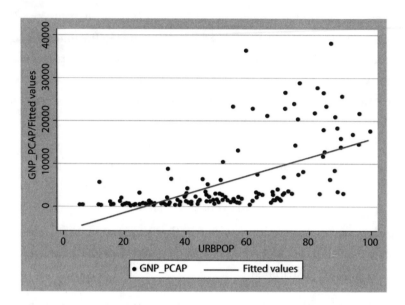

Note some possible assumption violations. First, in some areas of the data, the regression line almost always underestimates the relationship (for example, for urban populations under 30 million). Also, note that the spread of the actual values around the regression line is not consistent— or equally variable—for all values of urban population. For example, the GNP/capita values seem to vary more when urban population is greater than 50 million. We will eventually test the independence assumption (by looking at residuals), but we cannot check the normal distribution assumption because we would need all residuals (i.e., the population model and data) to determine this.

Still, we can see some possible violations. Though a linear model doesn't seem to be an ideal model for this relationship, let's proceed to build it anyway and study its attributes.

Measuring the Significance and "Fit" of the Regression Model

How do we actually determine the equation of our regression line (i.e., the slope and intercept)? And if we have them, how do we know whether our relationship between GNP/capita and urban population is statistically significant in the sense that urban population is a significant predictor of GNP/capita? Let's start by examining the basic numerical output from a regression model. (Note that similar output can be created using Microsoft Excel. Please see the tutorial in Appendix B.)

Source	SS	df	MS		Number of obs	=	154
					F(1, 152)	=	92.73
Model	3.9155e+09	1	3.9155e+09		Prob > F	=	0.0000
Residual	6.4183e+09	152	42225700.3		R-squared	=	0.3789
					Adj R-squared	=	0.3748
Total	1.0334e+10	153	67541338.7		Root MSE	=	6498.1

gnp_pcap	Coef.	Std. Err.	t	P>|t|	[95% Conf. Interval]	
urbpop	213.5579	22.17734	9.63	0.000	169.7423	257.3736
_cons	−5536.177	1253.778	−4.42	0.000	−8013.258	−3059.096

Note that the regression output has three sections. The box in the upper left is the *analysis of variance* of the model. Here, we obtain information on the explained ("model") and unexplained ("residual") errors (or variances) from our regression model. To the right is the *model significance* section where we have statistics about how "good" the model is and how well the regression line predicts or fits the data from our sample. Finally, at the bottom is the *parameter significance* portion of the output. Let's look at some key pieces of this output to understand the model, its significance, and how well it fits the data.

To start, what is the equation of the line that relates GNP/capita and urban population? This can be found in the bottom part of the output where we see the coefficients (*Coef.*) of the model. Note that the model we have built, based on a sample of 154 countries (see *Number of obs* in the upper right), is of the form

Predicted GNP/capita = y-Intercept + Slope × Urban Population

We can pull the y-intercept, which is a constant, and the slope from the output, above and get

Predicted GNP/capita = –5536.177 + 213.5579 × Urban Population

This is our sample regression model, or the equation of the line that best fits the points in our scatterplot, above. Note the positive slope—that is, as urban population increases so does GNP/capita. This is expected because the correlation between these two variables is also positive.

But does the input variable (urban population) significantly explain GNP/capita using this model? The key to this is to look at a ratio of two variances. Note that the numerator is the variance of the differences between the predicted values and the mean value of GNP/capita (or the explained difference) and the denominator is the variance of the residuals (or unexplained differences).

$$\frac{Explained\ Variance}{Unexplained\ Variance} = \frac{\sum (\hat{y}_i - \bar{y})^2}{\frac{1}{n-2}\sum (y_i - \hat{y}_i)^2} = F\text{-}ratio$$

Don't worry too much about the fractions in front of these sums; pay attention to the sum of squares pieces. This ratio of two variances is called the *F-ratio*, named for the agronomist and statistician R. A. Fisher. When we build a model, we would like this F-ratio to be quite large. That is, we want the amount of variance (in GNP/capita) that is explained (by urban population) to be very large compared to the amount of variability that is left unexplained. This sounds like a hypothesis test!

H_0:   Model has no linear explanatory or predictive power; $F \leq 1$
little explained variance.

H_A: Model has significant linear explanatory power; $F > 1$
significantly large explained variance.

Said differently, we want our model to have much more explained variance than unexplained variance. If this is true, this F-ratio will be significantly greater than one. Note, too, that if the alternative hypothesis holds true, then the slope will be significantly different from zero. That is, if our model has statistically more explained variance than unexplained— such that the F-ratio is significantly greater than one—then this implies that the slope in our model is significantly different from zero, and our regression line has nonzero slope. (This also indicates that the output variable "responds" to the input variable instead of the regression line being flat: slope = 0.)

But what is this ratio? The analysis of variance box in the output gives us the numerator (3.9155×10^9) and the denominator (42,225,700.3). These are the *mean squared model* errors and the *mean squared residual* errors. Note that these can be found under the *MS* or *mean squared* column in the table.

But the math has already been done for us! Look to the right—in the model significance output section. We see that the F-ratio, with one degree of freedom for the model and 152 degrees of freedom for the residuals, is 92.73. But is this F-ratio statistically significantly greater than 1?

To determine this, we need the p-value of this hypothesis test. Without going into details about the F-distribution of the ratio of variances, suffice it to say that we can determine if the ratio of 92.73 is significantly greater than 1 if we know the p-value of this one-tailed test. In our output above, the *Prob > F* is the p-value of this hypothesis test. (It is referred to as *Significance F* in Excel output.) Note that this p-value is 0.0000, far less than any reasonable alpha (Type I) error tolerance level.

Therefore, we can reject the null hypothesis that the model has no linear explanatory power. Instead, we believe the alternative hypothesis—that urban population is a significant predictor of GNP/capita—while running the risk of a Type I error (thinking that this model is significant when, in fact, it is not at the population level).

Thus, the F-ratio (sometimes called the *F-statistic*) gives us a measurement (and p-value) by which we can determine if our linear model is significant; that is, whether urban population significantly predicts or explains GNP/capita using a line.

How do we measure how well the line actually "fits" the points? Can we measure how much of the variability in GNP/capita is explained by urban population? Let's look at another couple of ratios. First, let's look at the unexplained variance as a ratio of the total variance (that is, the error between the mean GNP/capita and the actual GNP/capita value). We want this ratio to be quite small so that unexplained variance is a very small component of total variance.

$$\frac{\sum (y_i - \hat{y}_i)^2}{\sum (y_i - \bar{y})^2} = \frac{Unexplained\ Variance}{Total\ Variance} \qquad \longleftarrow \quad \textbf{You want this fraction to be very small!}$$

Again, don't worry about any constants or fractions in front of the numerator or denominator. Now, let's subtract this ratio from one. In doing so, we will get one minus this ratio, or the ratio of explained variance to total variance.

$$1 - \frac{\sum (y_i - \hat{y}_i)^2}{\sum (y_i - \bar{y})^2} = \frac{Explained\ Variance}{Total\ Variance} \qquad \longleftarrow \quad \textbf{Above 50\% is ideal}$$

Note that this ratio measures how much of the variability in GNP/capita is explained by urban population when using a line (or linear model) to relate the two variables. This is also known as the *coefficient of determination* or r^2.

The r^2 term can be interpreted in two ways.

1. *As a percentage*: The variance in output variable (GNP/capita) that is explained by the input variable (urban population) using a linear model.

2. *As a "goodness of fit" statistic*: Note that the closer the r^2 term is to 1, the more total variance is actually explained variance. Thus, the closer this term is to 1, the closer the actual values are to the regression line.

Let's look at our output. We have two r-squared terms—an *R-Squared* term and an *Adj. R-Squared* term. Notice that the adjusted one is less than the unadjusted one. Which one should we use and why?

The unadjusted r-squared term is 0.3789, or 37.89 percent. The adjusted r-squared is 37.48 percent. The adjustment takes into account the sample size relative to the number of input variables (in this case only one input variable is used to model GNP/capita). Thus, the adjusted r-squared term is always less than the unadjusted one. To be safe, always use the *adjusted r-squared* term when discussing explained variance.

From the output, we can see that, on an adjusted basis, urban population explains about 37.5 percent of the variability in GNP/capita when using a linear model (or straight line) to model their relationship.

Another interesting outcome that is not on the output is the following.

$\sqrt{r^2} = |r| \approx \rho \longleftarrow$ = correlation between input variable(s) and output variable

Thus, the correlation between GNP/capita and urban population is roughly 0.6, which is what we saw earlier in the correlation matrix.

Note that the F-statistic and r-squared are similar but different terms. The F-statistic gives us a sense of whether our line is a good *trend model* whereas the r-squared tells us whether the model *fits the actual values* well. It is possible to have a model with a good (significant) F-statistic but with a relatively poor r-squared. Our example is such a case. The model (or line) trends well—the line goes in the same direction as the data—but the line doesn't fit the points that well. The reverse—high r-squared and poor F-ratio—is impossible.

One question that always comes up is what represents a "good" correlation or r-squared? Practically speaking, we should always want at least half of the total variance in the output explained by the input. Thus, we should strive for r-squared terms greater than 50 percent. With this goal, we should strive for correlations between input and output variables of greater than 70 percent. This is because if correlation is 70 percent, then r-squared (unadjusted) will be approximately 49 percent. But as we have seen, such goals are not always achievable. Recall that urban population was the highest correlated variable with GNP/capita. Sometimes, we can only do the best job that our data allow!

The last component of the model significance section of the output is the *Root MSE* statistic. This stands for *root mean squared error* (which is 6,498.1, in this case). But what is this quantity? It's the *standard error of the regression line*. Recall that when we sampled means, we had a statistic that represented the variability of all possible sampled averages. Similarly, the *Root MSE* term—called *Standard Error* in Excel output—represents how variable our actual values are around the regression line. As such, if we know how variable our actual values are in relation to our regression line, we can use this standard error term to create *prediction intervals* for specific predicted values.

The *Root MSE* term is given by the square root of the unexplained variance.

$$S_{y|x} = \textit{Standard Error of Regression} = \textit{Root MSE} = \sqrt{\frac{1}{n-2}\sum (y_i - \hat{y}_i)^2}$$

Let's learn how to use this term to create prediction intervals.

Using a Regression Model to Make Predictions

Let's use this model to create a prediction. As we recall from Rule #2 of statistics, we pay a price for guessing or sampling. Therefore, we will need not just to create a single predicted value (for a given value of urban population) but rather a *range* of possible values given some confidence level. Pictorially, we can see this prediction interval as an interval around a predicted value along the y-axis (GNP/capita values).

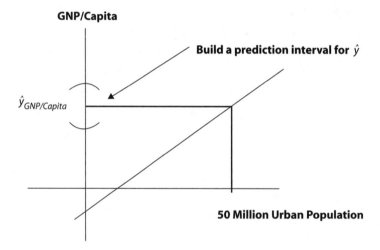

But how do we create this interval? First, we remember one of the most common errors in using regressions to make predictions. Remember: *Never made predictions outside the range of inputs used to build the model!*

If we look back to the scatterplot, we see no countries with urban populations of 150 million in our sample (100 million seems to be the largest.) But it is quite easy to plug in 150 million into our regression equation and get a predicted value of GNP/capita with urban population of 150 million.

This is incorrect! Our model is only as good as its input values, so we can only use the model to make predictions as long as our input value (urban population) is within the bounds of the sampled urban populations. We don't necessarily have to have an observation for GNP/capita at the urban population value we want to use, but this input value must be within the range of inputs used to create the model in the first place if we are to use this model for predictive purposes.

Now, let's use this model—including the equation of the predicted values and the standard error of the residuals—to create an estimate for the GNP/capita at an urban population equal to 50 million. Note that the creation of a prediction interval is similar to that of a confidence interval for a population mean.

95% confidence interval for $\mu : \bar{x} \pm (1.96)(S_x)$

95% prediction interval for $y_{50} : \hat{y}_{50} \pm (1.96)(S_{y|x})$

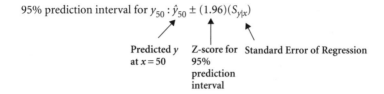

Predicted y at $x = 50$ 	 Z-score for 95% prediction interval 	 Standard Error of Regression

This is a relatively simple, "good enough" formula for prediction intervals. But why are we using a z-score as the multiplier of our standard error? Remember our assumptions: we have assumed that all the residuals (which create standard error) are normally distributed.[1] With this assumption, we can create this interval as follows:

Predicted GNP/Capita = $-5,536.177 + 213.5579 \times$ Urban Population

Using an urban population of 50 million, we get the predicted GNP/capita of

$$-5,536.177 + 213.5579 \times 50 = 5,141.72$$

Now we can use this predicted value and build a 95 percent prediction interval around it:

95% prediction interval = 5,141.72 +/- (1.96) (6,498.1)
= 5,141.72 +/- 12,736.28
= [−7,594.6 , 17,877.0]

Note that this prediction interval is quite wide. This is because of the high standard error, a result of the relatively low r-squared, or explained variance, of this model. Note that we can interpret this interval in a similar fashion as we did confidence intervals: if we were to resample over and over

---

[1] To be precise, we should use a t-statistic with $(n - 2)$ degrees of freedom here instead of a z-score. However, such differences only start to matter when the degrees of freedom are quite low. For sake of simplicity, we will simply use z-scores here and in future prediction interval examples.

again, and create similar prediction intervals, we would expect 95 percent of the prediction intervals to contain the actual population GNP/capita value for a country with urban population equal to 50 million.

This simple formula for creating prediction intervals technically creates the best "average" prediction interval around the predicted value. This interval formula is most accurate when the input (x) value is relatively close to the mean of all (sampled) x-values.

To be more precise, a 95 percent prediction interval for a y-value (GNP/capita) given an x-value (urban population) is given by

$$\hat{y}_{x=50} \pm 1.96 \left(S_{y|x} \sqrt{1 + \frac{1}{n} + \frac{(\dot{x} - \bar{x})^2}{\sum (x_i - \bar{x})^2}} \right)$$

where $\dot{x}$ is the x-value where we want to create the estimate (50 million in urban population, in this case). Also, the sum in the denominator under the square root is $(n - 1)$ times the variance of the x-values, which we can obtain from simple descriptive statistics of the urban population values. While this prediction interval formula is precise, the simpler one mentioned earlier is often good enough for models with relatively good fit and low standard error.

Measuring Input Variable (Slope) Significance

Now let's explore the bottom part of our regression output, the *input variable significance* section. Recall our output:

```
    Source  |      SS        df        MS            Number of obs   =      154
------------+---------------------------------       F(  1,  152)    =    92.73
     Model  |   3.9155e+09     1    3.9155e+09       Prob > F        =   0.0000
  Residual  |   6.4183e+09   152    42225700.3       R-squared       =   0.3789
------------+---------------------------------       Adj R-squared   =   0.3748
     Total  |   1.0334e+10   153    67541338.7       Root MSE        =   6498.1

------------------------------------------------------------------------------
  gnp_pcap  |     Coef.    Std. Err.       t     P>|t|     [95% Conf. Interval]
------------+-----------------------------------------------------------------
    urbpop  |   213.5579   22.17734      9.63    0.000     169.7423     257.3736
     _cons  |  -5536.177   1253.778     -4.42    0.000    -8013.258    -3059.096
```

Another way to test our model for significance is to see whether the input variable, *urbpop*, is a statistically significant input variable (that is, does urban population statistically significantly predict GNP/capita by having a nonzero slope?). In a one-variable model, this is equivalent to the F-ratio test from earlier where we tested the ratio of explained variance to unexplained variance to see if it was greater than one. When we get to multiple-input models, however, the distinction between these two significance tests will become clearer.

Note the statistics to the right of the urban population coefficient.

gnp_pcap	Coef.	Std. Err.	t	P>|t|	[95% Conf. Interval]	
urbpop	213.5579	22.17734	9.63	0.000	169.7423	257.3736

Here, we see that the slope of the regression line (213.5579) also has statistical properties because we obtained it via sampling. We have the standard error of the slope (22.17734), a t-statistic, a p-value, and a 95 percent confidence interval for the slope.

But what do all of these slope statistics mean? Remember, we have sampled some data to create an estimate (213.5579) for the true slope of the regression line that would fit the entire population of data. Thus, just like a sampled mean, there is room for error when we sample and compute the slope of a regression line.

The standard error of the slope is 22.17734, and if we divide the slope by its standard error, we get its t-statistic (9.63). We could compare this t-statistic of the slope to the t-statistic for a particular alpha value when testing whether this estimate of the population model slope is different from zero. *Do not confuse the standard error of the slope with the standard error of the regression model!* Be sure to use the proper standard error when creating prediction intervals (Root MSE in this case).

The p-value that follows is important. This (two-tailed) p-value helps us determine the result of the following hypothesis test for the slope coefficient:

- H_0: Input variable is insignificant (or population model slope = 0; GNP/capita does not respond to urban population).

- H_A: Input variable does significantly predict the output (or population model slope ≠ 0; GNP/capita does respond, with nonzero slope, to changes in urban population).

This is a two-tailed test because we don't care if the slope is positive or negative. We only care if it is zero—and thus no linear relationship exists—or nonzero.

We can assess this test in two ways. We can compare the t-statistic (9.63) to the t-statistic of the critical value for this hypothesis test. But this would require degrees of freedom computation, table lookups, and so on.

An easier way is to just look at the given p-value. Here, the p-value is 0.000, less than a standard alpha level (of 5 percent). Thus, we can reject the null hypothesis and conclude that the slope of our regression line (22.17734) is statistically different from zero. This result can be seen by looking at the 95 percent confidence interval for the slope. This interval does not contain zero; thus, the slope is not statistically equal to zero. This further confirms our result that the slope is nonzero and, thus, urban population is a significant predictor of GNP/capita. (In a one-variable model, the p-value of the slope test is identical to the p-value of the F-ratio test. In fact, the square root of the F-ratio is equal to the t-statistic of the slope!)

Thus, from this regression output, we see that urban population significantly predicts or explains GNP/capita, although the amount of explained variance is relatively low due to only a moderate fit of the regression line with the data points. Some of our underlying assumptions may have been violated—like the equal variance assumption. Is there a way to look at the part of the model that remains unexplained?

Regression Diagnostics: Looking at Residuals

An important part of postmodeling diagnostics is to look at all of the leftovers—the unexplained differences—that result from our model. To do so, most tools (including Excel) allow for the creation of *residual plots*.

Below is the residual plot from our GNP/capita and urban population model.

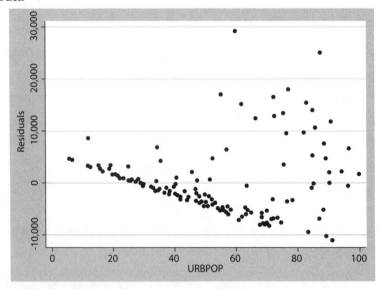

A few notes about this plot: the x-values are still urban populations, but the y-values are the residuals, or differences between the actual GNP/capita values in our dataset and what our regression model predicted. As such, the x-axis—or where all residuals are zero—is actually nothing more than the regression line laid down horizontally. By looking at this residual plot, we effectively "lay down" the regression line so we can look at differences between actual GNP/capita values and the values that our regression line would create.

This allows us to test our assumptions about our residuals. Although our assumptions are for the population regression model, we can still see if our sample data are generally obeying some of the assumptions. For example, from the residual plot, we can see that the equal variance assumption is likely violated. Higher-urban-population countries have more variable GNP/capita values than smaller-urban-population countries. This may indicate that we should break up our dataset into high- and low-population countries and model them separately. (Perhaps a different variable will be the best predictor for low-urban-population countries versus high ones.)

So what do we want from our plot of residuals? Ideally, we would like to see the residuals as random as possible (with equal spread around the x-axis and no bias). If they are randomly distributed (and obey our assumptions), then our residuals are said to be *homoskedastic* (or have the property of *homoskedasticity*). This is what we want—nothing but "noise" in our residuals with all the explanatory power, trends, and patterns modeled by our regression equation (and thus explained).

However, if our residuals have patterns or behavior that could be explained by our model, our residuals are said to be *heteroskedastic* (or have the property of *heteroskedasticity*). We should strive to explain this behavior with our model. For example, significant industrial investment may affect urban population (which in turn affects GNP/capita, as we've seen). Thus, if we see some patterns in our residuals, we may want to find a variable, like investment levels in industrial expansion, that helps explain these patterns. This will move the pattern to the model (and out of the residuals), increase our explained variance, and create a better fit and predictive power for our model and data.

Looking at the scatterplot, linear model, and regression output is not enough. Be sure to look at the residuals—that is, what your model *does not* explain—as part of your analysis.

STATISTICS IN ACTION

The following grid shows the reaction times (RT in seconds) and IQ scores of ten students.

	x	y
Student	RT (secs)	IQ Score
1	0.20	130
2	0.22	120
3	0.25	110
4	0.29	105
5	0.30	104
6	0.37	102
7	0.39	100
8	0.40	99
9	0.44	97
10	0.50	95

Find the regression equation that relates IQ score to reaction time. Calculate the standard error of the model and interpret it. Test the null hypothesis that the slope $\beta_1 = 0$. Find the coefficient of correlation and interpret it. Is there a strong linear relationship between reaction times and IQ scores?

Solution: From Excel, we get the following output:

SUMMARY OUTPUT

Regression Statistics	
Multiple R	0.889124062
R Square	0.790541597
Adjusted R Squa	0.764359297
Standard Error	5.355868584
Observations	10

ANOVA

	df	SS	MS	F	Significance F
Regression	1	866.1173736	866.1173736	30.19374102	0.000577219
Residual	8	229.4826264	28.68532829		
Total	9	1095.6			

	Coefficients	Standard Error	t Stat	P–value	Lower 95%	Upper 95%
Intercept	139.4133574	6.277220123	22.20941032	1.78552E-08	124.9380619	153.888653
RT (secs)	-98.84927798	17.98933207	-5.494883167	0.000577219	-140.3327521	-57.36580387

From the summary output, we find that our intercept is 139.41 and our slope is = −98.85. Therefore, the regression model is

$$\text{Predicted IQ Score} = 139.41 - 98.85 \times \text{Reaction Time}$$

Note that because $x = 0$ is not within the sampled range of reaction times, the statistical properties of the intercept have no value to us.

The standard error of the model (for prediction interval purposes) is 5.36. This implies that roughly 95 percent of the observed IQ scores should fall within approximately $2 \times 5.36 = 10.72$ points of their respective predicted values when using the regression model.

The model has a significant F-ratio as well as a significant slope. Note that 76.4 percent (adjusted) of the variability in IQ scores is explained by reaction time when using a linear model to relate the two variables. The square root of this explained variance will give us the absolute correlation between these two variables. The correlation is negative, as is the slope of the regression line.

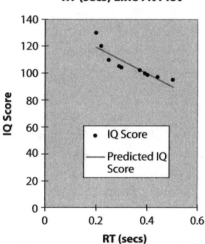

RT (secs) Line Fit Plot

Note, too, that while a line is a fairly good model for this relationship, a nonlinear (or curved) regression model may fit this relationship even better.

A 95 percent confidence interval for the slope is shown in the output to be $[-140.33, -57.37]$. Because 0 does not fall within this interval, the null hypothesis that we have a zero slope is rejected. The small p-value of .000577 is also indicative of a significant linear relationship between reaction times and IQ scores.

Looking at the residuals, we can see that a curved or parabolic pattern is present in the residuals; thus, we have some heteroskedasticity in them.

We should try to identify the variable that is causing this curvature and model this effect to remove it from the unexplained or residual errors.

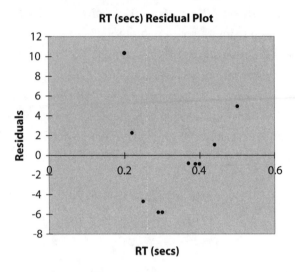

RT (secs) Residual Plot

TEST YOURSELF

You own a small manufacturing firm that makes various torture devices for use in the classroom. Your company, Sadistics, makes, in particular, a type of textbook that is impossible to read, difficult to understand, and offensive in the way it presents statistical theory. Of particular interest to us is the total cost of production: the sum of fixed and variable costs (where variable cost, recall, is marginal cost times quantity).

See the data below. These data represent the quantity of textbooks created along with the total costs required to create them. For example, in the first row, you can see that the total cost to make two textbooks was $30. However, we would like to get a better sense of the fixed versus variable cost components of our total cost. Assume, for purposes of your initial analysis, that a simple linear model can approximate total costs.

Data Item	Quantity (# of Books Produced)	Total Cost of Production
1	2	$ 30
2	5	$ 40
3	8	$ 73
4	10	$ 100
5	11	$ 130
6	12	$ 90
7	14	$ 150
8	15	$ 160
9	16	$ 155
10	17	$ 180
11	18	$ 240
12	19	$ 280
13	20	$ 180
14	21	$ 181
15	22	$ 185
16	23	$ 190
17	24	$ 200
18	25	$ 200
19	26	$ 275
20	28	$ 215
21	30	$ 220
22	31	$ 221
23	32	$ 225
24	33	$ 200
25	34	$ 205
26	35	$ 206
27	36	$ 210
28	37	$ 200
29	38	$ 388
30	40	$ 275
31	41	$ 400

(Continued)

(Continued)

Data Item	Quantity (# of Books Produced)	Total Cost of Production
32	42	$ 428
33	43	$ 415
34	44	$ 450
35	45	$ 460
36	46	$ 450
37	47	$ 471
38	48	$ 500
39	49	$ 476
40	50	$ 450
Use these sums to verify your data entry into Excel:	1,137	$ 10,104

Please answer the questions that follow. Don't forget to state any necessary assumptions!

1. Please describe, with words and numerical coefficients, your model for the *total* cost function (again assuming a linear model).

2. How much variance in *total* cost is explained by estimating it with number of units manufactured using this linear model?

3. What is your best point-estimate (single number) for *fixed* cost? What about *variable* cost of producing 20 textbooks (again, single number)?

4. Create a 90 percent confidence interval for the *marginal* cost, given this model.

5. Create a 95 percent prediction interval estimate for the *total* cost to produce 20 textbooks. Create a similar interval estimate for the *total* cost to produce 200 textbooks.

KEY POINTS TO REMEMBER

This chapter discussed how to perform basic statistical analyses and modeling for related, paired, or bivariate data. Key points to remember about regression modeling include the following:

- Always graph the data! If the relationship between the variables doesn't look linear, don't try to model it that way.

- Start with a correlation matrix and pick the best single correlated input variable to use to model your output variable. Don't disregard negative correlations—look for the highest absolute values.

- When you are ready to build the model, make sure your regression assumptions are clearly stated and make sure your scatterplot indicates some adherence to these assumptions (or if not, be sure to note any concerns or exceptions).

- After building the model, write the equation of the model in words so you can see how the input variable, slope, and intercept all work together.

- Assess the model significance first. Look at the F-ratio and see if it is significantly greater than 1. If so, you have a statistically significant model that "trends" well. This also implies that the slope of the regression line differs significantly from zero and that the input variable is a significant predictor of the output variable.

- Next, assess the "fit" of the model using the adjusted r-squared term. We want this term to be close to 1.

- Remember that the r-squared term is the amount of variability in the output that is explained by the input using a linear model.

- It is possible to have a significant "trend" model (based on an F-ratio) but not a terribly good "fit" model. Be sure to understand the distinction between these two statistics/inferences.

- If necessary, use the standard error of the model—not of the slope!—to create prediction intervals, but only create predictions for x-values in the range of the x-values used to create the model in the first place. No extrapolation!

- Assess the input variable (or slope) significance by looking at the p-value of the slope test and/or the confidence interval for the slope (which, if significant, should not contain zero). (For single-input models, this is equivalent to looking at the F-ratio/F-test, as discussed above.)

- Finally, be sure to look at what your model does not explain—the residual plot. Check assumptions here as well as for the presence of heteroskedasticity (or heteroskedastic residuals). If possible, try to use known information to explain any behaviors found in the residuals.

Creating Better Predictions and Modeling Relationships Using Several Continuous Variables

INTRODUCTION

In the previous chapter, we learned how to examine, construct, and assess the significance of a linear model through a set of bivariate data. But this only helps us so much. In our example, we only achieved a small explained variance using just urban population to predict or model gross national product (GNP) per capita. Can we do better? Can we create a better prediction model using more information?

We can by extending the concept of simple (or one input variable) linear regression to include more input variables. By including more information in our model, we should be able to explain more variance and to make better (and less volatile) predictions.

But adding data or variables comes with a potential price. If we aren't careful, we may put highly correlated information into the model that results in a *false fit*. That means our r-squared term may increase but not necessarily because we are explaining more variability in the output. Also, by adding variables to a regression model, some variables that were significant predictors in simpler models may not be significant when other variables are added. Thus, we must be cautious when creating multi-input models. Throwing all the variables into the model is exactly the wrong place to start! Regression models should be improved by adding variables carefully, not by taking them out of a very complex model that may not even have enough data to support itself.

WHAT'S AHEAD

In this chapter, you'll learn how to:

- Describe relationships among several input variables and an output variable
- Use more data to improve predictive power and "fit" and figure out what data should be added
- Make the assumptions required for multiple linear regression modeling
- Measure the significance and fit of the multiple regression model
- Determine if the improved fit is really the result of the inputs predicting the output better

- Spot when using more data gives a false sense of fit: multicollinearity
- Use multiple regression models to make predictions
- Measure input variable significance
- Perform regression diagnostics: looking at residuals when multiple inputs are involved
- Avoid common pitfalls of multiple variable linear regression

IN THE REAL WORLD

You're in charge of marketing for a hotel chain. Your firm is considering expanding into new geographic areas. Executives in your company wish to know what factors most influence the profitability (or profit margin) of a new hotel. Is it the competition? What about the types of customers (such as vacationers, business travelers, and so on), the income level of the community in which the hotel is built, or the hotel's proximity to the downtown or business district? While all of these may drive hotel profitability, we'd like to understand which factors are most important. That way, when we study a new area, we can quickly identify which marketing mix elements—and real estate decisions—will have the most impact on the success of our new hotel.

Is there a way to do this? Is there a way to look at several critical factors that affect profitability and determine which have the most significant impact?

Once we perform this analysis, can we determine how sensitive profitability is to a change in any factor? What does it cost us, in terms of hotel profit, to move closer to town versus further away? What influence does competition actually have? Are there factors that we think are important that may not be?

The tools from Chapter 9 are helpful, but simple linear regression only allows us to look at one input variable at a time. Our profitability structure is more complicated, so we need a tool or framework to help us model several factors at the same time and to assess their individual and collective impacts on profitability. If we build such a tool, we could also use it to study the relative profitability (and influence of these various factors) on our *existing* hotels, not just new ones planned. How do we extend the concepts from the previous chapter to include more input variables? Are there any potential risks in doing so? In fact, why not build a model with all the data we have? Wouldn't that be the best model?

THE KEY CONCEPTS

Describing Relationships among Several Input Variables and an Output Variable

Previously, we used simple linear regression to find a linear relationship between a response or outcome variable (GNP/capita) and an input or predictor variable (urban population). Now we would like to expand this framework to incorporate more inputs into our model to better estimate our output. For example, if we could predict GNP/capita with both urban population and birth rate, perhaps this model would have a higher explained variance (r-squared) and thus give us better predictions (because the standard error of the regression should be less).

When we use multiple input variables (simultaneously) to predict an output variable, this is called *multiple (linear) regression modeling*. Let's review the model-building process. The best way to build regression models is to start with the *simplest* model (one input variable) and then add information (variables) carefully to see if the model improves. Yet there is a risk that comes with adding too many (redundant) variables—or *overfitting* the model—and we should be careful in terms of which variables we add and why.

Recall from simple linear regression (one input variable) that building a predictive model is an iterative process:

1. State any necessary assumptions (e.g., the ones regarding the distribution of residuals).

2. Build a correlation matrix and find the input variable that is best correlated with the output variable (regardless of the sign of the correlation).

3. *Graph the data!* Look at a scatterplot of these variables and see if a linear model even makes sense. If it does, proceed. If not, it may be helpful to contact a professional data analyst for assistance with nonlinear regression methods.

4. If it appears that a linear model makes sense, construct the best single-input model (based on highest *absolute* correlation).

5. Check for model significance (F-ratio and its p-value) and explained variance or fit (r-squared).

6. If the model is significant, graph the residuals and look for heteroskedasticity (or unmodeled patterns or behaviors).

7. If required, use the standard error of the regression model to build prediction intervals—while staying within the range of the input variable!

Earlier, we found that urban population had the strongest correlation with GNP per capita, our output variable. Yet urban population is not the only factor that has an impact on GNP per capita. Let's recall how we built this simple model and then try to improve it by adding more information.

First, we look at the correlation matrix for all of our input and output variables, and we select the best input variable based on absolute correlation. (Note: matrix below is slightly different from the one in Chapter 9.)

	gnp_pcap	pop	urbpop	popgrow	birth_rt	inf_mort	life_exp
gnp_pcap	1.0000						
pop	−0.0340	1.0000					
urbpoop	0.6143	−0.0878	1.0000				
popgrow	−0.4062	−0.0420	−0.5102	1.0000			
birth_rt	−0.5893	−0.0852	−0.7286	0.7473	1.0000		
inf_mort	−0.5496	0.0019	−0.7172	0.5545	0.8746	1.0000	
life_exp	0.5918	0.0212	0.7307	−0.5356	−0.8685	−0.9595	1.0000

Urban population is the most correlated variable, so we look at the scatterplot to see if a linear model makes sense.

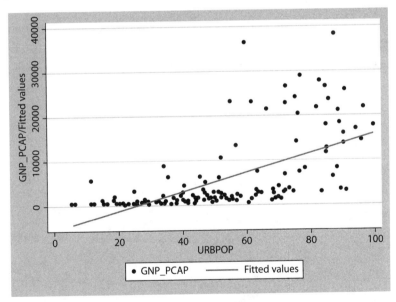

Because a linear model may make sense here, we state the four required assumptions for the residuals of the population regression model:

1. Residuals have mean equal to zero.

2. Residuals have equal variance for all values of the input variable.

3. Residuals are independent.

4. Residuals are normally distributed around the regression line.

Using a statistical tool (STATA, for example), we get the following output for this simple model.

Source	SS	df	MS			
Model	3.9155e+09	1	3.9155e+09	Number of obs	=	154
Residual	6.4183e+09	152	42225700.3	F(1, 152)	=	92.73
				Prob > F	=	0.0000
				R-squared	=	0.3789
Total	1.0334e+10	153	67541338.7	Adj R-squared	=	0.3748
				Root MSE	=	6498.1

gnp_pcap	Coef.	Std. Err.	t	P>|t|	[95% Conf. Interval]	
urbpop	213.5579	22.17734	9.63	0.000	169.7423	257.3736
_cons	−5536.177	1253.778	−4.42	0.000	−8013.258	−3059.096

We see that we have a significant model based on the p-value of the F-ratio and/or the p-value of the slope, but it has a relatively high standard error (6,498.1) and relatively low explained variance or fit (adjusted r-squared is only 37.5 percent).

A look at the residuals doesn't reveal any patterns, but some potential assumption violations are present, including that the model is biased in some ranges of inputs and the spread of the residuals around the regression line is not consistent across all values of the inputs.

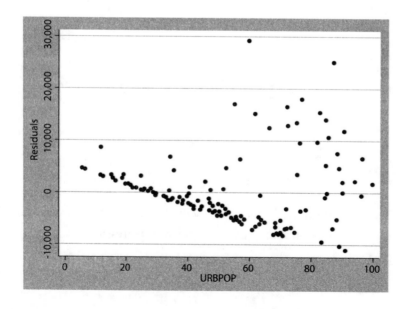

So how can we add more information to this model, improve the fit and explained variance in GNP/capita, and create a small standard error of the regression model for prediction purposes?

Using More Data to Improve Predictive Power and Fit—What Data Should Be Added?

With our GNP/capita model, which variable should we add? Does it matter? Practically speaking, we only want to add variables to the model that are different from—or uncorrelated with—information and variables already in the model. If we add a variable that basically gives us the same information as urban population, we will have collected and added redundant information that won't really help us explain GNP/capita any better.

In general, however, adding *any information or variable* to a model—even random numbers—will likely improve the r-squared term! Thus, adding just about anything to a single-variable model will give the appearance of improving our explained variance in the output. So how can we tell when we're adding new and not redundant information to a model? We look back at the correlation matrix. By doing so, we can see if the next variable we wish to add is already highly correlated with the input variable we've already used.

A simple example: Let's say you are building a model to predict the age of a person if you know his weight. This can easily be done by collecting a random sample of ages and weights. Let's assume this model has an adjusted r-squared of 70 percent.

If we've also collected the respondents' heights, should we add the height variable into the model? No! By doing so, we would be adding information that is redundant and likely to be highly correlated with the weight data already in the model. A check of the correlation between height and weight shows that these two input variables have a correlation of 0.80. This is quite high. Note that the model—with both height and weight used to estimate age—will likely have a higher adjusted r-squared (maybe 85 percent), but this higher fit and explained variance, while mathematically accurate, is not really reflecting the relationship between the inputs and the output. Instead, the adjusted r-squared is likely higher because the two inputs explain *each other* more than they explain age, the output variable.

Let's apply this logic to our GNP/capita model. According to the correlation matrix, life expectancy is the second most highly correlated variable with GNP per capita ($r = 0.5918$). However, life expectancy is also very highly correlated with urban population ($r = 0.7307$), which is already in the model.

```
            | gnp_pcap      pop    urbpop  popgrow   birth_rt  inf_mort  life_exp
------------+--------------------------------------------------------------------
   gnp_pcap |  1.0000
        pop | [-0.0340]   1.0000
     urbpop |   0.6143   [-0.0878]   1.0000
    popgrow |  -0.4062    -0.0420   -0.5102   1.0000
   birth_rt |  -0.5893    -0.0852   -0.7286   0.7473    1.0000
   inf_mort |  -0.5496     0.0019   -0.7172   0.5545    0.8746    1.0000
   life_exp |  [0.5918]    0.0212   [0.7307] -0.5356   -0.8685   -0.9595    1.0000
```

Ideally, the independent variables that we choose should not be highly correlated with each another. In fact, the variable with the lowest correlation to urban population is total population ($r = -0.0878$). The only problem with this choice is that population is also the worst correlated variable with GNP/capita ($r = -0.0340$). Thus, we have some tough choices to make. We want to additional inputs that are highly correlated with GNP/capita while not being highly correlated with the input variable already in the model (urban population). This looks difficult to achieve in this case.

Let's go ahead and see what happens when we add the two inputs that are most correlated with GNP/capita: urban population and life expectancy.

```
   Source  |    SS         df       MS              Number of obs =     147
-----------+------------------------------          F(  1,  144)  =   52.30
    Model  | 4.3233e+09     2    2.1616e+09          Prob > F      =  0.0000
  Residual | 5.9519e+09   144    41332454.9          R-squared     =  0.4208
-----------+------------------------------          Adj R-squared =  0.4127
    Total  | 1.0275e+10   146    70377699.3          Root MSE      =    6429

-----------+----------------------------------------------------------------
  gnp_pcap |    Coef.    Std. Err.      t    P>|t|      [95% Conf. Interval]
-----------+----------------------------------------------------------------
    urbpop |  136.8366   32.28392     4.24   0.000     73.02504    200.6482
  life_exp |  249.1021   76.26414     3.27   0.001     98.36028    399.8439
     _cons | -17859.21   3973.003    -4.50   0.000    -25712.15   -10006.27
-----------+----------------------------------------------------------------
```

By adding the second independent variable, the percentage of variance in GNP/capita explained by our model as measured by adjusted r-squared increases from roughly 37.5 percent to about 41.3 percent, or by about 3.8 percent.

Before we go much further, let's outline the framework we've used here for multiple input variable linear regression modeling. Simply put, multiple regression is just regression using more than one input variable to predict an output.

Recall the single input variable population and sample models. Here, an actual value (y) is the intercept (β_0) plus the slope (β_1) times the input variable (x) plus the error (ε):

$$y = \beta_0 + \beta_1 x_1 + \varepsilon$$

Said another way, an actual value of the output (y) is created by the sum of a predicted value ($\beta_0 + \beta_1 x_1$) and error (ε).

The sample version of this model simply gives us the predicted values and estimates for the population slope and y-intercept parameters:

$$\hat{y} = b_0 + b_1 x_1$$

Here, the input variable (x) is urban population, and the predicted $\hat{y}$-value is GNP/capita. Also, the sample slope (b_1) and intercept (b_0) are estimates of the population slope (β_1) and intercept (β_0).

Now, let's extend these models to allow for multiple (linear) inputs. Here's the model at the population level, which shows an output (GNP/capita) being modeled by two input variables:

$$y = \beta_0 + \beta_1 x_1 + \beta_2 x_2 + \varepsilon$$

Here, an actual GNP/capita value (y) is modeled with a predicted value in two variables (x_1 = urban population and x_2 = life expectancy) plus an error term. In fact, we could extend this multiple input model to create an equation that gives us actual GNP/capita values using k input variables.

$$y = \beta_0 + \beta_1 x_1 + \beta_2 x_2 + \dots + \beta_k x_k + \varepsilon$$

From this, we can see that the sample multiple linear regression model has this form:

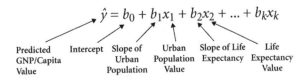

Using this form of the regression model, we can construct the two-variable model for GNP/capita from the regression output we obtained earlier:

Predicted GNP/Capita = −17,859.21 + (136.8366 × Urban Pop.)
+ (249.1021 × Life Expectancy)

Collecting and adding this additional life expectancy data increased our fit or explained variance in GNP/capita by only 3.8 percent. Is this small increase significant?

Also, take a look at the slope of urban population, the first variable we used to estimate GNP/capita. In our single-variable model, the slope was 213.6. In this revised (two-variable) model, the impact of urban population on GNP/capita is substantially less because the slope has decreased to 136.8. This is a fairly significant decrease. The addition of life expectancy, which has a slope of 249, seems to have greatly *reduced* the effect of urban population on GNP/capita.

Let's step back and review the steps we've added to our regression modeling process and checklist. If we want to try to improve the model—that is, to increase the explained variance (adjusted r-squared)—we can perform the following additional steps:

8. If needed, add variables that are *not* highly correlated with the input variables already in the model.

9. Assess overall fit and model significance (r-squared and F-ratio significance) to see if the r-squared has increased. If only a small increase is seen, perhaps it is not worth modeling this additional data. The prior (simpler) model may suffice.

10. Assess large changes in the coefficients and impacts of individual inputs (p-values of the individual slopes).

11. If required, use the standard error of the multiple regression model to build prediction intervals—while staying within the ranges of each and every input variables!

Measuring the Significance and Fit of the Multiple Regression Model

Let's assess the overall significance of the model and the explained variance or fit with the regression line as we did when only one input variable was used.

Source	SS	df	MS		Number of obs	=	147
					F(2, 144)	=	52.30
Model	4.3233e+09	2	2.1616e+09		Prob > F	=	0.0000
Residual	5.9519e+09	144	41332454.9		R-squared	=	0.4208
					Adj R-squared	=	0.4127
Total	1.0275e+10	146	70377699.3		Root MSE	=	6429

gnp_pcap	Coef.	Std. Err.	t	P>|t|	[95% Conf. Interval]	
urbpop	136.8366	32.28392	4.24	0.000	73.02504	200.6482
life_exp	249.1021	76.26414	3.27	0.001	98.36028	399.8439
_cons	−17859.21	3973.003	−4.50	0.000	−25712.15	−10006.27

When using both urban population and life expectancy to predict GNP/capita, we see that the F-ratio is now only 52.3, but it is still significant (p-value of 0.0000). The adjusted r-squared, as mentioned earlier, increases almost 4 percent to 41.3 percent. Together, these two variables significantly model GNP/capita—because the ratio of explained to unexplained variance is statistically larger than 1—and we've improved the fit somewhat. Note that the standard error of the regression model is now 6,429 compared to 6,498.1. This is not a huge improvement, especially if it is expensive to collect life expectancy data for all countries in the sample.

Thus, we can be skeptical about the necessity—and economic practicality—of adding this variable.

Is the Improved Fit a Result of the Inputs Predicting the Output Better?

This is an important question to answer. We see a small improvement in the adjusted r-squared, but is this really the result of the two inputs variables doing a better job of predicting the output? Not really. The standard error didn't decrease much, and the slope of our urban population variable decreases quite a bit in the multi-input model.

Recall that these two input variables are highly correlated. Thus, this small increase in r-squared (and decrease in the standard error of the model) is likely due to a relationship between the two inputs instead of these inputs doing a better job of predicting GNP/capita.

When Using More Data Gives a False Sense of Fit: Multicollinearity

This falsely higher adjusted r-squared is often referred to as a *false sense of fit* or the outcome of *overfitting* the model by using redundant information (highly correlated inputs) to model the output. Statisticians refer to this as the effect of *multicollinearity*. While multicollinearity can never be completely eliminated—spurious correlations will always exist among variables—it can be controlled by choice of input variables. But how can we spot multicollinearity? Although not all of these effects are evident when multicollinearity is present, we can look for these telltale signs:

- High correlations between/among input variables
- Small changes in explained variance with large changes in the coefficient(s) of variable(s) compared to the previous model
- Counterintuitive signs in front of slopes (coefficients), such as correlation between the input and output being positive but the slope being negative
- All possible input variables used to model the output without an assessment of possible input variable correlations

As a result of overfitting the model or getting a falsely high adjusted r-squared, we might claim to have gotten a more explanatory model when, in fact, the inputs are explaining each other, not the output!

Let's make this mistake on purpose. Assume we build a model that predicts age based on height and weight. We may get a model that looks like this:

$$\text{Age} = b_0 + b_1 \times \text{Height} - b_2 \times \text{Weight}$$

Look carefully. Does it make sense that age will be positively correlated with height (the taller a person is, the older she is) but that age will be *negatively* correlated with weight? This would imply that the lighter a person is, the older he is. The sign of the weight slope (or coefficient of weight) seems counterintuitive; we would expect it to be positive. Thus, this model is likely suffering from multicollinearity between the height and weight input variables.

Using Multiple Regression Models to Make Predictions

The precise formula for the standard error of a predicted value gets fairly complicated in multiple regression models. Yet a good estimate of a prediction interval is simply to use the predicted value plus or minus a number of standard errors of the regression model, depending on the error tolerance you choose. And in multiple regression models, a prediction interval can only be created using input values within the bounds of *each and every input variable*. Again, this is a logical extension of our single-variable model.

For example, to predict a country's GNP/capita using an urban population of 40 million and a life expectancy of 60 years, we can create the following 95 percent prediction interval using the same technique we developed in the previous chapter (but this time with two input variables).

$$\hat{y}_{40million\ 60\ years} \pm (1.96)^*S_{y|x}$$
$$= [-17,859.21 + (136.8366^*(40) + 249.1021^*(60)] \pm (1.96)^*(6,429)$$
...*and so forth.*

This formula works best only when all inputs are close to their respective means.[1] To create more precise prediction intervals, using common statistical packages/software is highly recommended.

Measuring Input Variable Significance

Another common use of multiple regression modeling is to determine the variables that significantly affect or "drive" the output variable. What are the significant drivers of hotel profitability in our example at the beginning of the chapter? Is it the number of rooms in a competitive hotel or how close your hotel is to downtown? What about our GNP/capita model—if we look at all contributing (input) variables, can we determine which ones significantly influence or affect GNP/capita?

If an input variable does not contribute significantly to predicting the value of the output variable, the slope of the input will not be significantly

---

[1]As we noted in Chapter 9, a t-statistic using $(n - k - 1)$ degrees of freedom, where k is the number of input variables, would be more precise. But again, this is best used when the degrees of freedom are quite small. We use a simple z-statistic here for illustrative purposes.

different from zero. Using the hypothesis-testing framework from Chapter 9, we observe the p-values of our multiple-input model. From the output above, we can see that

- the coefficient of urban population is 136.8366 and the p-value, for the null hypothesis of this slope (or coefficient) being zero, is 0.000; and

- the coefficient of life expectancy is 249.1021 and the p-value, for the null hypothesis of this slope (or coefficient) being zero, is 0.001.

Based on these results, we conclude that both of these inputs—urban population and life expectancy—significantly predict GNP/capita when modeled simultaneously because the slopes of both of these variables are statistically different from zero. Yet we cannot know the relative impact of one variable versus another using the slopes because the units of the variables may cause the slopes to be larger or smaller, not the real statistical impact of the input variable.

What would happen if we put *all possible inputs* in the model at the same time? First and foremost, we worry about multicollinearity. And though we may be able to determine the most significant input variables, we have to depend on all variables interacting at once (and with minimal interaction or multicollinearity). Because we can't eliminate these annoyances, it is best not to start modeling by throwing all the data into the regression model at the same time.

Instead, build the model from the bottom up: start with one variable and add variables carefully, while always watching out for the effects of multicollinearity.

Just for illustrative purposes, let's see what the output looks like when we use all possible inputs to model GNP/capita (don't try this at home!).

Source	SS	df	MS			
Model	4.5342e+09	6	755696814	Number of obs	=	146
Residual	5.7143e+09	139	41109716.5	F(6, 139)	=	18.38
				Prob > F	=	0.0000
				R-squared	=	0.4424
Total	1.0248e+10	145	70678837.8	Adj R-squared	=	0.4184
				Root MSE	=	6411.7

gnp_pcap	Coef.	Std. Err.	t	P>|t|	[95% Conf. Interval]	
pop	−2.63e−06	4.48e−06	−0.59	0.558	−.0000115	6.23e−06
urbpop	119.9058	34.25474	3.50	0.001	52.17808	187.6335
popgrow	86.80082	605.0101	0.14	0.886	−1109.412	1283.013
birth_rt	−184.2134	123.8101	−1.49	0.139	−429.0081	60.58123
inf_mort	92.84224	49.41295	1.88	0.062	−4.855934	190.5404
life_exp	440.1041	194.6965	2.26	0.025	55.15454	825.0538
_cons	−28745.33	15240.12	−1.89	0.061	−58877.76	1387.095

Only two variables significantly predict GNP/capita: urban population (p-value of 0.001) and life expectancy (p-value of 0.025)—the same two variables that we used before! But we know these two variables are highly correlated, so we suspect multicollinearity.

Note the model equation with all inputs included:

$$
\begin{aligned}
\textit{Predicted GNP/Capita} \quad = \quad & -2.63 \times 10^{-6} \times \textit{population} \\
+ \quad & 119.9058 \times \textit{urban population} \\
+ \quad & 86.80082 \times \textit{population growth} \\
- \quad & 184.2134 \times \textit{birth rate} \\
+ \quad & 92.84224 \times \textit{infant mortality} \\
+ \quad & 440.1041 \times \textit{life expectancy} \\
- \quad & 2,8745.33
\end{aligned}
$$

Did you notice anything different? When we compare these coefficients to the initial correlation matrix, we find that some signs have mysteriously reversed. For example, population growth, birth rate, and infant mortality are all *negatively* correlated to GNP/capita. However, our model gives us *positive* coefficients for population growth and infant mortality. This is a clear indication of multicollinearity in our model.

With all these variables in the model, our adjusted r-squared is only 41.5 percent. Recall that our one-input model had an r-squared of 37.5 percent. Thus, collecting all these additional variables and data only improves our explained variance by 4 percent. This additional data collection and modeling not only leads to multicollinear inputs but doesn't really improve the predictive power or estimability of our model that much.

Finally, note that the standard error of the model (Root MSE, or *mean squared error*) is 6,411.7. This is not appreciably less than our one-input model standard error of 6,498.1. Thus, in this case, all these additional variables and data *do not* do a significantly better job at predicting GNP/capita than urban population alone.

Regression Diagnostics: Looking at Residuals When Multiple Inputs Are Involved

We can examine the residuals of a multiple regression model—and check for any heteroskedasticity—but we have to perform this diagnostic check one input variable at a time. Most tools—like Excel and STATA—will automatically create a residual plot for each input variable used in a multiple input model.

For example, if we go back to our two-input model, where we predicted GNP/capita with urban population and life expectancy, we observe the following residual plot, respectively:

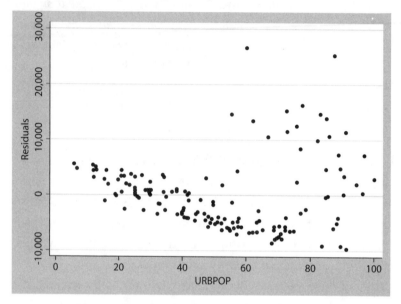

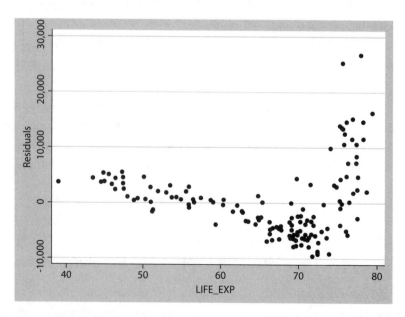

In both cases—especially in the case of life expectancy—we see some potential assumption violations (such as lack of consistent variance around the regression line) as well as some potentially unmodeled behavior. There seem to be differences in GNP/capita for countries with less than 50 million in urban population and with life expectancy less than 70 years when compared to countries with higher life expectancies and urban populations. One possible solution is to separate the countries into more meaningful subsets—mostly rural, low-life-expectancy countries versus more urban, higher-life-expectancy countries—and repeat the correlation, single-input, and multiple-input analyses to see if the same variables are the most significant predictors.

Common Pitfalls of Multiple Variable Regression Modeling

Let's review some of the common errors and pitfalls that analysts make when creating multiple variable linear regression models:

- *Parameter estimability*: This is a fancy way of saying that if you want to use more input variables in your model, make sure you have more data to create it. Otherwise, you will be spreading the explained (and unexplained) variances over fewer and fewer data points (and more and more input variables). That means an outlier in any input variable could have a profound impact in your modeling. Samples should be random, and if at all possible, each input variable should have more than 30 observations. This will help with the normality assumption of the residuals and reduce the impact of outliers. The more data the better when creating multiple input models. If you don't have enough data points, a multiple model will be misleading or simply won't make sense.

- *Beware of multicollinearity*: Avoid placing highly correlated independent variables in the same model. This can often, but not always, be seen by coefficients whose signs don't make sense (a negative coefficient in the model versus a positive one expected), significant movement in variable coefficients (slopes), and/or the use of all possible input variables with no initial correlation analysis to detect possible multicollinearity.

- *Look at the residuals in all dimensions*: Watch the residuals; examine one input variable at a time against the output. Residuals must be random; if you see a pattern, your model is not explaining all of the behavior in the data.

- *Remember Rule #3 of statistics*: Predictions are not forecasts. Don't make predictions outside the range of inputs. Don't pick an input value outside the range used in the model for prediction purposes. If the input values range from 50 to 100, for example, don't use a model to get a prediction with an input of 25 or 150. Also don't use basic regression tools for time series forecasting (i.e., using time as an input variable). If a dataset has any time-sensitive behavior, simple regression models may not adequately explain time-dependency behaviors (or so-called *autocorrelation*).

STATISTICS IN ACTION

Let's recall our example from the beginning of this chapter. We want to figure out what really drives a hotel's profitability or profit *margin*. (Here, when speaking about profitability, we will use net profit margin, or net operating income divided by total sales or revenue). Management knows that hotel profitability is driven by the following key variables, but they don't know the magnitude or priority of influence that each variable has.

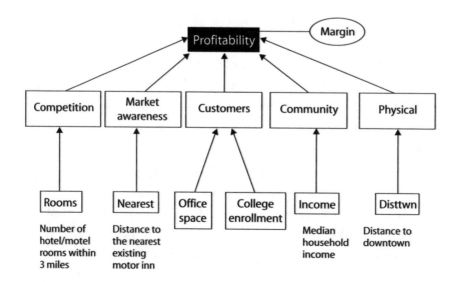

Data were collected in random samples of 100 existing hotels. A few rows of the spreadsheet used for this analysis are shown below.

INN	MARGIN	ROOMS	NEAREST	OFFICE	COLLEGE	INCOME	DISTTWN
1	55.5	3,203	0.1	549	8.0	37	12.1
2	33.8	2,810	1.5	496	17.5	39	0.4
3	49.0	2,890	1.9	254	20.0	39	12.2
4	31.9	3,422	1.0	434	15.5	36	2.7
5	57.4	2,687	3.4	678	15.5	32	7.9
6	49.0	3,759	1.4	635	19.0	41	4.0

Using Microsoft Excel, we get the following correlation matrix:

	MARGIN	ROOMS	NEAREST	OFFICE	COLLEGE	INCOME	DISTTWN
MARGIN	1						
ROOMS	-0.470329396	1					
NEAREST	-0.160251533	-0.081679711	1				
OFFICE	0.501430771	-0.093475216	-0.042761633	1			
COLLEGE	0.123012456	0.063908076	-0.071236621	-0.00103044	1		
INCOME	-0.247500311	-0.037142757	-0.045322352	-0.152614011	0.11263169	1	
DISTTWN	0.09227191	-0.07300932	0.091286693	-0.032855396	-0.097323583	-0.051541365	1

From this matrix, we can see that the best correlation with margin comes from the amount of office space around the hotel. This variable is followed closely by the number of competing hotel rooms in the area.

Did you notice that the input variables generally don't appear to be highly correlated with each other? The largest (absolute) correlation between two possible input variables is r = −0.1526, which comes from office space and median income. Thus, our risk of multicollinear effects is relatively low. Because we want to model these variables to determine which ones have the most significant impact, not to estimate profit margin, let's look at all of the variables in the model at once. From Excel, we get the following regression output, from which we can determine the regression model (intercept, slope of each input variable, and so on).

Given the tiny p-value of the F-ratio, we conclude that all of these variables together significantly predict hotel margin. The explained variance of this model is 49.4 percent. This compares quite favorably to the r-squared we would have achieved had we just modeled margin with office space (r-squared would be approximately only 25 percent). Thus, all of the additional information in the model appears not to be redundant and helps us improve our explained variance.

SUMMARY OUTPUT

Regression Statistics	
Multiple R	0.724611358
R Square	0.52506162
Adjusted R Square	0.494420435
Standard Error	5.512084373
Obsevations	100

ANOVA

	df	SS	MS	F	Significance F
Regression	6	3123.832006	520.6386676	17.1358127	3.03382E-13
Residual	93	2825.625894	30.38307413		
Total	99	5949.4579			

	Coefficients	Standard Error	t Stat	P-value	Lower 95%	Upper 95%
Intercept	72.4546114	7.893103745	9.179482968	1.11388E-14	56.78047202	88.12875077
ROOMS	-0.007617867	0.00125527	-6.068708019	2.7662E-08	-0.01011058	-0.00512515
NEAREST	-1.646237091	0.632836913	-2.601360726	0.010803327	-2.90292575	-0.389548431
OFFICE	0.019765541	0.003410442	5.79559419	9.24331E-08	0.012993078	0.026538003
COLLEGE	0.211782942	0.133427935	1.587245893	0.115851278	-0.05317849	0.476744372
INCOME	-0.413122112	0.139552395	-2.960336947	0.003898802	-0.69024551	-0.135998719
DISTTWN	0.225258099	0.178708888	1.260475074	0.210651417	-0.12962233	0.580138524

> MARGIN = **72.455** - **0.008***ROOMS - **1.646***NEAREST +
> **0.02***OFFICE + **0.212***COLLEGE -
> **0.413***INCOME + **0.225***DISTTWN

Let's now interpret the slopes or coefficients of each variable:

$b_0 = 72.5$ —> This is the intercept, the value of y when all the input variables take the value zero. We won't focus on the intercept—or its statistical properties—because the case where all the input variables are zero is probably not a value inside the ranges of all our inputs.

$b_1 = -0.0076$ —> In this model, for each additional competitor room within three miles of the hotel, the operating margin decreases by 0.0076 percent.

$b_2 = -1.65$ —> For each additional mile that the nearest competitor is to the hotel, the operating margin decreases by 1.65 percent.

$b_3 = 0.02$ —> For each additional 1,000 square feet of office space (assumes units given are in 1,000s of square feet), the increase in operating margin will be 0.02 percent.

$b_4 = 0.21$ —> For each additional 1,000 students (assumes units are given in 1,000s of students), margin increases by 0.21 percent.

$b_5 = -0.41$ ---> For each additional $1,000 increase in median household income (assumes units are thousands of dollars), margin decreases by 0.41 percent.

$b_6 = 0.23$ ---> For each additional mile to the downtown center, margin increases by 0.23 percent.

Now let's answer the key question—what inputs are really driving profit margin? Because different units are involved, we need to look at the statistical significance of each input variable to answer this question.

If we use an alpha of 5 percent, we see that the only variables with p-values smaller than this—and thus significantly different from zero, as evidenced by their confidence intervals—are *rooms, nearest,* and *income.* Note that the most highly correlated variable, *office,* is *not significant* with all these other variables in the model.

Thus, the number of competitors' rooms, the distance to a competing hotel, and the relative income of the hotel's geographical area are the key drivers of margin when all variables are in the model simultaneously. This may be surprising to management, as a correlation analysis shows that hotels may be best situated near office buildings but away from competitors' rooms and hotels. Management may want to consider placing new hotels away from other hotel clusters (lots of rooms) but not in the most affluent of ZIP codes (as this likely drives up rents and eats into margins). Apparently, a strategy of locating closer to outlying office complexes, away from the saturated (and expensive) big cities, may be the right strategy.

We can also use the model to predict the margin of a hotel in an area that management has targeted for new construction. Assuming all values are within the ranges of inputs (for each variable) used to create this model, let's find the margin when there are

- 3,815 rooms within 3 miles
- Closest competitor 3.4 miles away
- 476,000 sq. ft. of office space
- 24,500 college students
- $39,000 median household income
- 3.6 miles to downtown

To create this prediction, we simply insert these quantities into the regression equation:

$$\text{Margin} = 72.455 - 0.008(3,815) - 1.646(3.4) + 0.02(476)$$
$$+ 0.212(24.5) - 0.413(39) + 0.225(3.6) = 37.1\%$$

To create a prediction interval around this predicted value, we could approximate such an interval—say at the 95 percent level—using the standard error of the regression model. A 95 percent prediction interval for *Margin* given specific input values above is as follows:

$$37.1\% \pm (1.96) \times s_{y|x} \approx 37.1\% \pm 2(5.5\%) = [26.1\%, 48.1\%]$$

The review of residuals for unmodeled behaviors is left as an exercise for the reader.

TEST YOURSELF

Using the "Test Yourself" problem from Chapter 9, construct a multiple-input linear regression by adding two new input variables, Economic Factor 1 and Economic Factor 2

Data Item	Quantity (# of Books Produced)	Economic Factor 1	Economic Factor 2	Total Cost of Production
1	2	21	17	$ 30
2	5	41	45	$ 40
3	8	67	65	$ 73
4	10	91	90	$ 100
5	11	146	142	$ 130
6	12	81	86	$ 90
7	14	152	142	$ 150
8	15	189	180	$ 160
9	16	141	138	$ 155
10	17	169	164	$ 180
11	18	233	241	$ 240
12	19	290	285	$ 280
13	20	158	162	$ 180

Continued

14	21	206	196	$ 181
15	22	186	185	$ 185
16	23	178	188	$ 190
17	24	193	192	$ 200
18	25	187	194	$ 200
19	26	279	271	$ 275
20	28	226	236	$ 215
21	30	224	226	$ 220
22	31	217	214	$ 221
23	32	231	221	$ 225
24	33	226	216	$ 200
25	34	214	205	$ 205
26	35	193	201	$ 206
27	36	194	201	$ 210
28	37	198	194	$ 200
29	38	389	390	$ 388
30	40	285	287	$ 275
31	41	406	407	$ 400
32	42	423	418	$ 428
33	43	411	420	$ 415
34	44	454	456	$ 450
35	45	464	454	$ 460
36	46	465	462	$ 450
37	47	466	461	$ 471
38	48	519	517	$ 500
39	49	462	471	$ 476
40	50	469	463	$ 450
Sums to Check Data Entry	1,137	10,144	10,103	$ 10,104

Answer the following questions using the output from your multivariable linear regression:

1. Describe, in words with numerical coefficients, this model for *total* cost estimation.

2. How much variance in *total* cost is explained by estimating it with these three input variables? Is this model, as a whole, "significant" at the 95 percent level?

3. Now, assume that this cost control estimation model has to be *three-sigma* in nature. That is, coefficients (or input parameters) are only considered to be statistically significant if we reject the null hypothesis (that coefficient = 0) at a level of three standard errors above or below their expected mean value (of zero). Given this constraint, which input variable(s) would you now *discard* from this model, if we were to abide by this three-sigma requirement? Briefly explain why, using p-values.

4. Finally, let's assume we learn that Economic Factor 1 is a share-price index for paper companies and that Economic Factor 2 is an indexed price for paper. What concerns, if any, do you have about these two variables being in this model at the same time?

KEY POINTS TO REMEMBER

This chapter reviewed how to construct and to interpret a single-input regression model and then how to add data carefully to try to improve the explained variance or fit of the model. To start, let's review the key steps to building single-input or multiple-input linear regression models.

1. State any necessary assumptions (such as those regarding the distribution of residuals).

2. Build the correlation matrix and find the input variable that is best correlated with the output variable (regardless of the sign of the correlation).

3. *Graph the data!* Look at a scatterplot of these variables and see if a linear model even makes sense. If it does, proceed. If not, it may be helpful to contact a professional data analyst for assistance with nonlinear regression methods or approaches.

4. If it appears that a linear model makes sense, construct the best single-input model (based on highest *absolute* correlation).

5. Check the model for model significance (F-ratio and its p-value) and explained variance or fit (r-squared).

6. If the model is significant, graph the residuals and look for heteroskedasticity (or unmodeled patterns and behaviors).

7. If required, use the standard error of the regression model to build prediction intervals—while staying within the range of the input variable!

8. If needed, add variable(s) that are *not* highly correlated with the input variable(s) already in the model.

9. Assess overall fit and model significance (r-squared and F-ratio significance) to see if the r-squared has increased. If only a small increase is seen, perhaps it is not worth collecting or modeling this additional data. The prior (simpler) model may suffice.

10. Assess large changes in the coefficients and assess impacts of individual inputs (p-values of the individual slopes). Watch out for multicollinearity!

11. If required, use the standard error of the multiple regression model to build prediction intervals—while staying within the ranges of all input variables!

12. Don't forget to look at the residuals—one input variable at a time—to see if any unmodeled behaviors exist.

13. Finally, recall some of the guiding principles of regression modeling—both dos and don'ts—that will hopefully make your predictive modeling successful no matter how much—or how little—information you have at your disposal.

Acknowledgments

I confess that I've wanted to write this book for years—especially after so many of my students and I became fed up with expensive, confusing, "academic" textbooks. Numerous teaching assistants, consulting clients, and friends suggested that I put together a good set of lecture notes that really "cut to the chase" on business data analysis topics. Thanks to an incredible group of teaching and course assistants, these notes have been constantly refined, edited, enhanced, and improved through my years at Columbia. But I never got around to turning them into a book until one of those friends, who is also a former student, joined Kaplan Publishing and encouraged me to write the first text in Kaplan's *MBA Fundamentals* series. Thanks so much, Ken Stern, for getting in touch with me and for encouraging me finally to do what so many family members, friends, and colleagues had been suggesting for years.

It all started back in the seventh grade with my algebra teacher, Mr. Lee Easton, and his TRS-80 Model I computer. At Chaffin Junior High School, in Fort Smith, Arkansas, Mr. Easton brought it into the classroom, and I was instantly hooked. Learning to program in BASIC and learning the principles of structured thinking, logic, and attention to detail were engrained in me, and I was hooked on mathematics and all that was quantitative from then on. At Northside High School, Mrs. Elizabeth Haupert became my first mentor. She taught me trigonometry, calculus, and, perhaps most importantly, she let me teach a class for the first time. Thanks to Mrs. Haupert, I was infected with the teaching virus, and I owe much of my teaching philosophy still to her. Thankfully, too, at Northside, Mr. Thomas Hon taught me how to write. He was the strictest editor I ever had, and he forced me to do with paragraphs what I had loved to do with numbers: make them organized, clear, concise, and complete. Mr. Earl Zechiedrich, my chemistry and physics teacher at Northside, taught me the scientific method and discovery through data and analysis.

At Stanford, I learned perhaps the most important lesson of all from my advisor, Professor Brad Osgood: although I loved mathematics and majored in it, I wasn't cut out to be a professional mathematician. Fortunately, I met and worked with many colleagues who were made of the right mathematical "stuff," and I learned what I knew well and what I needed to learn more about. I learned to know what I didn't know and how to be humble about it.

At New York University, where I studied mathematics, statistics, and operations research, Professor Ed Melnick gets all the credit (or all the blame) for getting me interested in statistics, a course I admittedly really wasn't looking forward to because it wasn't "theoretical enough" for me. However, Ed taught me to appreciate data analysis—and its applications—from both a theoretical and practical perspective: how to "think it" and how to "do it." A few more statistics classes and software programs later, I was enamored with how data analysis could help (and hurt) in business contexts, and providing and teaching practical data analysis and inference became my (completely unplanned) career.

But I couldn't finish my master's at NYU because I took my first consulting job with Booz Allen Hamilton. Thankfully, I spent most of my six years there with Gil Irwin, who taught me innumerable skills that I use and cherish to this day. Not only did Gil teach me the craft of consulting—including how to write for clients, how to perform sound qualitative and quantitative analyses and make results understandable to them, and how to maintain long-lasting advisory roles with them—he also was instrumental in convincing me to get an MBA from his alma mater, the Columbia Business School.

When I arrived at Columbia in 1997, Peter Garrity taught preterm "Math Camp" and showed me how to make business math practical, fun, exciting, and challenging—all at the same time. During my first semester, the very first class I took was B7401: Managerial Statistics. Professor Don Pardew taught the course, and Don remains a good friend and mentor to me today. Don gave me the practical approach to data analysis—and to teaching it—and he also gave me my first teaching job as his teaching assistant. Professor Don Sexton also hired me, and thanks to the two Dons, I was hooked on making the introductory course as practical, understandable, and fun as possible.

After I graduated from Columbia in 1998, the dean of Executive MBA Programs at the time, Dr. Dina Consolini, hired me to the adjunct faculty of the Columbia Business School to help revive/improve a two-semester course in research methods and team project work. After two years of doing this and assisting Professors Pardew and Sexton, I received my first lecturing/graduate teaching job at Columbia—teaching B7401 to incoming Executive MBA students. I owe a lifelong debt of gratitude to Senior Vice Dean Awi Federgruen and Professor Paul Glasserman, chair of the department of Decision, Risk, and Operations, for hiring me to teach statistics at the graduate level and for letting me develop and test a new approach to the course. Without their support during the five years I spent at the business school, my current full-time faculty appointments—and this book—would have not been possible.

Professor Zeger Degraeve, of the London Business School, and Professor Andy Shogan, of the Haas School of Business at the University of California—Berkeley, deserve thanks for letting me teach in their Executive MBA Programs (as part of Columbia joint MBA efforts) and for letting me expand my course to include more international elements and technology and entrepreneurship examples. Dr. Geof Mills, formerly dean of the faculty and vice president of the American College of Greece, also gets many thanks for betting on me in 2003 by bringing me to Greece to teach a semester's worth of data analysis in just two weeks! (Thanks to that first group of students, too, for working so hard!)

In 2004, I moved over to Columbia's School of International and Public Affairs (SIPA), thanks to Rob Garris and Dean Lisa Anderson, and I also took an appointment at Columbia's Mailman School of Public Health, thanks to my business school strategy professor, Dr. Tom Ference. Rob and Lisa let me adapt my data analysis course for international affairs and public affairs graduate students, and Tom helped get me a job teaching strategic management. These opportunities opened up many new ways for me to explain, apply, and reinforce data analysis in business, public policy, international affairs, and health care contexts. Today at SIPA, Dan McIntyre continues to counsel, mentor, and guide me as we continue to enhance SIPA core courses and support for analytical methods and learnings. Professors Sherry Glied and Linda Green also deserve thanks for letting me take the helm of Columbia's Alliance for Healthcare Management, where I've been able to work with and learn from so many graduate students of business, public health, and medicine in a variety of data analysis and policy contexts.

But the Columbia story is only part of my story. Thanks to my work in the executive MBA programs, I have been able to interact with a number of business leaders, managers, and researchers. In particular, two of my students in the inaugural Global Executive MBA Program, a two-degree MBA program from Columbia and the London Business School, asked me to apply my course and its tools to sophisticated business and laboratory science applications. Ron Boire, former senior executive at Sony Electronics and Best Buy and current president of Toys "R" Us North America, and Dr. William D. "Doug" Figg, of the Center for Cancer Research at the National Cancer Institute, have been invaluable colleagues, mentors, supporters, and personal friends both inside and outside the classroom. Many thanks to them for letting me "go nuts" in their respective organizations. Lou Magnan and Bruno Graizzaro (an MBA classmate of mine), of Magnan Graizzaro & Associates, CPAs, also deserve big thanks for letting me apply my data analysis skills to the world of forensic accounting on behalf of many of their clients.

I owe Mr. Leonidas Phoebus Koskos, executive vice president of the Hellenic American University in Athens, Greece, much gratitude for hiring me as a visiting professor and senior research fellow there. Dr. Daphne Halkias and Dr. Nick Harkiolakis deserve thanks for putting up with my late-night research rants (and statistics) as they have been instrumental in giving me an outlet for data analysis case studies and research on immigration, health care, and information technology trends in Europe.

Denise Caruso, author of the terrific book *Intervention*, forced me to explain probability, risk management, and sampling theory in such a way that she could use it in her research and writing. (And she made me explain it all over the phone, too—no pictures!). Thanks to Denise, I discovered a whole new way of explaining these often dry concepts in a refreshing way that appeals to policy analysts and business leaders alike.

Speaking of refreshing approaches, I wish to thank my good friend, fellow Cessna pilot, and, for my money, the best data analyst in the world, Dr. Bill Kahn. Bill has always helped me "get it right" without ever reminding me that he's infinitely better at statistical reasoning than anyone else on the planet.

To be sure, I owe infinite thanks to all the teaching and course assistants I have been blessed with over the past ten years at Columbia. Of particular note are Stacey Schinder, Julia Hook, Dmitry Nikitin, Thalia Tzanetti, William Panlilio, Grant Milthorpe, Dhurva Ganesan, and Megan Good—the initial architects, editors, and housekeepers of the course notes, lecture slides, lab aids, and practice problems and solutions that formed the basis of this text. Thanks to them and to all the other wonderful assistants I've had for making every course, lecture, and example so much more relevant, significant, compelling, and palatable than I ever could have alone.

In terms of making my writings and scribbles immeasurably better, I owe Shannon Berning and Joshua Martino of Kaplan Publishing a huge debt of gratitude. They provided encouragement when I thought writing this book was too hard, far too much leniency when I fell behind the deadlines, and a never-ending supply of good counsel and "customer feedback" about the readability and practicality of the material. Thank you both for all your patience, guidance, and terrific feedback. I also thank Fred Urfer, my production editor at Kaplan, for cleaning up my manuscript and for making it much more readable than I could have alone.

Finally, my family deserves the most credit. My wife, Andrea, deserves the highest level of love and praise for she put up with my working on this book on so many late nights and weekends, always at the expense of being a less-than-available husband, friend, and father while locked in my office typing, drawing, and editing. Our four-year-old, Lisa, deserves tremendous credit, too, for always being patient and understanding when I would answer, "Not yet, but soon." when she would repeatedly ask, "Daddy, are you done with your book yet?" Our one-year-old, Vanessa, didn't have much to say during the time this book was written, but when she would spy me at my desk typing away, she always crawled over, pulled herself up on the side of my desk and smiled or giggled at me. That, alone, kept me focused and writing during some of the tough times. So did the memory of my mother,

Velma Joyce Thurman. She never pushed me, but she always encouraged me. She never lectured me, but she always taught me. Thank you, Mother, for always telling me I could accomplish anything I put my mind to. And for always believing it to be true.

Columbia University
New York, New York
June 30, 2007

Test Yourself Answers

CHAPTER 1

1. Expenditures are on a per capita basis because if they were on a gross basis, large states, with more students, would distort the data by making it appear that they spend more on students' education when, in fact, they may simply have more students.

2. Descriptive statistics (from STATA):

Expenditure per Student

	Percentiles	Smallest		
1%	5571.3	5571.3		
5%	6117.58	5669.75		
10%	6447.625	6117.58	Obs	50
25%	7309.57	6257.05	Sum of Wgt.	50
50%	8037.35		Mean	8191.414
		Largest	Std. Dev.	1529.902
75%	9138.28	10395.06		
90%	10017.29	11530.56	Variance	2340600
95%	11530.56	12087.1	Skewness	.7462728
99%	12428.71	12428.71	Kurtosis	3.484248

The data are slightly skewed to the right, as evidenced by positive skewness. Kurtosis is high at 3.48. (Recall that in Excel, a kurtosis greater than zero is high. However, in most other tools, a kurtosis greater than 3 is considered high.) These facts can be seen when looking at the histogram of the data.

The range is $6,857—largest value (12,428.71) minus smallest value (5,571.3).

The data are not normally distributed. If they were, then skewness would be 0 and kurtosis would be 3 (or 0 in Excel).

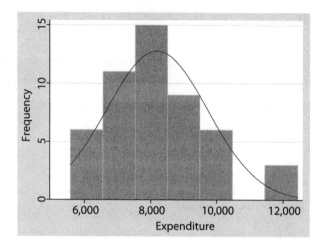

3. There are several outliers at the right-hand side of the distribution. They are New Jersey and New York with $12,428 and $12,087, respectively. (You can find this by sorting the data file in Excel.)

4. I chose a bin size of 500 because the range was relatively small and I wanted to see differentiation among states in the distribution. Any bin size up to 1,000 would have been appropriate. You cannot compare histograms of different bin sizes. The bin size will affect the shape of the distribution.

CHAPTER 2

1. P(buying BMW) = P(sale) × P(BMW/sale) = 0.1 × 0.2 = 0.02 = 2%
   P(buying Skoda) = P(sale) × P(Skoda/sale) = 0.1 × 0.1 = 0.01 = 1%

2. Number buying Ladas = 200 × P(sale) × P(Lada/sale) = 200 × 0.1 × 0.4 = 8.

3. P(Profit more than $1,000) = S × P(sale) × profit of those vehicles with profits >$1,000

$$= 0.1 \times (0.15 + 0.15 + 0.2 + 0.1)$$

$$= 0.06 \text{ (or 6\%)}$$

4. Expected profit (with 400 customers) = 400 × (Expected profit per sale)

$$= 400 \times 313 \text{ (see table below for detail)}$$

$$= \$125,200$$

Car	P(Sale)	% Sold per Sale	Profit per Sale($)	Expected Profit per Customer
VW Golf	0.1	0.15	1,000	15
Saab	0.1	0.15	2,000	30
BMW Z4 Roadster	0.1	0.20	12,000	240
Skoda Octavia	0.1	0.10	1,200	12
Lada Niva	0.1	0.40	400	16
Σ (sum)		1		313

5. We cannot accurately tell from the data provided—although figures tend to indicate that it is much more cost-effective to sell BMWs compared to Ladas (that is, $12,000 profit compared to $400 profit per sale).

6. Expected profit (with 400 customers) = 400 × (Expected profit per sale)

$$= 400 \times 96 \text{ (see table below for detail)}$$

$$= \$38,400$$

Car	P(Sale)	% Sold per Sale	Profit per Sale($)	Expected Profit per Customer	Expected Profit Given Sale
VW Golf	0.1	0.20	1,000	20	$ 200.00
Saab 92X	0.1	0.20	2,000	40	$ 400.00

(Continued)

(Continued)

Car	P(Sale)	% Sold per Sale	Profit per Sale($)	Expected Profit per Customer	Expected Profit Given Sale
Skoda Octavia	0.1	0.15	1,200	18	$ 180.00
Lada Niva	0.1	0.45	400	18	$ 180.00
Σ (sum)		1		96	$ 960.00

CHAPTER 3

1. We assume that the population of data (commuting times) is normally distributed. Making this assumption allows us to use the mean commuting time and standard deviation reported from the survey. Without this assumption, we would not know what the population of commuting times looks like, and we would not be able to solve the problem.

$$\text{z-score calculation: } z = (x - \mu) \div \sigma$$
$$= (37 - 49) \div 6$$
$$= -12 \div 6 = -2$$

The z-table shows that this z-score corresponds to 0.0228. Thus 2.28 percent of commuters have commutes shorter than 37 minutes.

2. We assume that the population is normally distributed. In this case, we already know the z-score (which is easily calculated from the percentile), and we are looking for its corresponding commuting time.

$$\text{z-score of 95th percentile: } 1.64$$
$$\text{Calculation: } z = (x - \mu) \div s$$
$$1.64 = (x - 49) \div 6$$
$$x = 58.84$$

The 95th percentile of commuting times is 58.84 minutes.

3. We assume that the population is normally distributed. From the z-score tables we know the 65th percentile corresponds to 0.39.

$$\text{Calculation: } z = (x - \mu) \div s$$
$$0.39 = (x - 49) \div 6$$
$$x = 51.34$$

So 65 percent of commuters commute for less than 51.34 minutes.

4. This question asks us for a percentile of average commuting times. However, we can only know how averages are distributed—by the central limit theorem (CLT) for large, representative samples—if we know the mean and standard error of the averages. Because the standard error is the standard deviation of the data (6) divided by the square root of the sample size—which is unknown from the problem—we cannot figure out how averages are distributed. Thus, we don't have enough information to answer this question.

5. Possible biases with the results include the following:

   a. Commuters at these subway stations may not be representative of the "average" commuter for a variety of reasons including (but not limited to) the nature of jobs around those subway stations, or the time of day, or the subway stations themselves. It may not be possible to apply the results found in this survey to commuters on lines that do not pass through these stations.

   b. The summer months are probably not good months to conduct this type of survey because many people are on vacation. It is possible that the absence of people who can afford to take a vacation in the peak season may skew your results.

CHAPTER 4

1. We need not assume any shape of the data distribution because we have a large random sample of students ($n > 30$ and sampled randomly). However, we can only talk about average behaviors using the central limit theorem, which tells us that sample averages are normally distributed (not data). Also, note that you are given the variance of the data, not the standard deviation. The standard deviation will be the square root of 36, or 6 hours.

$$\text{SE of the mean} = \sqrt{36} \div \sqrt{36} = 6 \div 6 = 1$$
$$Z = (9 - 8) \div 1 = 1$$

Thus, we need the area less than nine hours or less than $z = 1$ on the standard normal distribution (of averages). A table gives this as approximately 84 percent.

2. People may give biased answers for average weekly hours spent as higher or lower than actuality to give a certain implication of their intelligence or effort put forth. Also, the subjects in the sample may have actually wrongly estimated their time commitment.

3. This problem cannot be solved! This problem asks us to compute the percentage of students who spend less than two hours studying for statistics. This would require us to know how hours spent studying are distributed. This question *does not* ask about average behavior; it asks about data behavior. Because we can only know about average behavior when we sample (Rule #2), we cannot answer this question. Assuming the population of hours spent studying is normal is not appropriate; we have no basis for this assumption based on our sample.

CHAPTER 5

1. CI (95%) $= 89.25 \pm (1.96)(13.44 \div \sqrt{49})$

   $= 89.25 \pm 3.76 = [85.49, 93.01]$

2. CI (90%) $= 89.25 \pm (1.64)(13.44 \div \sqrt{49})$

   $= 89.25 \pm 3.15 = [86.10, 92.40]$

3. This problem cannot be solved! We don't know how the training hours are distributed. We only know how average numbers of training hours are distributed.

4. This problem can be solved because we are asked for the probability of resampling and getting an average of 85 hours or fewer. The standard error for this distribution is $13.44 \div \sqrt{49} = 1.92$ hours. The z-score for 85 hours is: $(85 - 89.25) \div 1.92 = -2.21$. From the z-table, we see the area below this z-score is 1.36 percent.

CHAPTER 6

Reworking problems 1, 2, and 4 from Chapter 5 with a (random) sample size of only 19 requires us to assume the population of training hours (per year) is normally distributed. We can then use the t-distribution, with $19 - 1 = 18$ degrees of freedom, to create the interval estimates required.

1. Confidence interval is $89.25 \pm (2.101)(13.44 \div \sqrt{19}) = 89.25 \pm 6.48 =$ [82.77, 95.73].

2. Confidence interval is $89.25 \pm (1.734)(13.44 \div \sqrt{19}) = 89.25 \pm 5.35 =$ [83.90, 94.60].

3. Standard error is 3.083. The t-score for 85 hours is $(85 - 89.25) \div 3.083$ $= -1.38$. This number, at 18 degrees of freedom, is not on the t-table, but we can say that the probability is between 5 percent and 10 percent because this t-score sits between the t-scores for 5 percent and 10 percent in one tail.

CHAPTER 7

1. Hypotheses are as follows:

   $H_0: \mu \geq \$92,411$ (initial research claim is believed)

   $H_A: \mu < \$92,411$ (new claim challenges the validity of the *Non-Profit Times* study)

2. This is a single-sample test, and we are comparing the new mean to a prior sampled/believed one. Because the sample is random and representative, we can apply the central limit theorem and assume that the distribution of sample averages is normally distributed.

   We use the z-table to arrive at critical value to test whether the test value (\$87,566) is significantly lower than \$92,411.

   $z_{5\% \text{ in left tail}} = -1.645 = (CV - \mu) \div SE$ (need negative z-score due to a left-tail test)

   $SE = s \div \sqrt{n} = 2,256.22$

   $-1.645 = \rightarrow (CV - 92,411) \div 2,256.22$

   CV (left of mean) = \$88,700

   Here, the new mean, \$87,566, is lower than the left-hand critical value. Thus, the competing newspaper's research team has found a significantly lower average salary than expected (at total alpha = 5%). Thus, it does appear that the new information proves that the initial survey overestimated the average executive director salary. We reject the null but run the risk of a Type I error because outliers in our sample could have caused us to reject the null, not necessarily a statistically signifi-cantly lower average salary for nonprofit executive directors.

CHAPTER 8

1. Hypotheses are as follows:

H_0: Mean difference (post – pre) ≤ 0 (product placement didn't in-crease view time)
H_A: Mean difference (post – pre) > 0 (product placement did increase view time)

This is a one-tailed paired test. Because we have only 20 readings, the CLT does not apply. We must use t-distributions, but only if we assume the population of differences is normally distributed.

Using a software package (like Excel), we can obtain the one-tailed p-value of this test (with 19 degrees of freedom) to be 0.06 (or 6%). Be-cause this p-value is less than alpha (10%), we reject the null and believe the product placement did significantly increase viewing times of the TV show. However, we may have made a Type I error, because outliers in our differences could cause us to reject the null, not an actual increase in viewing time.

2. Hypotheses are as follows:

H_0: Male mean – Female mean $= 0$ (no difference in average male ver-sus female minutes)
H_A: Male mean – Female mean $\neq$ (significant difference in average male versus female minutes)

This is a two-tailed test of differences of means (independent samples). Also, looking at the dataset, each subset has more than 30 observations. Thus, we use a difference of means test without assum-ing anything about the population distribution or about population variances.

From Excel, we can perform this test and get the following output. Note that the two-tailed p-value is 0.004. Because this is less than our alpha level of 1 percent, we reject the null hypothesis and conclude that males and females have different average minutes of TV viewing after our product is placed. Note that the females have a higher average number of minutes.

t-Test: Two-Sample Assuming Unequal Variances

	Males – After Placement	Females – After Placement
Mean	25.86956522	29.25
Variance	39.84927536	17.62142857
Observations	46	36
Hypothesized Mean Difference	0	
df	78	
t Stat	-2.903214444	
P(T<=t) one-tail	0.002400502	
t Critical one-tail	1.664624645	
P(T<=t) two-tail	0.004801004	
t Critical two-tail	1.990847036	

CHAPTER 9

Here's the regression output from Excel along with the line-fit plot and residuals.

Regression Statistics	
Multiple R	0.902892598
R Square	0.815215043
Adjusted R Square	0.810352281
Standard Error	57.67014172
Observations	40

ANOVA

	df	SS	MS	F	Significance F
Regression	1	557559.4806	557559.4806	167.6444451	1.65117E-15
Residual	38	126382.1194	3325.845246		
Total	39	683941.6			

	Coefficients	Standard Error	t Stat	P-value	Lower 95%	Upper 95%	Lower 90.0%	Upper 90.0%
Intercept	1.655063236	21.41921016	0.07727004	0.938814151	-41.70586231	45.01598879	-34.4567198	37.76684627
Quantity	8.828317916	0.681841421	12.9477583	1.65117E-15	7.448002075	10.20863376	7.678765282	9.97787055

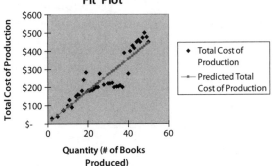

Quantity (# of Books Produced) Line Fit Plot

Quantity (# of Books Produced)
Residual Plot

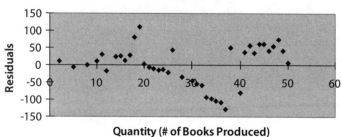

Quantity (# of Books Produced)

1. Total cost = $1.655 + $8.828 × Quantity

2. The explained variance is given by the adjusted r-squared term, or 81.04 percent.

3. Fixed cost is just the intercept: $1.655. The variable cost of 20 textbooks is the marginal cost (or the slope, in this case) multiplied by the quantity. Here, the variable cost of 20 textbooks would be $8.828 × 20, or $176.56.

4. We can use Excel (or any tool) and find a 90 percent confidence interval for the slope by specifying a different confidence (or alpha) level. In the output above, we see that the 90 percent confidence interval for the slope (or marginal cost, in this case) is given by [$7.679, $9.978]. We can also use the standard error of the slope and a z-score (or t-score) to approximate this interval. In this case, using the output from Excel, a 90 percent confidence interval for the slope would be approximately the following: $8.828 +/− 1.645 − $0.682.

5. We can only create prediction intervals using input (quantity) values that are within the range of the values used to build the model. Note that 20 textbooks is inside the range but 200 textbooks is not. Thus, we will not be able to use this model to create a prediction interval for 200 textbooks. A 95 percent prediction interval for the total cost of 20 textbooks is given by

$$\hat{y}_{x=20} \pm 1.96 \times \left(s \times \sqrt{1 + \frac{1}{n} + \frac{(x^* - \bar{x})^2}{\Sigma(x_i - \bar{x})^2}} \right)$$

where x^* is the x-value where we want to create the estimate (20 books, in this case) and s is the standard error of the regression model (57.67, from the Excel output, above).

$$= (1.655 + 8.828 \times 20) \pm 1.96 \times \left(57.67 \times \sqrt{1 + \frac{1}{40} + \frac{(20 - \bar{x})^2}{\Sigma(x_i - \bar{x})^2}}\right)$$

Now, the average number of textbooks is 28.425 (found from descriptive statistics of just the number of textbooks values). The sum in the denominator under the root sign is just $(n - 1)$ times the variance of all x-values, which is $39 \times 183.430 = 7,153.77$.

Putting all of these values in gives us a 95 percent prediction interval for the total cost of 20 textbooks of [$63.22, $293.20].

Note, too, that a reasonable approximation to this interval is given by simply creating the prediction interval using only the standard error of the regression model:

$$\hat{y}_{x=20} \pm 1.96 \times s_{y|x}$$
$$= (1.655 + 8.828 \times 20) \pm 1.96 \times 57.67$$
$$= [\$65.18, \$291.25]$$

CHAPTER 10

Here is the regression output from Excel:

Regression Statistics	
Multiple R	0.997192651
R Square	0.994393184
Adjusted R Square	0.993925949
Standard Error	10.32087238
Observations	40

ANOVA					
	df	SS	MS	F	Significance F
Regression	3	680106.8654	226702.2885	2128.252186	1.46121E-40
Residual	36	3834.734643	106.5204067		
Total	39	683941.6			

	Coefficients	Standard Error	t Stat	P-value	Lower 95%	Upper 95%	Lower 95.0%	Upper 95.0%
Intercept	5.215980291	3.83632847	1.359628179	0.18240316	-2.56445441	12.99641499	-2.56445441	12.99641499
Quantity (# of Books Produced)	0.13670991	0.289211518	0.472698705	0.639281516	-0.449838231	0.723258051	-0.449838231	0.723258051
Economic Factor 1	0.078963861	0.251581706	0.313869647	0.75543164	-0.431267484	0.589195206	-0.431267484	0.589195206
Economic Factor 2	0.885121906	0.247065599	3.582538037	0.000998907	0.384049651	1.386194162	0.384049651	1.386194162

1. Total cost = $5.216 + $0.137 × (Quant) + $0.079 × (E. Factor 1) + $0.885 × (E. Factor 2).

2. Explained variance is given by adjusted r-squared, or 99.39 percent. The model is significant because the p-value of the F-statistic, or Significance F, is quite small (1.5×10^{-40}).

3. From a z-table, we can see that at three-sigma—or three standard errors away from the mean slope—only 0.0013, or 0.13 percent, is left in each tail. The only input variable with a p-value smaller than this is Economic Factor 2. Thus, we would discard Economic Factor 1 and Quantity under this criterion.

4. These two Economic Factor inputs are likely to be highly correlated because the stock prices of paper companies are likely highly correlated with the price of paper. Thus, we may have put two highly correlated input variables into the model at the same time. This causes multicollinearity, or a false sense of fit. Thus, the very high r-squared, or explained variance, may be a result of these two inputs explaining each other, not from the three inputs explaining total cost.

Appendix A: Distribution Tables

TABLE A.1 STANDARD NORMAL DISTRIBUTION— POSITIVE Z-SCORES

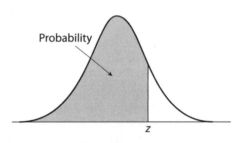

Table entry for z is the area under the standard normal curve to the left of z.

Probability

z

Standard normal probabilities									
z	.00	.01	.02	.03	.04	.05	.06	.07	.08	.09
0.0	.5000	.5040	.5080	.5120	.5160	.5199	.5239	.5279	.5319	.5359
0.1	.5398	.5438	.5478	.5317	.5587	.5596	.5636	.5675	.5714	.5753
0.2	.5793	.5832	.5871	.5910	.5948	.5987	.6026	.6064	.6103	.6141
0.3	.6179	.6217	.6255	.6293	.6331	.6368	.6406	.6443	.6480	.6517
0.4	.6554	.6591	.6628	.6664	.6700	.6736	.6772	.6808	.6844	.6879
0.5	.6915	.6950	.6983	.7019	.7054	.7088	.7123	.7157	.7190	.7224
0.6	.7257	.7291	.7324	.7357	.7389	.7422	.7454	.7486	.7519	.7549
0.7	.7580	.7611	.7642	.7673	.7704	.7734	.7764	.7794	.7823	.7852
0.8	.7881	.7910	.7939	.7967	.7995	.8023	.8051	.8078	.8106	.8133
0.9	.8159	.8186	.8212	.8238	.8264	.8289	.8315	.8340	.8365	.8389
1.0	.8413	.8438	.8461	.8485	.8308	.8531	.8554	.8577	.8599	.8621
1.1	.8643	.8665	.8686	.8708	.8729	.8749	.8770	.8790	.8810	.8830
1.2	.8849	.8869	.8888	.8907	.8925	.8944	.8962	.8980	.8997	.9015
1.3	.9032	.9049	.9066	.9082	.9099	.9115	.9131	.9147	.9162	.9177
1.4	.9192	.9207	.9222	.9236	.9251	.9265	.9279	.9292	.9306	.9319
1.5	.9332	.9345	.9357	.9370	.9382	.9394	.9406	.9418	.9429	.9441
1.6	.9452	.9463	.9474	.9484	.9495	.9505	.9515	.9525	.9535	.9545
1.7	.9554	.9564	.9573	.9582	.9591	.9599	.9608	.9616	.9625	.9633
1.8	.9641	.9649	.9656	.9664	.9671	.9678	.9686	.9616	.9699	.9706
1.9	.9713	.9719	.9726	.9732	.9738	.9744	.9750	.9693	.9761	.9767
2.0	.9772	.9778	.9783	.9788	.9793	.9797	.9803	.9756	.9812	.9817
2.1	.9821	.9826	.9830	.9834	.9838	.9842	.9846	.9808	.9854	.9837
2.2	.9861	.9864	.9868	.9871	.9875	.9878	.9881	.9830	.9887	.9890
2.3	.9893	.9896	.9898	.9901	.9904	.9906	.9909	.9884	.9913	.9916
2.4	.9918	.9920	.9922	.9925	.9927	.9929	.9931	.9911	.9934	.9936

(Continued)

(Continued)

Z	.00	.01	.02	.03	.04	.05	.06	.07	.08	.09
2.5	.9938	.9940	.9941	.9943	.9945	.9946	.9948	.9932	.9951	.9952
2.6	.9953	.9955	.9956	.9957	.9959	.9960	.9961	.9949	.9963	.9964
2.7	.9965	.9966	.9967	.9968	.9969	.9970	.9971	.9962	.9973	.9974
2.8	.9974	.9975	.9976	.9977	.9977	.9978	.9979	.9972	.9980	.9981
2.9	.9981	.9982	.9982	.9983	.9984	.9984	.9985	.9979	.9986	.9986
3.0	.9987	.9987	.9987	.9988	.9988	.9989	.9989	.9985	.9990	.9990
3.1	.9990	.9991	.9991	.9991	.9992	.9992	.9992	.9989	.9993	.9993
3.2	.9993	.9993	.9994	.9994	.9994	.9994	.9994	.9992	.9995	.9995
3.3	.9995	.9995	.9995	.9996	.9996	.9996	.9996	.9996	.9996	.9997
3.4	.9997	.9997	.9997	.9997	.9997	.9997	.9997	.9997	.9997	.9998

TABLE A.2 STANDARD NORMAL DISTRIBUTION—NEGATIVE Z-SCORES

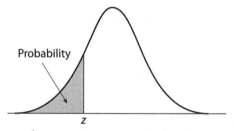

Probability

Table entry for *z* is the area under the standard normal curve to the left of *z*.

Standard normal probabilities

Z	.00	.01	.02	.03	.04	.05	.06	.07	.08	.09
−3.4	.0003	.0003	.0003	.0003	.0003	.0003	.0003	.0003	.0003	.0002
−3.3	.0005	.0005	.0005	.0004	.0004	.0004	.0004	.0004	.0004	.0003
−3.2	.0007	.0007	.0006	.0006	.0006	.0006	.0006	.0005	.0005	.0005
−3.1	.0010	.0009	.0009	.0009	.0008	.0008	.0008	.008	.0007	.0007
−3.0	.0013	.0013	.0013	.0012	.0012	.0011	.0011	.0011	.0010	.0010
−2.9	.0019	.0018	.0018	.0017	.0016	.0016	.0015	.0015	.0014	.0014
−2.8	.0026	.0025	.0024	.0023	.0023	.0022	.0021	.0021	.0020	.0019
−2.7	.0035	.0034	.0033	.0032	.0031	.0030	.0029	.0028	.0027	.0026
−2.6	.0047	.0045	.0044	.0045	.0041	.0040	.0039	.0038	.0037	.0036
−2.5	.0062	.0060	.0059	.0057	.0055	.0054	.0052	.0051	.0049	.0048
−2.4	.0082	.0080	.0078	.0075	.0073	.0071	.0069	.0068	.0066	.0064
−2.3	.0107	.0104	.0102	.0099	.0096	.0094	.0091	.0089	.0087	.0084
−2.2	.0139	.0136	.0132	.0129	.0125	.0122	.0119	.0116	.0113	.0110
−2.1	.0179	.0174	.0170	.0166	.0162	.0158	.0154	.0150	.0146	.0143
−2.0	.0228	.0222	.0217	.0212	.0207	.0202	.0197	.0192	.0188	.0183
−1.9	.0287	.0281	.0274	.0268	.0262	.0256	.0250	.0244	.0239	.0233
−1.8	.0359	.0351	.0344	.0336	.0329	.0322	.0314	.0307	.0301	.0294
−1.7	.0446	.0436	.0427	.0418	.0409	.0401	.0392	.0384	.0375	.0367
−1.6	.0548	.0537	.0526	.0516	.0505	.0495	.0485	.0475	.0465	.0455
−1.5	.0668	.0655	.0643	.0630	.0618	.0606	.0594	.0582	.0571	.0559
−1.4	.0808	.0793	.0778	.0764	.0749	.0735	.0721	.0708	.0694	.0681
−1.3	.0968	.0951	.0934	.0918	.0901	.0885	.0869	.0853	.0838	.0823
−1.2	.1151	.1131	.1112	.1093	.1075	.1056	.1038	.1020	.1003	.0985
−1.1	.1357	.1335	.1314	.1292	.1271	.1251	.1230	.1210	.1190	.1170
−1.0	.1587	.1562	.1539	.515	.1492	.1469	.1446	.1423	.1401	.1379
−0.9	.1841	.1814	.1788	.1762	.1736	.1711	.1685	.1660	.1635	.1611
−0.8	.2119	.2090	.2061	.2033	.2005	.1977	.1949	.1922	.1894	.1867
−0.7	.2420	.2398	.2358	.2327	.2006	.2266	.2236	.2206	.2177	.2148
−0.6	.2743	.2709	.2676	.2643	.2611	.2578	.2546	.2514	.2483	.2481
−0.5	.3085	.3050	.3015	.2981	.2946	.2912	.2877	.2845	.2810	.2776
−0.4	.3446	.3409	.3372	.3336	.3300	.3264	.3228	.3192	.3156	.3121
−0.3	.3821	.3783	.3745	.3707	.3669	.3632	.3594	.3557	.3520	.3483
−0.2	.4207	.4168	.4129	.4090	.4052	.4013	.3974	.3936	.3897	.3859
−0.1	.4602	.4562	.4522	.4483	.4443	.4404	.4364	.4325	.4286	.4247
−0.0	.5000	.4960	.4920	.4880	.4840	.4801	.4761	.4721	.4681	.4641

TABLE A.3 T-DISTRIBUTION (T-SCORES AND AREAS FOR SMALL SAMPLES WITH ASSUMPTIONS STATED)

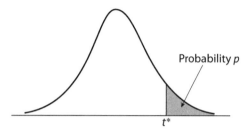

Table entry for p and C is the critical value t^* with probability p lying to its right and probability C lying between $-t^*$ and t^*.

Probability p

t^*

t–Distribution critical values

df					Upper tail probability p							
	.00	.20	.15	.10	.05	.025	.02	.01	.005	.0025	.001	.0005
1	1.000	1.376	1.963	3.078	6.314	12.71	15.89	31.82	63.66	127.3	318.3	636.6
2	0.816	1.061	1.386	1.886	2.920	4.303	4.849	6.965	9.925	14.09	22.33	31.60
3	0.765	0.978	1.250	1.638	2.353	3.182	3.482	4.541	5.841	7.453	10.21	12.92
4	0.741	0.941	1.190	1.533	2.132	2.776	2.999	3.747	4.604	5.598	7.173	8.610
5	0.727	0.920	1.156	1.476	2.015	2.571	2.757	3.365	4.032	4.773	5.893	6.869
6	0.718	0.906	1.134	1.440	1.943	2.447	2.612	3.143	3.707	4.317	5.208	5.959
7	0.711	0.896	1.119	1.415	1.895	2.365	2.517	2.998	3.499	4.029	4.785	5.408
8	0.706	0.889	1.108	1.397	1.860	2.306	2.449	2.896	3.355	3.833	4.501	5.041
9	0.703	0.883	1.100	1.383	1.833	2.262	2.398	2.821	3.250	3.690	4.297	4.781
10	0.700	0.879	1.093	1.372	1.812	2.228	2.359	2.764	3.169	3.581	4.144	4.587
11	0.697	0.876	1.088	1.363	1.796	2.201	2.328	2.718	3.106	3.497	4.025	4.437
12	0.695	0.873	1.083	1.356	1.782	2.179	2.303	2.681	3.055	3.428	3.930	4.318
13	0.694	0.870	1.079	1.350	1.771	2.160	2.282	2.650	3.012	3.372	3.852	4.221
14	0.692	0.868	1.076	1.345	1.761	2.145	2.264	2.624	2.977	3.326	3.787	4.140
15	0.691	0.866	1.074	1.341	1.753	2.131	2.249	2.602	2.947	3.286	3.733	4.073
16	0.690	0.865	1.071	1.337	1.746	2.120	2.235	2.583	2.921	3.252	3.686	4.015
17	0.689	0.863	1.069	1.333	1.740	2.110	2.224	2.567	2.898	3.222	3.646	3.965
18	0.688	0.862	1.067	1.330	1.734	2.101	2.214	2.552	2.878	3.197	3.611	3.922
19	0.688	0.861	1.066	1.328	1.729	2.093	2.205	2.539	2.861	3.174	3.579	3.886
20	0.687	0.860	1.064	1.325	1.725	2.086	2.197	2.528	2.845	3.153	3.552	3.850
21	0.686	0.859	1.063	1.323	1.721	2.080	2.189	2.518	2.831	3.135	3.527	3.819
22	0.686	0.858	1.061	1.321	1.717	2.074	2.183	2.508	2.819	3.119	3.505	3.792
23	0.685	0.858	1.060	1.319	1.714	2.069	2.177	2.500	2.807	3.104	3.485	3.768
24	0.685	0.857	1.059	1.318	1.711	2.064	2.172	2.492	2.797	3.091	3.467	3.745
25	0.684	0.856	1.058	1.316	1.708	2.060	2.167	2.485	2.787	3.078	3.450	3.725
26	0.684	0.856	1.058	1.315	1.706	2.056	2.162	2.479	2.779	3.067	3.435	3.707
27	0.684	0.855	1.057	1.314	1.703	2.052	2.158	2.473	2.771	3.057	3.421	3.690
28	0.683	0.855	1.056	1.313	1.701	2.048	2.154	2.467	2.763	3.047	3.408	3.674
29	0.683	0.854	1.055	1.311	1.699	2.045	2.150	2.462	2.756	3.038	3.396	3.659
30	0.683	0.854	1.055	1.310	1.697	2.042	2.147	2.457	2.750	3.030	3.385	3.646
40	0.681	0.851	1.050	1.303	1.684	2.021	2.123	2.423	2.704	2.971	3.307	3.551
50	0.679	0.849	1.047	1.299	1.676	2.009	2.109	2.403	2.678	2.937	3.261	3.496
60	0.679	0.848	1.045	1.296	1.671	2.000	2.099	2.390	2.660	2.915	3.232	3.460
80	0.678	0.846	1.043	1.292	1.664	1.990	2.088	2.374	2.639	2.887	3.195	3.416
100	0.677	0.845	1.042	1.290	1.660	1.984	2.081	2.364	2.626	2.871	3.174	3.390
1000	0.675	0.842	1.037	1.282	1.646	1.962	2.056	2.330	2.581	2.813	3.098	3.300
z^*	0.674	0.841	1.036	1.282	1.645	1.960	2.054	2.326	2.576	2.807	3.091	3.291
	50%	60%	70%	80%	90%	95%	95%	98%	99%	99.8%	99.8%	99.9%
						Confidence level C						

Appendix B: Microsoft Excel Tutorials

TUTORIAL 1: CREATING DESCRIPTIVE STATISTICS

This tutorial discusses how to use the Data Analysis add-in in Excel to compute various descriptive statistics for data ranges.

Adding the Add-Ins to the Tools Menu

To use the Data Analysis toolkit, you'll need to add it to your Tools menu.

Step	Action	Result
1	Run Excel and select the Tools menu from the menu bar.	Tools menu displays starting with Spelling..., Auditing, and so on.
2	See if the option Data Analysis... appears at the bottom of the menu (after Options...).	If you see the Data Analysis... menu option, skip to the next section, "Computing Descriptive Statistics for Spreadsheet Data." If not, continue with step 3.
3	Select the Add-Ins... option in this menu (about halfway down the list).	After several seconds, a new window, titled *Add-Ins*, will appear with several checkbox entries in a list.

(Continued)

(Continued)

Step	Action	Result
4	Check the boxes next to the Analysis Toolpak and Analysis Toolpak—VBA add-ins.	Boxes next to these add-ins will be checked with a checkmark.
5	Also, it's a good idea to check the AutoSave add-in so that Excel prompts you to save your work periodically.	Box next to the AutoSave add-in will be checked.
6	Push the OK button to the right of the list of add-ins.	Excel will now add in the functionality of these toolpaks. This may take a few seconds.
7	Repeat steps 1 and 2 in this list.	You should now see the Data Analysis... option in the Tools menu.

Note: If you don't see the Analysis Tookpak add-ins, you may not have performed a complete install of Microsoft Office (or Excel). Reinstall Office (or Excel) with a full installation, or work with your IT department if you use Office over a network.

Now, we're hopefully ready to use this toolpak to do some statistical analyses!

Computing Descriptive Statistics for Spreadsheet Data

Let's start by entering some data into a blank spreadsheet to use for this (and future) tutorials. Input the information below into Sheet1 in Excel.

Monthly Rates of Return

Date	S&P	Viacom	AT&T	GM	Coke
01/30/98	0.8799	0.7541	2.1407	-4.6296	-18.8406
02/27/98	7.5187	14.9701	-2.5948	18.9860	6.6964
03/31/98	5.5580	11.9792	7.7869	-1.7226	-3.3473
04/30/98	1.3716	7.9070	-8.5551	-0.5535	5.8442
05/29/98	-1.6289	-5.1724	1.2474	6.6790	1.9427
06/27/98	2.4171	3.4091	0.8214	1.8261	2.1063

These are monthly rates of return for the stocks shown in the first half of a past year. Now, let's compute some simple descriptive statistics for these data, such as maximum, minimum, range, mean, median, variance, and standard deviation. To compute these, we could use the Function Wizard and insert formulas for these statistics below the columns of data. But there's an easier way to do more with less effort!

Let's use our newfound Data Analysis toolkit and look at some descriptive statistics for the S&P 500 data in the B column of the data. To do this, follow the steps below.

Step	Action	Result
1	Select the Tools menu and then the Data Analysis... menu item. (Note: You don't need to select a data range yet.)	A new window, titled *Data Analysis*, appears with several options listed, including Anova: Single Factor.
2	Select the Descriptive Statistics option and either double-click or press the OK button on the upper right.	A new window, titled *Descriptive Statistics*, appears with several fields and checkboxes.
3	Now we select the data range to analyze. Select the range B3:B9 on the original Sheet1. Note that this includes the column label S&P.	The Input Range field in the Descriptive Statistics window now contains the range B3:B9.
4	Next, because the S&P data are in a column, select the Grouped by Columns option. Also, because we have included labels with our data, check the Labels in First Row selection.	Grouped by Columns option should be bulleted, and the Labels in First Row option should be checked.
5	Select the Summary Statistics box at the bottom of the window so that the toolpak will give us descriptive statistics. Also, if you want the results in a particular sheet (with a name), select the New Worksheet Ply: option and provide a name in the blank to the side (e.g., *S&P Stats*)	Summary Statistics box is checked, and the New Worksheet Ply: option is selected (with a name for the new worksheet, if applicable).
6	Select no other options or features and press the OK button in the upper right.	Descriptive statistics should appear in a new worksheet!

The mean, (sample) variance, standard deviation, range, minimum, and maximum are now shown in the output. Other statistics, such as the kurtosis, skewness, and standard error are also provided.

Note: In some versions of Excel, the ampersand in the label *S&P* may cause errors. If this happens, simply change the column title to *S and P*. Also change the *AT&T* label to *ATT*.

Finally, note that we could have performed the steps above on all of our stock data at the same time. That is, if we had selected all of our data—that is, the range B3:F9—Excel would have created summary statistics for all of the data as shown below:

S&P		Viacom		ATT		GM		Coke	
Mean	2.686066667	Mean	5.641183333	Mean	0.141083333	Mean	3.4309	Mean	-0.93305
Standard Error	1.357493856	Standard Error	3.044844991	Standard Error	2.215493992	Standard Error	3.476072202	Standard Error	3.865040584
Median	1.89435	Median	5.65805	Median	1.0344	Median	0.6363	Median	2.0245
Mode	#N/A	Mode	#N/A	Mode	#N/A	Mode	#N/A	Mode	#N/A
Standard Deviation	3.325167276	Standard Deviation	7.458316575	Standard Deviation	5.426829808	Standard Deviation	8.514603203	Standard Deviation	9.467377265
Sample Variance	11.05673741	Sample Variance	55.62648613	Sample Variance	29.45048177	Sample Variance	72.4984677	Sample Variance	89.63123228
Kurtosis	-0.674386392	Kurtosis	-0.937691407	Kurtosis	1.183192445	Kurtosis	2.252482256	Kurtosis	3.205729052
Skewness	0.391898632	Skewness	0.227195286	Skewness	0.415749762	Skewness	1.492009576	Skewness	-1.74979474
Range	9.1476	Range	20.1425	Range	16.342	Range	23.6156	Range	25.537
Minimum	-1.6289	Minimum	-5.1724	Minimum	-8.5551	Minimum	-4.6296	Minimum	-18.8406
Maximum	7.5187	Maximum	14.9701	Maximum	7.7869	Maximum	18.986	Maximum	6.6964
Sum	16.1164	Sum	33.8471	Sum	0.8465	Sum	20.5854	Sum	-5.5983
Count	6	Count	6	Count	6	Count	6	Count	6

Creating Histograms

The Data Analysis toolpak also has a Histogram function that can be used to create simple frequency distributions. When using this function, be sure to select Chart Output so you get a picture of the histogram. Also, if you do not specify your bin ranges, Excel will create them for you automatically (using a formula that finds the optimal number of bins for your histogram). However, you can select the Bin Range option to specify a range of cells in your spreadsheet that contain the bins to be used. This is important when comparing histograms of different datasets visually. Bins must be kept the same, or you cannot accurately compare the pictures across datasets.

Try creating some histograms—with and without your own defined bins. Note that options exist to create cumulative frequency distributions as well as Pareto or sorted histograms (where the bars are arranged from left to right in descending order of height/frequency).

The Excel help function is a good resource to use when using this and other Data Analysis tools.

TUTORIAL 2: CONDUCTING ONE-SAMPLE AND TWO-SAMPLE HYPOTHESIS TESTS OF MEANS

This tutorial discusses how to use the Data Analysis add-in in Excel to test hypotheses of means and of mean differences. To complete this tutorial, you will need to have the Data Analysis add-in in your Tools menu. If you do not, please refer to "Tutorial 1: Creating Descriptive Statistics" for help on installing and accessing this tool kit. In addition, you should have the stock data shown below (from the first tutorial) available for use.

Monthly Rates of Return

Date	S&P	Viacom	AT&T	GM	Coke
01/30/98	0.8799	0.7541	2.1407	-4.6296	-18.8406
02/27/98	7.5187	14.9701	-2.5948	18.9860	6.6964
03/31/98	5.5580	11.9792	7.7869	-1.7226	-3.3473
04/30/98	1.3716	7.9070	-8.5551	-0.5535	5.8442
05/29/98	-1.6289	-5.1724	1.2474	6.6790	1.9427
06/27/98	2.4171	3.4091	0.8214	1.8261	2.1063

Testing Mean Differences and Differences of Means Hypotheses

Hypothesis testing is one of the core topics of this text. One of the most common hypothesis tests performed is one comparing average values or means of two sets of sample data. Data can be paired. For example, the data above could be considered paired if we were to sample dates randomly and then collect stock returns for all stocks on the randomly selected dates. We could also do before/after analyses in which we look at the same random sample of customers, for example, before and after we run a marketing promotion. This is a test of *mean difference* and reduces to a single-sample test.

Also, we can compare two unpaired means from two separate, independent random samples. In this case, we are testing the *difference of means*. For example, if we have product defect information on two similar or comparable products—one that we use extensively today and another that we are considering adding to our inventory—it would be nice to know if, statistically, the mean number of failures of the two products are, based on a sample, the "same" or if they differ by a predetermined amount (subject, of course, to some experimental tolerance or *Type I* or *alpha error*).

Thus, if one product, on average, fails as much as the other, we may be led not to switch suppliers (if one product is currently our preferred choice). However, if the new product that we are examining appears to fail less often than our current one, we may be led to switch suppliers. If Product A is our current choice, Product B is the new product that we are examining, and Mean Number of Failures$_A$ is the mean number of failures for Product A (and similarly for Product B), then the hypothesis that we are testing is a *difference of means*:

H_0: Mean Number of Failures$_A$ = Mean Number of Failures$_B$
(our null hypothesis)
H_A: Mean Number of Failures$_A$ ≠ Mean Number of Failures$_B$
(our alternative)

Note here that our null or "going in" assumption is that the products are similar and, thus, fail at about the same average rate. Our alternative hypothesis is that they fail at different rates. Note that this is a two-tail hypothesis test. If we wanted to test Failures$_A$ < Failures$_B$, we could use a one-tail test, instead.

If we rewrite these hypotheses, we can see that we are testing *differences of means*:

H_0: (Mean Number of Failures$_A$) − (Mean Number of Failures$_B$) = 0
H_A: (Mean Number of Failures$_A$) − (Mean Number of Failures$_B$) ≠ 0

Fortunately, we can use Excel to "do the math" with respect to these hypothesis tests of mean differences and help us understand if we should reserve judgment (not reject the null hypothesis) or reject the null hypothesis. The Data Analysis toolkit has four options devoted to helping us test mean difference hypotheses; care should be taken to ensure that the proper one is used.

Data Analysis Option	Use When You Have...[1]
• T-Test: Paired Two-Sample for Means	• Dependent samples/outcomes (i.e., paired observations, such as before and after measurements from an ad campaign) • Small or large random sample sizes • An assumption that population of differences is normally distributed is required if using a small sample • Note: This tool can also be used for single sample tests of hypotheses (of one mean).
• T-Test: Two-Sample Assuming Unequal Variances	• Independent samples/outcomes (i.e., unpaired observations) • Large sample sizes (more than 30 items in both samples/lists) • Both samples random and representative
• T-Test: Two-Sample Assuming Equal Variances	• Independent samples/outcomes (i.e., unpaired observations) • Small sample sizes (30 or fewer items in one or both samples/lists) • An assumption that both populations sampled are *normal* and that the population variances are *equal* (even if sample variances are not)
• Z-Test: Two Sample for Means— *generally not used!*	• Independent samples/outcomes; (i.e., unpaired observations, such as market returns from two different portfolios/managers) • Large sample sizes (more than 30 items in both samples/lists) • Known *population* variances of both data sets, but only if you have populations of data! • Because we rarely have population data, this test is generally not used, and we will ignore it in this tutorial.

[1] Note that in each case, a Type I or alpha error threshold will be required by the add-in. An alpha level of 5 percent is the default.

We will now discuss how to use the "Data Analysis" add-in to apply each of these tests in turn. Note that we will show the general mechanics and sample output here based on our stock return data.

T-Test: Paired Two Sample for Means

In this test, we assume that the two data sets are dependent or paired in some way (e.g., average bank balances before and after you eliminate ATM fees for your bank's customers). We can randomly sample some of our bank's customers and measure their balances before and after this policy is implemented. We can then compare these paired data sets—which are paired by randomly chosen customer—to see if our policy had a significant impact.

With our stock data, let's assume the dates chosen have been randomly selected. Thus, all of our various stock returns are paired by the date they were sampled. Let's do a paired test using Excel. Note, though, that because we have small samples, we must assume the population of differences (between Viacom and GM stock, for example) is normally distributed.

To set up the paired test, perform the following steps.

Step	Action	Result
1	Select Data Analysis from Tools menu.	Window appears with various data analysis tools listed.
2	Select the T-Test: Paired Two Sample for Means option and press the OK button.	A new window, titled *T-Test: Paired Two-Sample for Means*, appears.
3	Now fill in the data ranges. First, fill in the Variable 1 Range with Viacom's returns (and label) (C3:C9). Next, fill in Variable 2 Range with GM's (E3:E9). Next, enter 0 for the Hypothesized Mean Difference because we are testing strict inequality. Finally, enter an Alpha level of 0.05 (*not 5!*).	The Variable 1 Range, Variable 2 Range, Hypothesized Mean Difference, and Alpha fields should be filled in with the appropriate values.
4	Because we have included labels in the ranges entered in step 3, we need to check the Labels checkbox.	Labels checkbox should contain a checkmark.
5	Let's put our output in a new worksheet ply titled *T-Test, Paired Means*	New Worksheet Ply: option is selected with the name *T-Test, Paired Means* entered.

(*Continued*)

Step	Action	Result
6	Now, let's get the results! Press the OK button and watch Excel work its magic.	Hypothesis/t-test results appear in a worksheet ply named, *T-Test, Paired Means* (see below).

Here's the output from this test:

t-Test: Paired Two Sample for Means

	Viacom	*GM*
Mean	5.641183333	3.4309
Variance	55.62648613	72.4984677
Observations	6	6
Pearson Correlation	0.350437967	
Hypothesized Mean Difference	0	
df	5	
t Stat	0.592077573	
P(T<=t) one-tail	0.28977785	
t Critical one-tail	2.015049176	
P(T<=t) two-tail	0.5795557	
t Critical two-tail	2.570577635	

Note here that the degrees of freedom is 5, or the number of pairs minus one. Again, this test is only valid if we assume the population of differences is normal. Note the one-tail and two-tail p-values in the output. The two-tail p-value is simply twice the one-tail p-value. Also, if we have an alpha of 5 percent, we see that both the one-tail and two-tail p-values are greater. Thus, regardless of whether we use a one-tailed or two-tailed test, these two stocks do not have statistically different average returns when compared by a paired data test. Thus, we would not reject the null that the averages are equal, and we risk a Type II error by making this conclusion.

Using Paired Test Tool to Perform Single-Sample Means Tests

While there is no single-sample test tool in Excel, we can use the two-sample paired test effectively to perform a one-sample means test. The way to do this is as follows. Suppose you have a null hypothesis that the historical average call-wait time in your customer service center is 90 seconds. You collect some random call data and see that the sample average wait time is 105 seconds. Is this significantly different from our prior belief (or policy, if 90 seconds is the maximum hold time we should allow our operators)?

This is a one-sample test comparing the sample mean of 105 to the perceived or historical mean of 90. To use the paired test tool to solve this problem, simply create two columns of (paired) data. Let one of them be your sample data points, and make the other one a constant with the null mean (90) in every cell.

Historical Mean (Sec)	Randomly Sampled Wait Times (Sec)
90	100
90	105
90	95
90	80
90	90
...	...

We can use the paired test tool to determine the p-value of this single-sample test. By making one column—our null belief about the mean—a constant, we effectively create a second sample to compare our random sample with (in a paired fashion).

Note that the same test tool is used for both small and large paired samples. Thus, be sure to have your assumptions clearly stated and in place if using the paired test tool for small sample testing.

T-Test: Two-Sample, Assuming Unequal Variances

This test is used for large independent (unpaired) sample tests. Note that the name of the test, which always appears at the top of the output so you can check to make sure you picked the right test, says *Assuming Unequal Variances*. This implies that we aren't concerned about having equal variances, so we must have large (random) samples from both populations. The steps to perform this test are effectively the same as with a paired test, except that no small-sample assumptions are needed.

If we treat our Viacom and GM stock returns as independent (and large) samples, we would perform the following steps to complete this test.

Step	Action	Result
1	Select Data Analysis from Tools menu.	Window appears with various data analysis tools listed.
2	Select the T-Test: Two-Sample Assuming Unequal Variances option and press the OK button.	A new window, titled *T-Test: Two-Sample Assuming Unequal Variances,* appears.
3	Now fill in the data ranges. First, fill in the Variable 1 Range with Viacom's returns (and label) (C3:C9). Next, fill in Variable 2 Range with GM's (E3: E9). Next, enter 0 for the Hypothesized Mean Difference because we are testing strict equality. Finally, enter an Alpha level of 0.05 (*not 5!*).	The Variable 1 Range, Variable 2 Range, Hypothesized Mean Difference, and Alpha fields should be filled in with the appropriate values.
4	Because we have included labels in the ranges entered in step 3, we need to check the Labels checkbox.	Labels checkbox should contain a checkmark.
5	Let's put our output in a new worksheet ply titled *T-Test, Unequal Vars.*	New Worksheet Ply: option is selected with the name *T-Test, Unequal Vars* entered.
6	Now let's get the results! Press the OK button and watch Excel work its magic.	Hypothesis/t-test results appear in a worksheet ply named *T-Test, Unequal Vars* (see below).

Here's the output from this test:

t-Test: Two-Sample Assuming Unequal Variances

	Viacom	GM
Mean	5.641183333	3.4309
Variance	55.62648613	72.4984677
Observations	6	6
Hypothesized Mean Difference	0	
df	10	
t Stat	0.478306974	
P(T<=t) one-tail	0.321358277	
t Critical one-tail	1.812461505	
P(T<=t) two-tail	0.642716555	
t Critical two-tail	2.228139238	

Notice that neither the one-tail or two-tail p-value is lower than our alpha of 5 percent, so again, we cannot reject the null that on an independent sample basis, the mean returns for Viacom and GM are the same. We risk a Type II error again, because they could be different but outliers in our sample led us to believe otherwise.

Note that Excel doesn't provide an error or warning because we used a large-sample tool for a small sample. This is up to you, the analyst, to see and to correct! Note the degrees of freedom is: 6 + 6 - 2, or 10, as expected.

T-Test: Two-Sample Assuming Equal Variances

To perform a two-sample hypothesis test when you have one or two small independent samples, can assume the population variances are equal, and can assume that the populations, themselves, are both normal, conduct the following steps via the Data Analysis toolpak.

Step	Action	Result
1	Select Data Analysis from Tools menu.	Window appears with various data analysis tools listed
2	Select the T-Test: Two-Sample Assuming Equal Variances option and press the OK button.	A new window, titled *T-Test: Two-Sample Assuming Equal Variances*, appears.
3	Now fill in the data ranges. First, fill in the Variable 1 Range with Viacom's returns (and label) (C3:C9). Next, fill in Variable 2 Range with GM's (E3: E9). Next, enter 0 for the Hypothesized Mean Difference because we are testing strict equality. Finally, enter an Alpha level of 0.05 (*not 5!*)	The Variable 1 Range, Variable 2 Range, Hypothesized Mean Difference, and Alpha fields should be filled in with the appropriate values.
4	Because we have included labels in the ranges entered in step 3, we need to check the Labels checkbox.	Labels checkbox should contain a checkmark.

(*Continued*)

Step	Action	Result
5	Let's put our output in a new worksheet ply titled *T-Test, Equal Vars*.	New Worksheet Ply: option is selected with the name *T-Test, Equal Vars* entered.
6	Now let's get the results! Press the OK button and watch Excel work its magic.	Hypothesis/t-test results appear in a worksheet ply named *T-Test, Equal Vars* (see below).

Here's the output from this test:

t-Test: Two-Sample Assuming Equal Variances

	Viacom	GM
Mean	5.641183333	3.4309
Variance	55.62648613	72.4984677
Observations	6	6
Pooled Variance	64.06247691	
Hypothesized Mean Difference	0	
df	10	
t Stat	0.478306974	
P(T<=t) one-tail	0.321358277	
t Critical one-tail	1.812461505	
P(T<=t) two-tail	0.642716555	
t Critical two-tail	2.228139238	

Here, we still have large p-values (both one-tailed and two-tailed), so we cannot reject the null that these two means are equal (Viacom average return and GM average return). This is the proper test to use if both key assumptions are in place (normal populations and population variances assumed equal) and if data are unpaired. This test *should not* be used for small paired data sets! Again, Excel will not warn you if you use the wrong test; it's up to you to pick the right one and to state any required assumptions.

Final Thoughts

The hypothesis tests that we've outlined are relatively simple yet very powerful. For the most part, you will use the paired test or the t-tests assuming either equal or unequal variances. The z-test, while helpful, is only used with large sample datasets where population variances are known (which is rare, in general). Remember, too, that with a little clever spreadsheet management, you can use the paired test tool to perform single-sample tests of means.

TUTORIAL 3: CREATING CORRELATIONS, SINGLE-VARIABLE, AND MULTIPLE-VARIABLE LINEAR REGRESSION MODELS

This tutorial discusses how to use the Data Analysis add-in in Excel to create correlation tables and both simple and multiple (variable) linear regression models. To complete this tutorial, you will need to have the Data Analysis add-in in your Tools menu. If you do not, please refer to "Tutorial 1: Creating Descriptive Statistics" for help on accessing this tool kit.

In addition, you should have the stock data shown below (from the first tutorial) available for use.

Monthly Rates of Return

Date	S&P	Viacom	AT&T	GM	Coke
01/30/98	0.8799	0.7541	2.1407	-4.6296	-18.8406
02/27/98	7.5187	14.9701	-2.5948	18.9860	6.6964
03/31/98	5.5580	11.9792	7.7869	-1.7226	-3.3473
04/30/98	1.3716	7.9070	-8.5551	-0.5535	5.8442
05/29/98	-1.6289	-5.1724	1.2474	6.6790	1.9427
06/27/98	2.4171	3.4091	0.8214	1.8261	2.1063

Correlation Analysis

A useful technique to employ when beginning a regression analysis is to analyze the *correlations* among the potential independent variables and the dependent variable. The correlation between two variables is a unitless number between -1 and 1 that indicates the relative linear relationship or movement of the variables. For example, if variable Y moves in the same direction and proportionally to variable X, the X and Y are *perfectly positively correlated*; that is, their correlation coefficient is 1. Note that the correlation is *not* the slope of the regression line that represents their relationship!

However, if Y moves in proportion to X but in the *opposite* direction, then X and Y are *perfectly negatively correlated;* that is, their correlation coefficient is -1. (Think of a demand curve, which relates price and quantity; in other words, a line with a negative slope.) Finally, if the correlation of two variables is zero (or near zero), then a change in one variable is not indicated by a change in the other; that is, there is no response or *no correlation* between them. (Think of the horizontal line $y = 4$; any change in x causes no change in y.)

The reason that correlations among variables are important in the development of regression models is that independent variables that are highly correlated with dependent variables produce better, more accurate regression models. This should make intuitive sense because if a dependent variable, say *sales*, is more highly correlated with the independent variable *age of salesperson* than it is with *years with company*, then we would expect to be more accurate in predicting sales using the salesperson's age—as opposed to years of service—as an input. Thus, we would *reduce uncertainty* by using a more highly correlated input/independent variable.

Excel's Data Analysis tools provide a way for us to calculate correlations among multiple variables. To create a *correlation matrix*, which shows the correlations of one variable with all others, we perform the following steps.

Step	Action	Result
1	Select the Data Analysis option from the Tools menu.	Data Analysis window appears with various options.
2	Select the Correlation option and press the OK button.	A new window, titled *Correlation*, appears.
3	Now fill in the data ranges. First, fill in the input range in the Input Range: field. Here, we want to correlate each variable with all other variables; thus, the entire data range (with labels) should be entered or selected (B3:F9).	The Input Range: field should contain the entire data range—all returns (B3:F9).

(Continued)

(Continued)

Step	Action	Result
4	Because our data are organized by columns and we have included labels in the ranges entered in step 3, we need to select the Columns option and check the Labels checkbox.	Columns option should be selected, and the Labels checkbox should contain a checkmark.
5	Let's put our output in a new worksheet ply titled *Correlations*. To do this, select the New Worksheet Ply: option and enter the worksheet ply name in the field to the right.	New Worksheet Ply: option is selected with the name *Correlations* entered in the field to the right.
6	Now let's get the results! Press the OK button and observe the results.	A correlation matrix appears in a worksheet ply named *Correlations* (see below).

	S&P	*Viacom*	*AT&T*	*GM*	*Coke*
S&P	1				
Viacom	0.938662	1			
AT&T	0.128558	-0.098933	1		
GM	0.470349	0.350438	-0.263711	1	
Coke	0.255053	0.342337	-0.50149	0.627514	1

Note that only half of the matrix is filled in due to the symmetry of these correlations—AT&T is correlated to the S&P the same way the S&P is correlated to AT&T. Now, by examining these correlations, we can develop a good first guess as to which independent variable (Viacom, AT&T, GM, or Coke returns) might best predict the dependent variable, S&P return. In this case, we see that Viacom returns correlate at the 0.9387 level with S&P returns. AT&T returns, on the other hand, only correlate with S&P returns at the 0.1286 level. Thus, Viacom returns might be a good input variable to use to predict the response variable, or S&P returns.

Note also that highly negatively correlated variables make good predictors as well; that is, the *magnitude* of the correlation is often more important than the *sign* of it.

Simple Linear Regression Models

Regression models are helpful because they give us a way to use historical data to predict behaviors (with appropriate caveats for error estimations). The simplest regression model is given by the one-variable equation of the line

$$\hat{Y} = mX + b$$

where X is the *independent* or *benchmark* variable, $\hat{Y}$ is the predicted *dependent* variable, and m and b are the slope and intercept of the line, respectively. Also, note that m is the *coefficient of X* in this equation.

Now let's assume that we would like to predict or determine Viacom's monthly return based on the S&P's return in the same month. That is, if we know the S&P return in a given month (*independent* variable), can we predict (with some level of certainty) what Viacom's return (*dependent* variable) will be in that month?

Regression analysis helps us do this, assuming, of course, that there is some simple, linear relationship (with nonzero slope) between these two return variables. To see this, we can graph a scatterplot of S&P returns and Viacom returns.

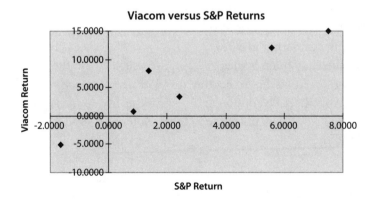

Note that if we had graphed AT&T versus S&P, no obvious (nonzero slope) relationship would have been seen, thus making a simple linear regression not useful. Our goal, now, is to determine the line that best "fits" these Viacom-S&P points and that will allow us, for a given S&P return, to predict the Viacom return. To use Excel to help us determine the equation of the regression line—the slope and intercept of it—we use the Regression function in the Data Analysis toolpak.

Step	Action	Result
1	Select the Data Analysis option from the Tools menu.	Data Analysis window appears with various options.
2	Select the Regression option and press the OK button.	A new window, titled *Regression,* appears.
3	Now fill in the data ranges. First, fill in the *dependent* variable range in the Input Y Range: field. We are trying to predict Viacom returns; thus, the range (and label) of Viacom's returns should be entered or selected (C3:C9). For the *independent* variable, enter the range (and label) including the S&P data (B3:B9) in the Input X Range: field.	The Input Y Range: field should contain the Viacom return range (C3:C9), and the Input X Range: field should contain the S&P return range (B3:B9).
4	Because we have included labels in the ranges entered in step 3, we need to check the Labels checkbox.	Labels checkbox should contain a checkmark.
5	Let's put our output in a new worksheet ply titled *Simple Regression.* To do this, select the New Worksheet Ply: option and enter the worksheet ply name in the field to the right.	New Worksheet Ply: option is selected with the name *Simple Regression* entered in the field to the right. (Note: it's a good idea to check the Line Fit Plots and Residual Plots boxes. See Chapter 9 for more detail as to what these tell you about your model.)
6	Now let's get the results! Press the OK button and watch Excel work its magic.	Regression results appear in a worksheet ply named *Simple Regression* (see below).

SUMMARY OUTPUT

Regression Statistics	
Multiple R	0.938661647
R Square	0.881085687
Adjusted R Square	0.851357109
Standard Error	2.875496778
Observations	6

ANOVA

	df	SS	MS	F	Significance F
Regression	1	245.0585038	245.0585038	29.63766651	0.005528201
Residual	4	33.07392688	8.268481719		
Total	5	278.1324306			

	Coefficients	Standard Error	t Stat	P-value	Lower 95%	Upper 95%	Lower 95.0%	Upper 95.0%
Intercept	-0.014084478	1.567540082	-0.008985083	0.993261301	-4.36628248	4.338113524	-4.36628248	4.338113524
S&P	2.105408582	0.386735808	5.444048724	0.005528201	1.031655617	3.179161547	1.031655617	3.179161547

This is a lot of data to analyze! However, we will focus only on a couple of pieces of this output for now: the R-Square term and the Coefficients. The R-Square term, or *coefficient of determination*, tells us how good a fit our regression line is to the data points. In this case, r-squared is 0.881085687, but we should always use the Adjusted R-Square, because it takes into account the sample size and degrees of freedom. The adjusted r-squared is 0.851357109. One way of interpreting this is as explained *variance*. That is, the input variable (S&P return) predicts or *explains* roughly 85 percent of the variance in the Viacom's stock return when using a linear model. Thus, roughly 85 percent of the Viacom return prediction is explained by the independent (S&P) variable/return.

The Coefficients section at the bottom actually gives us the two pieces of information we were searching for: the slope and intercept of the regression line. In this case, the intercept is -0.014084478. The slope, or coefficient of the *independent* variable (S&P return) is 2.105408582. Thus, putting all of this information together, we see that a regression equation of

Predicted Viacom Return = (2.105408582) × (S&P Return)
+ (-0.014084478)

gives us a prediction that explains approximately 88 percent of the variance in Viacom returns (based on S&P returns).

Note: The other 12 percent of the variance is known as *unexplained variance*. Our goal with regression analysis is to minimize this unexplained variance while not putting too many variables in the model to make it cumbersome or expensive to use.

Great! Now we have a way to predict returns. Note that the regression equation is not perfect—that is, if we input one of the known returns for the

S&P, say 2.4171 for 6/27/98, the resulting predicted Viacom return is 5.0749. This is not 3.4091 as we see in the dataset. (This is because this data point is not on the regression line.) Note that we can only use regression models to create predictions within the bounds or limits of the input variable used to construct the model. That is, we cannot extrapolate or use an x-value (an S&P return) to estimate a Viacom return if the S&P return was not inside the range of our data to start. For example, an S&P return of 10 percent could not be put into our model to predict Viacom's return. Ten percent is not inside the range of input values (S&P returns) used to build this model.

Multiple Linear Regression Modeling

What if we want to predict a (dependent) variable with more than one (independent) variable? For example, what if we turn the problem above around and want to predict S&P returns based on Viacom, AT&T, and GM returns? That is, what if we want to use *multiple* independent variables to predict another (dependent) variable?

The answer is to use the same tool but with more independent variables! In general, we can extend our one-variable model above to include more variables. We can create a simple (still linear) multiple regression model of the form

$$Y = m_1 X_1 + m_2 X_2 + m_3 X_3 + \ldots + m_n X_n + b$$

where Y is still the predicted/dependent variable, m_1 to m_n are the coefficients of the independent variables or observations X_1 to X_n, and b is the constant or intercept of this regression line.

In the case of this problem, let's assume we want to predict the S&P monthly return based on monthly returns of three stocks: Viacom, AT&T, and GM. Mathematically, we want to create a *multiple regression model:*

Predicted *S&P Return* = $m_1 \times$ *(Viacom return)* + m_2
$\times$ *(AT&T return)* + $m_3 \times$ *(GM return)* + b

Our goal, again, is simple: determine the coefficients or slopes m_1, m_2, and m_3 and the constant or intercept b. To do this, we follow the same steps as with single-variable regression, but we slightly modify steps 3, 5, and 6 above (see bolded text below for changes).

Step	Action	Result
1	Select the Data Analysis option from the Tools menu.	Data Analysis window appears with various options.
2	Select the Regression option and press the OK button.	A new window titled *Regression* appears.
3	Now fill in the data ranges. First, fill in the *dependent* variable range in the Input Y Range: field. We are trying to predict **S&P** returns; thus, the range (and label) of **S&P** returns should be entered or selected (**B3:B9**). For the *independent* variable, enter the range (and label) including the **Viacom, AT&T, and GM data (C3:E9)** in the Input X Range: field.	The Input Y Range: field should contain the **S&P** return range (**B3:B9**), and the Input X Range: field should contain the **Viacom, AT&T, and GM** return range (**C3: E9**).
4	Because we have included labels in the ranges entered in step 3, we need to check the Labels checkbox.	Labels checkbox should contain a checkmark.
5	Let's put our output in a new worksheet ply titled *Multiple Regression*. To do this, select the New Worksheet Ply: option and enter the worksheet ply name in the field to the right.	New Worksheet Ply: option is selected with the name *Multiple Regression* entered in the field to the right. (Note: No other options or checkboxes should be selected.)
6	Now let's get the results! Press the OK button and watch Excel work its magic.	Regression results appear in a worksheet ply named *Multiple Regression* (see below).

The results of this regression analysis appear on the following page. Note that from this we can make two observations. First, by using Viacom, AT&T, and GM returns, we can explain almost 94 percent (adjusted r-squared) of the variance in S&P returns using this simple, linear, multivariable regression model. This should not be surprising because these three stocks are used to compute the S&P return! However, notice that with just these three stocks and their returns—instead of all 500—you can make a pretty accurate prediction (based on historical data) of the S&P return.

Second, by looking at the coefficients, we see that the regression equation that we can use to predict S&P returns is as follows:

$$\text{Predicted S\&P Return} = (0.3942 \times \text{Viacom}) + (0.1701 \times \text{AT\&T}) + (0.0913 \times \text{GM}) + 0.1251$$

But wait: Our input variables (Viacom, AT&T, and GM) are likely highly correlated with each other! In this case, we have highly correlated input variables in the model at the same time. This is the effect of multicollinearity, and as a result, we may have a *false sense of fit*. Our r-squared is high not because the three inputs explain the output better but because the three inputs explain each other well. We have to be careful with this in multiple variable regression model building.

Notice also from this equation that Viacom has the most "influence" of the three stocks on the S&P return because its coefficient is largest. A large swing in Viacom's return, therefore, may affect the S&P more than a large swing in GM's return. This does not necessarily imply, though, that Viacom is the most statistically significant predictor of the S&P return (although it is in this case). Check out Chapter 10 for a more thorough discussion of this topic.

SUMMARY OUTPUT

Regression Statistics	
Multiple R	0.987732311
R Square	0.975615119
Adjusted R Square	0.939037796
Standard Error	0.821001266
Observations	6

ANOVA

	df	SS	MS	F	Significance F
Regression	3	53.9356009	17.97853363	26.67267746	0.036353424
Residual	2	1.348086157	0.674043079		
Total	5	55.28368705			

	Coefficients	Standard Error	t Stat	P-value	Lower 95%	Upper 95%	Lower 95.0%	Upper 95.0%
Intercept	0.1250621	0.44169756	0.283139667	0.803685895	-1.775410434	2.025534635	-1.775410434	2.025534635
Viacom	0.394220806	0.052563186	7.49994124	0.017317591	0.168059513	0.620382098	0.168059513	0.620382098
AT&T	0.170135064	0.070141633	2.425593151	0.136110167	-0.131660234	0.471930362	-0.131660234	0.471930362
GM	0.091267454	0.047497875	1.921506033	0.194617419	-0.113099551	0.295634458	-0.113099551	0.295634458

Some Caveats

A few caveats should be mentioned regarding the use—and often *abuse*—of linear regression analysis.

- *Not all relationships are linear!* Some relationships involve variables of higher powers and/or other functions (e.g., log x). This is why it is critical to *graph the data* first! In this way, you can see if a linear relationship will be helpful or not.

- *Not all data are related!* If the slope of the (linear) regression equation is near zero, then a linear regression analysis may not be that helpful. Again, *graph the data* to see what's going on! (Remember, a line with zero slope does not vary regardless of what happens to the independent variable.)

- *Adding more variables doesn't always help!* The model with the most variables is not always the best one. In fact, if there are costs associated with collecting addition data or variables, a simpler model may make more sense (especially if multicollinearity is apparent). Start with simple models and then construct ones with more than one variable only if substantially more variance is explained.

- *Variables can be multicollinear!* Sometimes independent variables in a regression model will depend on each other or will highly correlate with each other (such as height and weight). This can often lead to erroneous results and conclusions, leading you to believe that you have a better (linear) model than is really the case.

- *Correlation is not causation!* Just because two variables are correlated—or have a high r-squared when modeled with a regression tool—does not mean that one *causes* the other. All too often, analysts use the terms *correlated* and *caused* interchangeably. Please do not!

- *Correlation is not slope, either!* The correlation between two variables is not the slope of the regression line. Slopes can be larger than 1 or smaller than -1. Correlations cannot!

Index

About the Author

Paul W. Thurman, a Columbia MBA valedictorian, service award winner, and multiple teaching award recipient, has extensive management consulting and line management experience helping a variety of start-ups and Fortune 500 companies realize value from innovative and coordinated business, operations, and technology strategies. He has held senior positions at Booz Allen Hamilton and American Express, and he has served public and private sector clients on five continents.

Paul has consulted to several global financial services, health care, retail, and consumer products firms across a broad set of business disciplines. His consulting work has focused mostly on analytical modeling to support strategic planning and decision making, corporate cost management, and technology and business integration. He has also developed solutions around customer segmentation, demand modeling, profitability, and experience mapping. Paul currently runs his general management and executive education consultancy, Thurman and Associates, and is a frequent academic and business conference presenter.

Paul teaches strategic management and data analysis courses at Columbia University's School of International and Public Affairs and at its Mailman School of Public Health. He also serves as Executive Director of the Columbia University Alliance for Healthcare Management, where he coordinates research, academic, and industry programs among Columbia's graduate schools of Public Health, Physicians and Surgeons, and Business. Paul has also taught courses in decision, risk, and operations in the full-time and Executive MBA Programs at the Columbia, London, and University of California—Berkeley business schools.

In addition to his full-time faculty appointments, Paul serves as a clinical professor and affiliated researcher at the National Cancer Institute's Center for Cancer Research at the National Institutes of Health. His recent peer-reviewed research has focused on scientific collaboration and its effect on research quality and on cancer drug patents, FDA approvals, and market pricing. He is also a visiting professor and senior research fellow at the Hellenic American University in Athens, Greece, where he teaches a variety of MBA courses, conducts research, and has coauthored several refereed papers and conference presentations on immigrant entrepreneurship in emerging markets.

Paul is on the boards of the Greenburgh (New York) Nature Center, the Scarsdale (New York) Teen Center, and a New York City–based charity. He also serves on the advisory boards of a number of entrepreneurial ventures, including a cancer drug development and marketing alliance, a Web security software company, and a regional sports marketing and advertising firm.

Paul received his BS in mathematics from Stanford University and his MBA from Columbia University (with highest honors). He and his wife, Andrea, and their two daughters, Lisa and Vanessa, live in Scarsdale, New York. Paul can be contacted at Paul.Thurman@Columbia.edu.

2 sample hypothesis testing 143
tables 232